Reviewer's comments about the author's Final Cut Pro Editing Workshop books.

"It takes a pro to teach Final Cut Pro, and Tom Wolsky delivers. His years of TV and film experience make him uniquely qualified to demystify Final Cut Pro and teach good editing techniques. Every editor needs this book."

— Jim Heid, 'Mac Focus' columnist, *Los Angeles Times*

"If you want to learn editing with Final Cut Pro, look no further. Tom Wolsky brings a depth of experience to digital editing that few others share. He has proven himself an excellent teacher at Stanford University's Academy for New Media, and I will encourage, if not require, future students of the Academy to read this book."

— Phil Gibson, Executive Director, Digital Media Academy

"Tom has done a terrific job of putting it all together here — editing, compositing, effects, compression — and even better, he tosses in liberal doses of solid craft advice that can come only from a seasoned pro."

— Ralph Fairweather, Final Cut Pro development team member and 2-pop.com Final Cut Pro forum co-developer

"Tom Wolsky's longtime professional career with ABC News in London — and his later teaching position and full-time studio work in California — takes this work far beyond the simple "how to" books that address Final Cut. In Tom's hands, the subject becomes a look into the process of professional editing and project management as well. Because of this, we believe that he knows Final Cut in many ways better than the people that write the program."

— Ron and Kathlyn Lindeboom, founders, creativecow.net

"I have been reading Tom's post at 2-pop for years and I have learned a great deal from him at the Boards. He always writes clearly, his instructions are detailed and thorough."

— Ken Stone, photographer and FCP web host

"Easy reading, well-organized, thoughtful, and incisive. If you want to edit with Final Cut Pro, this is the book to get. With his years of experience on the network frontlines at ABC, Tom Wolsky gives readers not only the basics of Final Cut Pro　　　　　　　　　　　　points of technique that differentiate the good editor from the 　　　　　　　　　　　today the new media tools we'll all be using to communicate tom

— Jack Smith, former ABC News corresponde　　　　　　　　Marsteller

D1361633

FINAL CUT EXPRESS EDITING WORKSHOP

Tom Wolsky

San Francisco, CA • New York, NY • Lawrence, KS

Published by CMP Books
an imprint of CMP Media LLC
Main office: 600 Harrison Street, San Francisco, CA 94107 USA
Tel: 415-947-6615; fax: 415-947-6015
Editorial office: 1601 West 23rd Street, Suite 200, Lawrence, KS 66046 USA
www.cmpbooks.com
email: books@cmp.com

Acquisitions editor:	Dorothy Cox
Technical editor:	Steve Martin
Managing editor:	Michelle O'Neal
Copyeditors:	Madeleine Reardon Dimond
Layout design:	Madeleine Reardon Dimond
Cover design:	Damien Castaneda

Distributed to the book trade in the U.S. by:
Publishers Group West
1700 Fourth Street
Berkeley, CA 94710
1-800-788-3123

Distributed in Canada by:
Jaguar Book Group
100 Armstrong Avenue
Georgetown, Ontario M6K 3E7 Canada
905-877-4483

For individual orders and for information on special discounts for quantity orders, please contact:
CMP Books Distribution Center, 6600 Silacci Way, Gilroy, CA 95020
Tel: 1-800-500-6875 or 408-848-3854; fax: 408-848-5784
email: cmp@rushorder.com; Web: www.cmpbooks.com

Printed in the United States of America
03 04 05 06 07   5 4 3 2 1

ISBN: 1-57820-223-X

CMP**Books**

For B.T.
With All My Love

Table of Contents

Introduction

What is Editing?

The French film director Jean-Luc Godard called cinema "truth 24 times a second." For the film editor, the moment of the truth is choosing which 24 instances in a second to change the image from one to another. In the case of a video editor, that moment of truth comes every 29.97th of a second. An edit is that precise, that fraction of a moment in time, which may not seem that important, but a moment that has a fundamental effect on the way the viewer perceives the scene.

The moment of the edit is dictated by rhythm, sometimes by an internal rhythm the visuals present, sometimes by a musical track, more often than not by the rhythm of language. All language, dialog or narration, has a rhythm, a cadence or pattern, dictated by the words and based on grammar. Grammar marks language with punctuation: commas are short pauses; semicolons are slightly longer pauses; periods are the end of an idea. The new sentence begins a new idea, a new thought, and it is natural that as the new thought begins, a new image is introduced to illustrate that idea. The shot comes, not on the end of the sentence, not in the pause, but on the beginning of the new thought. This is the natural place to cut, and it's this rhythm of language that drives the rhythm of film and video.

Films and videos are made in the moments when one shot changes into another, when one image is replaced by the next, when one point of view becomes someone else's point of view. Without the image changing, you just have moving pictures. The idea of changing from one angle to another or from one scene to another quickly leads to the concept of juxtaposing one idea against another. It soon becomes apparent that the impact of storytelling lies in the way in which the shots are ordered. Editing is about selection, arrangement, and timing. Editing creates the visual and aural juxtaposition between shots. That what this book is about, how to put together those pieces of picture and sound.

Who Am I To Write This Book?

I have been working in film and video production for longer than I like to admit, nearly 40 years. A few years ago I left ABC News, for whom I'd worked as an operations manager and producer for many years, first in London and then in New York, to take up teaching—video production, of course—at a small high school in rural northern California. I also have written curriculum for Apple's Video Journalism program as well as teaching training sessions for them, and in the summers I have had the pleasure of teaching Final Cut at the Digital Media Academy on the beautiful Stanford University campus.

The structure of this book follows that of my *Final Cut Pro Editing Workshop* books. It is organized as a series of tutorials and lessons that I hope have been written in a logical order to lead the reader from one topic to a more advanced topic. The nature of your work with Final Cut Express, however, may require the information for example in Lesson 6 right away. You can read that lesson by itself and edit your sound. There may, however, be elements in Lesson 6 that presuppose that you know something about using the **Viewer** in conjunction with the **Canvas**.

Who Is This Book For?

This *Editing Workshop* is intended for all FCE users. So the broader question should really be, Who is FCE itself intended for? It appeals, I think, to serious hobbyists, the so-called prosumer market, event producers, and even small companies with video production requirements. I also think it's a great product for education, fully featured, far beyond the frustration many students find in iMovie, but without the professional features in its older brother Final Cut Pro. Institutional education pricing make it affordable for schools even in penny-pinching times. Final Cut is not a simple application to use. It's not plug-and-play. It requires learning your way around the interface, its tools, and its enormous capabilities.

What's on the DVD?

The DVD included with this book is a hybrid DVD. It contains an introduction to Final Cut aimed at the iMovie user. If you have been using iMovie, I urge you to watch it. It will explain, compare, and contrast the two applications. I hope it will make the transition easier for you. The DVD also has a DVD-ROM portion which contains some of the lessons, projects, and clips used in the book. Not all of the lessons require materials from the DVD. For some, such as Lesson 2, you don't need any at all. For others you may want to substitute your own material, clips you want to work with or are more familiar with. I hope you find this book useful, informative, and fun. I think it's a good way to learn this kind of application.

Updates

Those of you who would like to sign up for e-mail news updates can send a blank e-mail to fcexpress@news.cmpbooks.com. If you have a suggestion or correction, please email your comments to tom@fcpbook.com.

Acknowledgments

First, as always, my gratitude to all the people at CMP Books who make this book-writing process relatively painless: Dorothy Cox, senior editor, and Paul Temme, associate publisher, for their thoughtful advice and guidance. Next in line must be Steve Martin of Ripple Training, who took on the chore of being my technical editor. Steve is a great teacher, and the book would have been far poorer without his input. Any errors or omissions that remain are the results of my oversights or misunderstandings, not his. Many thanks as always are due to Michelle O'Neal and Madeleine Reardon Dimond for working through the copyediting and layout, despite the vagaries of Microsoft Word. My thanks again to Damien Castaneda for his wonderful work on the covers.

So many helped in making this book possible: Sidney Kramer for his expert advice, David Bogie for his useful suggestions and comments, Brooks Collins for catching my mistakes, Hiroshi Kumatani for his film look technique, Rich Corwin and Anita Lupattelli for their gracious cooperation, Toby Malina of Avondale Media for her great help in making the DVD. To the creative software engineers who allowed me to put samples of their work on the DVD, especially Christoph Vonrhein, Joe Maller, and Klaus Eiperle; and Eric Fry, for his Timecode Calculator.

A great many thanks are due to my partner, B. T. Corwin, for her insights, her endless encouragement, her engineering technical support, and for her patience with me. Without her, none of this would have been possible. Finally, again my thanks the wonderful people of Damine, Japan, who welcomed us into their homes and whose lives provided the source material for many of these lessons.

Lesson 1

Installing Final Cut Express

Congratulations! You're about to install one of the most creative and affordable video tools available for a desktop computer, running on one of the most elegant, efficient, and stable operating systems yet devised. Welcome to Final Cut Express, Apple's video editing software for DV users.

Many video users have been frustrated by the limitations of iMovie, despite its improvements since it was first introduced. It's important to note that there are a few similarities between iMovie and FCE but many, many distinct differences, not only on the surface, but in the very format where the applications work. For more information about working between iMovie and Final Cut Express, see the DVD that comes with this book. It is a hybrid DVD, including a section that will play with your Mac's DVD player. There I'll explain a little about the differences between the two applications and moving up from one to the other.

I'm sure you want to dive right into it, but Final Cut Express first must be installed properly on a properly functioning system. Video editing software is not a simple piece of shareware that you can install onto your computer and hope it will run without problems. Video editing software requires your system to be running in optimal condition, with all the correct system software and only the correct system software. Your hard drives must be clean and running properly, ready for moving large amounts of data at high speed.

What You Really Need

Final Cut Express will only work with Apple's OS X 10.2.2 (called Jaguar) and higher. The application will run on any G3 or G4 Mac with built-in FireWire connection, though the faster the computer, the better. It will run on a 12-in. G4 PowerBook or on a iMac or an eMac, and of course it will run beautifully on a top-of-the-line Power Mac G4 tower. To achieve real-time preview capabilities, you'll need 500-MHz or faster single or any dual processor Power Mac G4 or at least a 667-MHz PowerBook G4. Final Cut Express allows processor based real-time transitions, graphics, and motion. The ability to see transitions and graphics in real time is a great boon, but remember this real-time display is only available on your computer screen and will not display on a video monitor or TV set without first being rendered.

Memory: How Much and What Kind

In addition to the actual computer, you will need at least 256MB of RAM with 384MB required for real-time preview. The more you can put in, the better, allowing you to have multiple applications open with ease. You'll also need 40MB of storage space available for installation. See the sidebar on RAM and drive space on page 2.

What computer you purchase for editing your videos is almost invariably dictated by your finances. My recommendation is always to get the biggest, fastest, most powerful computer you can afford. If you have budget constraints, get started on an iMac. If you need to be on the road a lot, get a PowerBook. If you have a larger budget, go for it: a multiprocessor G4, loaded with lots of RAM.

Multiple Drives

Storage memory is an essential part of any video system. DV in its simplest form consumes about 3.6MB per second of storage space. That translates to 216MB a minute, approximately 1G for five minutes, and almost 13G for an hour. Fortunately, cheap IDE hard drives for Macs are now available in ever-increasing sizes,

---

Memory and Memory

Applications have to deal with two distinct types of memory: RAM and storage. They perform quite distinct functions. RAM (Random Access Memory) are the chips on your computer's motherboard that hold the system and applications while they are running. FCE is stored in RAM while it's open, as is the operating system.

The other type of memory is storage. The platters of the hard drive store your data. In the case of media drives for your video, these are often very big—and very fast—hard drives. They can store huge quantities of data and access them very quickly. In Figure 1.1 the hard drives are on the left and the three strips of RAM are circled on the right.

1.1   Hard Drives and RAM

1.2   Connection Layout

with platter speeds and seek times ample for working with DV-quality material.

Because a digital video editing system needs to access and move large amounts of data at high speed, you should use separate drives purely for storing video data. You should have one internal hard drive dedicated to your operating system and applications, such as Final Cut Express, Photoshop or Photoshop Elements, your iLife applications, iTunes, iDVD, etc., and everything else from Internet access software to word processing and spreadsheets. All of these should be on one drive. Unlike video media, they usually don't take up a lot of space, so this drive doesn't need to be either exceptionally large or even exceptionally fast. You should also have at least one other hard drive, one that's large and fast. This drive—better still, drives—should carry only your media.

A separate drive is much more efficient at moving large amounts of data at high speed. The media drive needs to find that data off the drive very quickly and play it back. In addition, it needs to play back multiple tracks of audio from various places on the drive simultaneously. That's quite enough work for any one drive to be doing at any one time. To then have it be accessing the application and the operating system as well is often the straw that breaks the camel's back. You are much less likely to have video playback or capture failure through dropped frames and other issues if you have the media on a separate, dedicated hard drive.

Optimizing your Computer for FCE

There are other things you can do in **System Preferences** to optimize your computer for video editing with Final Cut, mostly switching off things that might interfere with its operations while it's running.

- Make sure **Software Update** is set to connect **Manually** and not on **Automatic,** so that there is no chance it will take off and try to run while you're working in FCE.

- The **Displays** should be set so that your computer monitor is running in **Millions of colors** and at the resolution settings the monitor recommends in the **Displays** panel of your **System Preferences.**

- The **Energy Saver** should be set so that the system never goes to sleep. It's less critical that the monitor doesn't go to sleep. I usually set it around 10 minutes, but the system and the hard drive should never shut down. This can cause havoc with slow renders.

- One last step I would recommend is to switch off **Apple-Talk.** This is simplest to do in OS X by going to **Network Preferences** and creating a new **Location** called **None.** Set up your **None** location without any active connections—no internal modem, no Airport, no Ethernet—everything unavailable and shut off. To reconnect to the network, simply change back to a location from the **Apple** menu that allows access to whatever connection you want to use.

Monitors

You should have a video monitor. A video monitor reproduces images differently than a computer monitor, which has much greater color depth, resolution, and contrast range, and does not have the interlaced scan lines that a television set or video monitor has. These are all critical to how your video will finally look. If your project will be shown on a television set, you must edit with a video monitor that shows true output. You may also want a second computer display for the large number of windows that video editing applications need.

To get the video out of your computer and onto the video monitor or TV set you're going to need to use some kind of digital to analog conversion device. The simplest one for most people is a camcorder. The video and audio comes out of the computer's FireWire port, which gets connected to the camcorder, or DV deck, or DV convertor box. The output of the camcorder in turn is connected to the video monitor. That's the best place to watch your movie while you work. The audio from the camera or from the video monitor is fed into speakers. Figure 1.2 shows a typical connection layout. The camera on top of the monitor is the hub that passes the digital signal back and forth to the analog video monitor and speakers.

Speakers

Good quality speakers are really important. They should be connected to the same source as the video you're monitoring. If you are looking at your video on a television monitor, you should listen to your audio from the same source. So if you have a deck or a DV camera that is feeding the signal from your computer to your TV monitor, then that should also be feeding your audio speakers. Switchable speakers would be ideal, with two inputs to monitor either the video source or the computer output.

🐾 *Note*_____

Updates: After installing the software it's probably a good idea to check the Apple Final Cut Express web page http://www.apple.com/finalcutexpress to see if there have been any updates to the application. Applications are constantly being refined and updated to fix problems or to accommodate developments in hardware or the operating system itself.

Also, don't forget to register your new software. Apple usually gives out a free effects filter for registering, one from Joe Maller's filter package. Filters and plugins should be copied, while the application is closed, into *Library/Application Support/Final Cut Express Support/Plugins*. They will then be available on start up.

Firing Up the Application

Now it's time to launch that program. Double-click on the icon in the *Applications* folder, or better yet make an alias in the **Dock** and just click on that (Figure 1.3). After you start up the application, the first window that greets you is one asking you to enter your name, organization, and serial number.

After a new installation, or after you have trashed your *Final Cut Preferences* file, you will next be greeted with the preferences screen in Figure 1.4.

1.3　Final Cut Express Icon

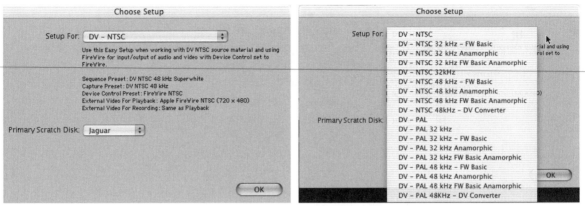

1.4 Start-up Dialogue   1.5 FCE Presets

The default setting is DV-NTSC with audio at 48kHz. In FCE the list of choices you have in the first popup are the setups available to you (Figure 1.5). For now, choose DV-NTSC. We'll look at the others in a bit more detail in the next lesson.

The second popup makes you choose a scratch disk. The popup defaults to your system partition and offers you the choice of any hard drives on your system. Accept the default for now; we'll change it later.

Understanding the Interface

Launching a new application for the first time is always an adventure, especially when it's as complex as Final Cut Express. Some software can be intimidating; some can be downright head-scratching. I particularly love those applications that open with the standard **Application** menu, **File**, **Edit**, a few other things, and nothing else. You're staring at your computer screen wondering where to start or what to do.

That's certainly not the case with Final Cut Express, which immediately fills your screen with windows, buttons, and tools to explore. Figure 1.6 shows what greets you when FCE is fully launched.

The Primary Windows

The screen is divided into four primary windows, with two large empty screens as your principal monitors:

- The **Viewer**, on the far left, allows you to look at individual video clips.

1.6   The Final Cut Express Interface

- The **Canvas,** in the center, is the output of your material as you edit it together. The **Canvas** is linked directly to the **Timeline.**

- The **Timeline** for your video is the window with the horizontal window in the bottom half of the screen. This is where you lay out your video and audio material in the order you want it.

- The **Browser** is the fourth window at the top right of the screen, the same location as the **Clips Pane** in iMovie.

Though the **Viewer** is your primary editor in traditional editing, you can also edit in the **Timeline** window, as well as control transitions and other effects. The project materials are listed in the **Browser.**

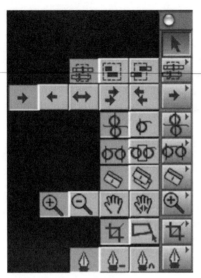

1.7   Tools Palette

Think of the **Browser** as a giant folder. You can nest folders within folders, just like you can on a Mac **Desktop**. This is not where your clips are stored; it is only a list. Your clips are physically stored on your media hard drives. In the **Browser** you can have a variety of different types of files: obviously video files, but also audio files and graphics or still images.

You'll also notice vertical bars that contain the **Tools** and **Audio Meters**. Some of the tools are hidden, nested inside the **Tools** palette. Figure 1.7 shows all the tools displayed. There is a **Selection** tool, the arrow at the top. There are **Edit** and **Range Selection** tools; **Track Selection** tools; editing tools such as **Roll**, **Ripple**, **Slip**, and **Slide**; **Blade** tools; **Zoom** and **Hand** tools; **Crop** and **Distort** tools; and various **Pen** tools for creating and editing keyframes.

▶ *Tip*

Open Sequence: Should your project ever open and you don't see a **Canvas** or **Timeline**, it means that there is no sequence open. There needs to be at least one sequence in a project. Simply double-click the sequence in the **Browser**, and it will open the **Timeline** together with its **Canvas**.

Figure 1.6 shows the default configuration, called **Cinema**. Many people like to work with larger screens, particularly when working on a PowerBook, where the computer screen is more likely to be your primary monitor. In the **Window** menu, select **Arrange> Standard** (Figure 1.8). This will bring up the arrangement in Figure 1.9, which is the default arrangement in Final Cut Pro. Final Cut Express' default arrangement was probably chosen because it most closely resembles the arrangement for the **Browser** that's used by iMovie's **Clips Pane**.

1.8   Window>Arrange> Standard

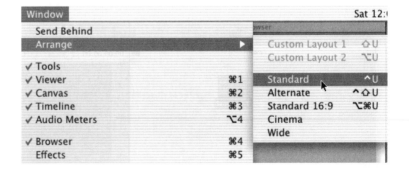

🐾 *Note*

Sequence: You'll notice that the **Browser** is not empty. When you create a new project, FCE creates a new sequence called *Sequence 1*. You can rename sequences just like you would any file in the Mac **Finder**. Click on the name to highlight it, and type in a new name. You can have as many sequences as you want in a project, and you can place, or nest, sequences within sequences. We'll look at nesting later (page 173 in Lesson 7).

🐾 *Note*

Custom Screen Setting: You can set the screen anyway you like and save it as a custom setting. When you've arranged the screen to your taste, hold down the **Option** key. From the **Window** menu, select **Arrange>Set Custom Layout 1** or **Set Custom Layout 2,** shown in Figure 1.8. Quickly return to these settings at any time using keyboard shortcuts (**Shift-U** for **Custom Layout 1** and **Option-U** for **Custom Layout 2**) or by choosing them from the **Windows>Arrange** menu.

Tabbed Palettes

You've probably also noticed that most of these windows have tabs with other windows behind them. Let's take a quick look at

1.9   Standard Arrangement

what's back there. Tabbed in the **Browser** is the **Effects** window. Video and audio effects, transitions, and generators are stored here, including any favorites you want to access frequently.

The **Viewer** has tabs behind it as well:

- **Audio** lets you see a video clip's audio waveform and manipulate the sound by raising and lowering the levels or panning the stereo from left to right.
- **Filters** is where you control effects applied to clips.
- **Motion** lets you view and change settings for properties like **Scale, Rotation, Center, Crop,** and others.

Most of these properties can be animated. You can also change the image's opacity, making it more transparent. At zero opacity it will be invisible. You can add a drop shadow that will appear on any underlying layers, and you can add **Motion Blur,** which simulates the amount of smearing, creating by a fast movement across the screen. We will look at these **Motion** tools in later lessons (see Lessons 7 and 8).

The **Canvas** and the **Timeline** window also have tabs. If you have more than one sequence open at a time, they will appear as tabs in the **Timeline** window and in the **Canvas.**

Browser

Now let's bring some material into the project so that we can look at each window in greater detail. We'll begin by opening a project I have already created for you.

If you have a project open, close it by clicking the red **Close** button in the upper left of corner of the **Browser.** You can have more than one project open at a time, which is very useful because it allows you to easily move elements from one project to another. However, you may get confused with which window belongs to which project, so I normally don't have more than one project open at a time unless I need to.

Let's begin by loading the book's DVD into your DVD drive. When you begin any lesson that needs material from the DVD, you should first drag the needed folders onto the media drive of your computer. The sound and video clips included in those folders will play much better and more smoothly from your computer's high-speed media drive than from any DVD drive. This is a hybrid DVD and will probably start up your DVD player when

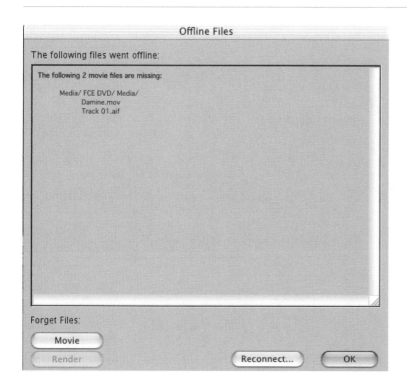

1.10 Offline Files Dialog Box

you mount the disk. The DVD portion contains a short introduction to FCE aimed at iMovie users, but if you double-click on the DVD itself you will find a folder called *FCE DVD-ROM Contents*. Inside that folder are a number of other folders. For this lesson you'll need the folder called *Media* and also the folder called *Lesson 1*, which is inside the *Projects* folder on the DVD.

1. Drag *Lesson 1* on to your internal system drive, either into the *Shared* folder inside the *Users* folder, or in your home *Documents* folder.

2. Drag the *Media* folder into your media drive. This may take a while to transfer.

You have to have both folders because some of the material is in the *Lesson 1* folder, while the media is in the *Media* folder.

3. After copying the material, before doing anything else, eject the DVD from your computer.

4. Open the *Lesson 1* folder on your hard drive and double-click the project file, *L1*, to open the project.

When the project finishes loading, you'll be greeted with the dialog box in Figure 1.10.

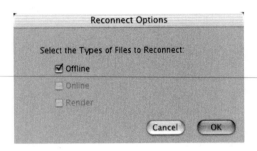

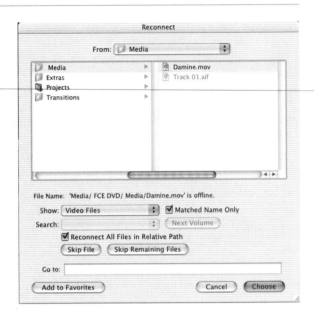

1.11 Reconnect Options Dialog Box (above)

1.12 Reconnect Selection Box (right)

5. Do *not* press **Enter** or click **OK**. Instead, click the **Reconnect** button.

Do not click the **Movie** button underneath **Forget Files** either, because the application will do exactly that: forget that it needs the media. After you click **Reconnect**, you will get the **Reconnect Options** dialog box in Figure 1.11.

The computer will now search through your hard drives looking for *Damine.mov*. When the file is found, you'll get a dialog box similar to the one in Figure 1.12.

6. If this is the correct file on your media drive, make sure the **Reconnect All Files in Relative Path** box is checked and click the **Select** button.

Final Cut will now reconnect all the material for the project, and then you're ready to go.

This project comes with material already in it. If it had been a new project you could have imported the various pieces. The easiest way to do this is to move the **Browser** to the left and then access your **Desktop**. You can simply drag and drop folders and files from anywhere on your drives directly into the **Browser**. This can be used for any material FCE uses—QuickTime movies, sound files, still images, etc. This is the simplest, quickest way to bring lots of material into your project. You can also use **Command-I** to import single items or the **File** menu under **Import>Folder** to bring a folder full of clips or other material.

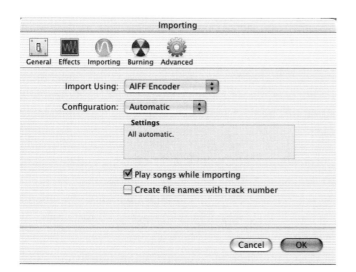

1.13 iTunes Importing Preference (left)

1.14 iTunes Custom Settings (below)

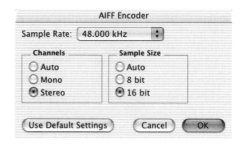

Importing Music

Importing from a music CD is slightly different from importing video. Final Cut can work with audio CD files, but they do raise some problems. Audio CDs use an audio sampling rate of 44.1kHz. This is not normally the sampling rate used by the DV format, which is either 32kHz or, more commonly, 48kHz. While FCE can deal with resampling the audio while it plays it back, this requires processor power and may limit your ability to do real-time effects or to play back video without dropping frames, i.e., the video stuttering. To avoid this, I would recommend re-sampling the audio to the correct sampling rate you want to use before importing it into FCE. Apple has already provided you with a simple tool to do this. It's called iTunes. This application may already have launched automatically when you loaded your audio CD. If it didn't, start it up.

1. Under the **iTunes** menu, go to **Preferences**, and in the **Preferences** window, select the **Importing** tab, which will look like Figure 1.13.

2. From the **Import Using** popup, select **AIFF Encoding**.

3. From the second popup, select **Custom**.

4. Set the sampling rate to 48,000Hz or whatever sampling rate you're working with.

5. Set the **Channels** to **Stereo** and the **Sample Size** to 16 bit, as in Figure 1.14.

Once you've set this preference, you shouldn't have to change it again. One more item in the **iTunes Preferences** that you will want to set is in the **Advanced** tab (Figure 1.15).

6. Click on the **Change** button and navigate to the media drive where you want to save your music. Again, you may only have to do this once for a project.

Now you're ready to import the music.

7. In the **iTunes** window, **Command**-click on one of the checked track boxes. This will deselect all the tracks.

8. Now check the tracks you want, and then click the **Import** button on the upper right corner of the window (Figure 1.16).

iTunes will then copy the track from the CD to your designated hard drive location and will resample as it does so.

The track you copied onto your hard drive will be inside a folder with the artist's name. If there was no name listed in iTunes, it will be inside a folder called *Unknown Artist*, inside a folder called *Unknown Album*. Now when you drag the track into your **Browser** or use **Command-I** to import it, the track will appear in the **Browser** appended with the suffix *aif* and will also be in the correct sampling rate that you chose in iTunes. Your system will be happy that you did this.

1.15 iTunes Advanced Window

1.16 iTunes Window

Importing CD Tracks Using the Browser

If you don't want to mess up your iTunes preferences, you can also use the FCE **Browser** as an import/export utility to bring audio CD tracks into the application.

1. Begin by inserting the CD into the CD drive.

2. Use **File>Import>Files (Command-I)**.

3. Select the track or tracks you want to import and hit **Choose**. The file is still linked to your CD, so do not eject it.

4. Next go to **File>Export>QuickTime**.

5. In the format popup, choose **AIFF**.

6. Click the **Options** button and set the **Compressor** to **None**.

7. **Size** should be **16 bit** and **Use** should be **Stereo**.

8. Set **Rate** to either **48,000** or **32,000** depending on which you're working in. (See the section on **Easy Setup** in the next lesson on page 31.)

9. Click **OK** and save the file onto your media drive and resample it from 44.1K to whatever you chose in the **Options** window.

10. All you have to do next is import the file from your media drive. You will now have the AIFF file available to use in your project. Eject the CD. and the original file you imported will become offline. Simply delete it from your **Browser**.

Bin Contents and Detail

When you start the **Browser**, the project called *L1* should look like Figure 1.17.

The default view for the **Browser** in Final Cut Express is to a medium-size Icon view. You'll see icons for video clips—notice the small speaker to indicate that the clip has audio—you'll see a sound track with its speaker icon, and you'll see a couple of folders. Though it uses a folder icon, in Final Cut–speak this folder is called a *bin*, an old film term. Think of long bits of processed film hanging from pins into a large, cloth-lined bin. Whatever you call it, it behaves like a folder.

You can change the **Browser** view by selecting **View>Browser Items** and choosing **List** or three different icon views, **Small**, **Medium**, and **Large**. **Small** is pretty useless while the large icons

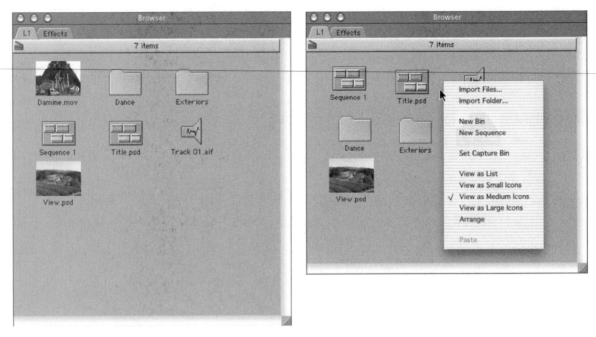

1.17 L1 Browser Window   1.18 Shortcut Menu in Browser

take up a lot of screen space. The keyboard shortcut **Shift-H** will cycle through the four **Browser** options.

Change the **Browser** to List view. To see the contents of the bins:

- Click the twirly disclosure triangle to expand the folder view or
- Double-click on the folder icon

If you double-click, a folder will open in a new window. To close the window, click on the little red **X** button in the upper left corner of the window or use the keyboard shortcut **Command-W**.

There are two sequences in the **Browser,** one called *Sequence 1* and another called *Title.psd.* A sequence is a timeline window in which you lay out your video, audio, and graphics clips. A sequence can have multiple tracks of video and audio. You can also place sequences within sequences, as we shall see later. Whenever you create a new project, FCE always creates a default empty sequence called *Sequence 1.* The *Title.psd* also has a **Sequence** icon because FCE imports Photoshop files as layered sequences; each of the layers in the PSD file appears as a separate

	Name		Duration	In	Out	Tracks	Good	Log Note	Frame Size	Vid Rate	Compressor	Data Rate	Aud Rate
	Damine.mov		00:08:02;28	Not Set	Not Set	1V, 2A			720 x 480	29.97 fps	DV/DVCPRO	3.6 MB/sec	48.0 KHz
▽	Dance												
	Dance1		00:00:08;16	00:00:49;05	00:00:57;20	1V, 2A			720 x 480	29.97 fps	DV/DVCPRO	3.6 MB/sec	48.0 KHz
	Dance2		00:00:17;27	00:00:57;21	00:01:15;19	1V, 2A			720 x 480	29.97 fps	DV/DVCPRO	3.6 MB/sec	48.0 KHz
	Dance3		00:00:16;14	00:01:15;20	00:01:32;03	1V, 2A			720 x 480	29.97 fps	DV/DVCPRO	3.6 MB/sec	48.0 KHz
▽	Exteriors												
	Stairs1		00:00:08;16	Not Set	Not Set	1V, 2A			720 x 480	29.97 fps	DV/DVCPRO	3.6 MB/sec	48.0 KHz
	Stairs2		00:00:08;29	Not Set	Not Set	1V, 2A			720 x 480	29.97 fps	DV/DVCPRO	3.6 MB/sec	48.0 KHz
	StoneBasin		00:00:05;08	Not Set	Not Set	1V, 2A			720 x 480	29.97 fps	DV/DVCPRO	3.6 MB/sec	48.0 KHz
	Temple1		00:00:07;29	Not Set	Not Set	1V, 2A			720 x 480	29.97 fps	DV/DVCPRO	3.6 MB/sec	48.0 KHz
	Temple2		00:00:18;13	Not Set	Not Set	1V, 2A			720 x 480	29.97 fps	DV/DVCPRO	3.6 MB/sec	48.0 KHz
	Sequence 1		00:00:00;00	Not Set	Not Set	2V, 4A			720 x 480	29.97 fps	DV/DVCPRO		48.0 KHz
	Title.psd		00:00:10;00	Not Set	Not Set	1V			2000 x 480	29.97 fps	DV/DVCPRO		48.0 KHz
	Track 01 .aif		00:00:17;27	Not Set	Not Set	2A				29.97 fps		187.7 K/sec	48.0 KHz
	View.psd		00:00:10.00	00:01:00:00	00:01:09;29	1V			720 x 480	29.97 fps		7.0 K/sec	

1.19 Browser List View

video layer in the Final Cut sequence, one stacked on top of the other. The other PSD file, *View.psd,* is a single-layer file and imports as single-layer graphic.

Using Shortcut Menus

Even more information can be displayed in the **Browser** with the **Control** key, one of the most powerful tools in the application. Throughout Final Cut Express, the **Control** key gives you access to shortcut menus. These menus change depending on where your cursor is. Using the shortcut menu (Figure 1.18), you have access to a huge amount of information about your media, which makes the **Browser** not only a list of your material but a very powerful tool for organizing and annotating your clips.

With the **Browser** in List view and the window arrangements set to **Wide**, stretch out the **Browser** window to the right, and you'll see just some of the many things the **Browser** displays in List mode (see Figure 1.19).

The **Browser** shows the duration of clips, the In and Out points, which are probably marked **Not Set** at this stage. You also see track types (whether video and/or audio) and how many audio tracks. Note that the Photoshop sequences tell you how many layers there are in the sequence. Also notice that *Sequence 1* by default as two video tracks and four audio tracks. Clips can be marked as **Good** in the **Browser.** This harks back to film days where good takes were placed in a separate bin for first consideration. Similarly in FCE, marking a clip **Good** lets you designate it for special attention. Comments can be added to clips in the **Log**

Hide Column
Edit Heading

Standard Columns
✓ Logging Columns

No hidden columns
Show Offline
Show Length
Show Alpha
Show Reverse Alpha
Show Composite
Show Tracks
Show Type
Show Source
Show Size
Show Last Modified
Show Thumbnail
Show Audio
Show In
Show Out
Show Good
Show Capture
Show Scene
Show Shot/Take
Show Reel
Show Log Note
Show Comment 1
Show Comment 2
Show Comment 3
Show Comment 4
Show Pixel Aspect
Show Anamorphic
Show Vid Rate
Show Frame Size
Show Aud Rate
Show Aud Format
Show Compressor
Show Data Rate

1.20 List of Browser Shortcut Menu Items

Note box or the four **Comments** boxes. You just click in the box and type.

Notice that the clips in the bin **Dance** have simple **Clip** icons, while those in the bin **Exteriors** have torn edges on the left and right. These are *subclips*. We'll look at subclips and how to use and create them in Lesson 3 on page 57.

The **Browser** also shows the type of audio, presence of stereo, frame size, and frame rate (in the case of these clips, 29.97 frames a second, the standard frame rate for all NTSC video).

Other information displayed in the **Browser** is:

- Type of video compression used
- Data rate
- Audio sampling rate
- And much, much information that you'll probably never need to look at

Only the **Name** column cannot be moved. It stays displayed on the left side of the window. You can move any of the other columns by grabbing the header at the top of the column and pulling it to wherever you want the column to appear.

☞ *Tip*

Ordering: You can arrange the order in which clips are shown in List view by selecting the column header. By clicking the green arrow that appears in the header, you can change the order from descending to ascending. Also, if you **Shift**-click on the header of other columns, a little blue arrow will appear and will be added as secondary ordering lists. Secondary sorting allows you to organize and arrange your material to suit your workflow. To clear secondary sort orders, just choose a new primary sort. Click on an unsorted column header without the **Shift** key.

Browser Columns

If your cursor is over the column headers in the **Browser** and you press the **Control** key while clicking the mouse, you get a shortcut menu. Figure 1.20 shows the whole list of available categories, except for **Name** and **Duration**, which are active columns in the **Browser**.

The **Comments** columns can be renamed anything you want by clicking in the **Comments** column header and choosing **Edit Heading** from the shortcut menu. These are the only columns you can rename.

One of the important items you can call up here is **Source**. This tells you the file path to a clip's location on your hard drive.

Another item hidden in the shortcut menu is **Show Thumbnail**. This cool feature brings up a thumbnail that shows the first frame of the video. Grab the thumbnail and drag the mouse. This is called *scrubbing*, and what you're doing is dragging through the video clip itself so you can actually see what's in it. Viewing

The FCE Facade

FCE and its entire interface is a facade. What you're bringing into the FCE project is the equivalent of aliases of your media (Figure 1.21). While you're working with these "aliases," you're using them to pass instructions to the computer about which pieces of video and audio to play when and what to do with them. The conveniences created for you in the **Browser** and in the **Timeline** are simply an elaborate way of telling the computer what to do with the media on your hard drives and how to play it back. All the clips in the project, either in the **Browser** or in the **Timeline**, are simply pointers to the media on the hard drive. This is a nondestructive, completely nonlinear, random-access artifice. This means that your media is not modified by anything you do in the application; it means you can arrange the media and work on any portion of your project at any time; and it means that you can access any piece of media from anywhere on your hard drive at any time. The clips are not "brought" into the **Browser** or placed on the **Timeline**. They never leave their place on the hard drives. They're never "in" the project at all except as a list. You can change the names in the list to anything more convenient that you like, and it has no effect at all on the data stored on your hard drive. All you're doing is changing how you give instructions to the data; you're not changing the data at all. On the other hand, if you change the names of the clips on your hard drive, that will throw FCE into confusion, and you'll have to reconnect each clip to establish the links between the two.

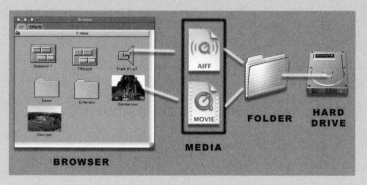

1.21 Media and FCE Workflow

1.22   Scrub Tool

1.23   Scrub Tool in Icon View

1.24   Browser Shortcut Menu

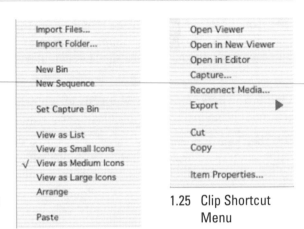

1.25   Clip Shortcut Menu

media like this in the **Browser** can save time. You can quickly scan through a shot to see if it's really the one you're looking for.

You can also change the Poster frame, the frame that appears in the thumbnail. The default is the first frame of the video (or the In point), but if you scrub through the video and find a new frame you would like to set as the thumbnail, press the **Control** key and release the mouse. A new Poster frame has been set. If you change the Poster frame for a clip here or in any other **Browser** window, the poster will change for each instance of that clip anywhere in the **Browser** and will also display as the poster when the **Browser** is set to Icon view.

When the **Browser** is in Icon view, the clips are shown with their Poster frame. Like the thumbnails we saw earlier in List view, these icons have the same scrubbable property.

You can also set the Poster frame as before by holding the **Control** key when you're over the frame you want to set and releasing the mouse.

You can select the **Scrub** tool from the **Tools** palette (Figure 1.22). Also, if you hold down **Control-Shift**, the cursor will change to the **Scrub** tool, which is the **Hand** tool with forward and reverse arrows that will let you scrub the icons (Figure 1.23).

In the **Browser**, the **Control** key again provides a useful shortcut menu. In the window it lets you change the views, make new bins and sequences, as well as import and arrange the material (Figure 1.24).

Clips themselves hold a shortcut menu that can do a variety of useful things (Figure 1.25).

✏ *Tip*

Shortcut Menus: Using shortcut menus in List view lets you change items for multiple clips with a few clicks of the mouse. For instance, to add a comment to the **Log Note,** I simply select a number of clips. Then I use the shortcut menu in the same column, the **Log Note** column. This will bring up a list with all my recent notes in that column. I select the one I want, and all the selected clips will have their log notes changed (Figure 1.26).

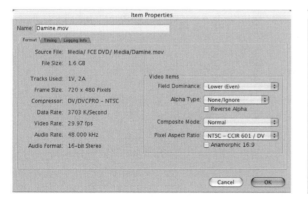

1.26 Log Note Shortcut Menu

With the clip shortcut menu open, a whole array of options is available. One very useful one is **Item Properties**.

Item Properties calls up an information window that tells you everything about a clip (Figure 1.27).

You can rename a clip here. There are popups that allow you to change properties such as pixel aspect ratio and field dominance. It also lets you change properties such as composite mode and alpha interpretation. "What in the world is he talking about?" you're thinking. They're all great tools that you'll soon learn about. Notice also the two panels in the back, **Timing** and **Logging Info**. **Timing** (Figure 1.28) allows you to change duration and actually set In and Out points, start and end points for the clip, though it would be very unusual to actually do it in this window.

Logging Info (Figure 1.29) gives you access to all the comments and notes for a clip. It's also a convenient place to add this material, especially if you're writing longer notes than just a few words.

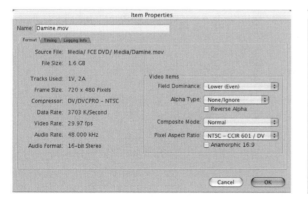

1.27 Item Properties

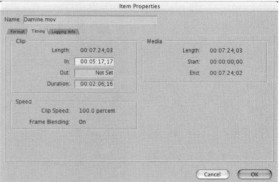

1.28 Timing Panel

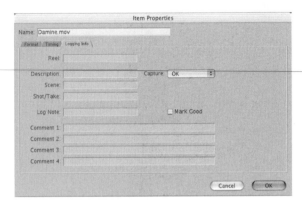

1.29 Logging Info (above)

1.30 The Viewer (right)

As you can see, the **Browser** window is not only full of important information about your video project, but its shortcut menu is actually a powerful tool for manipulating the clips and graphics you're working with.

Viewer

The **Viewer** is one of the primary editing tools within Final Cut Express. This is where you manipulate your clips, mark them, and prepare them for your timeline. To load a clip into the **Viewer,** just double-click on it or select it and hit the **Return** or **Enter** key. Start by double-clicking on the clip *Stairs1* in the **Exteriors** bin (Figure 1.30).

Viewer Buttons

Let's now take a look at that array of buttons clustered around the bottom of the **Viewer** so that you are familiar with them and what they do (Figure 1.31).

The **Shuttle** tab, on the left just below the video display in the **Viewer,** lets you shuttle the clip forwards and backwards. Grab it with the mouse and move right and left. The farther from the default center position you go, the faster the video will play.

The **Jog** wheel on the right, opposite the **Shuttle** tab, will let you roll back and forth through the frames slowly.

The central button in the middle is, of course, the **Play** button. Starting from the left in the group around the **Play** button, the first button is **Go to Previous Edit** (**Up** arrow). The next button is quite useful—it lets you play from your In point to your Out point. The keyboard shortcut is **Shift-**.

The next button to the right of the central **Play** button is **Play Around Current Point** (\). The default is for playback to start five seconds before where the playhead is, and play for two seconds past where the playhead is. We'll look at how to use these functions in later lessons.

The last button is **Go to Next Edit** (**Down** arrow).

Another cluster of smaller buttons sits at the bottom left of **Viewer**. From the left, the first button is **Match Frame** (**F**). This is a very useful tool, though it won't work for you at the moment. If you open a clip that's in a timeline, it allows you to match back to the same frame in the **Canvas**.

The next button is **Mark Clip** (**X**), which selects as the In and Out points the entire length of the clip.

The next button, the diamond shape, adds a keyframe, which you need when creating animation.

The next button adds a marker to the clip (**M**). Markers are useful. They let you set visible marks on clips that appear in the **Timeline** window. You can mark the beat of a piece of music, where a phrase appears in dialog, where a pan or zoom starts or ends. Practically anything you can imagine noting about a clip can be made to appear on the screen, like Post-It notes for video.

Next to the **Marker** button is a group of two buttons, first **Mark In** (**I**) and then **Mark Out** (**O**).

There are two more buttons at the bottom right of the **Viewer**. The one with the **Clip** icon lets you load recently opened clips. Next to that is a button with a large **A**. This opens a menu that

> **Tip**
>
> **Match Frame Variation:** Another useful tool to remember is **Shift-F**. This is a variation of **Match Frame**. It matches you back to the same frame of the original clip in the **Browser**. This is very useful if you've opened a clip from the **Timeline** and you want to find the original in the **Browser**.

1.34 Top of the Viewer

accesses the Generators, such as Bars and Tone, Render Gradients, Color Mattes, Slug, Text, Title 3D, and the Title Crawl tool. We'll delve into this button in latter lessons.

Put your cursor in the white bar directly below the video image. As you mouse down, the playhead will jump to where you are. The playhead is the little yellow triangle with a line hanging from it. There are other playheads in Final Cut Express. In addition to the **Viewer,** they're in the **Canvas** and the **Timeline,** every place where you can play video.

Top of the Viewer

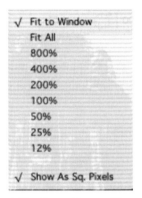

1.32 Zoom Popup Menu

Let's look at the top portion of the **Viewer** for a moment (Figure 1.34). In the center are two buttons, actually popup menus. The one on the left, the **Zoom** popup menu (Figure 1.32), adjusts the size of the image displayed in the **Viewer.** You can set to **Fit to Window (Shift-Z),** or to a percentage from very small to so large that you can see all the pixels at their blocky best.

The other button, the **View** popup menu, changes the view from **Image** mode to **Image+Wireframe** (Figure 1.33). You need this mode especially for compositing in the **Canvas** when you're combining and animating multiple layers of video. The popup also lets you turn on overlays, including the **Title Safe** overlay.

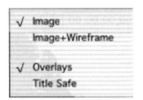

1.33 View Popup Menu

Viewer Time Displays

At the top of the **Viewer** are two sets of numbers. On the left is the duration of the clip from its marked In point to its marked Out point. If the In and Out are not set, it will show the duration of the media from start to finish.

The time display on the right shows the current time for the frame where its playhead is sitting. This is not the timecode for the clip, which FCE keeps track of internally. Timecode is crucial to video editing. It is a frame-counting system that is now almost universal to video cameras. A number is assigned to every frame of video and is physically recorded on the tape. We'll look at timecode more closely on page 33 in the next lesson on capturing. The **Time** window in the **Viewer** can be used to go to specific points in the clip just by typing in the appropriate number. You can also add and subtract time in the **Viewer**.

Playing Clips

There are a number of different ways of playing a clip to look at your video. The most apparent is the big **Play** button in the middle of the **Viewer** controls. If you like working with the mouse, this will be for you, but it is not the most efficient way to work by any means.

There are other ways to view your video besides at real speed. The buttons on the **Viewer** do this, but learn the keyboard. It's your friend, and it's really a much simpler, easier way to control your editing than the mouse.

Spacebar

Press the spacebar to play the clip. To pause, press the spacebar again. Spacebar to start, spacebar to stop. To play the clip backwards, press **Shift**-spacebar. This method is much quicker and keeps your hands on the keyboard and off the mouse. You can play and manipulate clips in the **Viewer** with great efficiency using only the keyboard.

Keyboard Shortcuts

Another common way to play the clip is with the **L** key.

- **L** is play forward.
- **K** is pause.
- **J** is play backwards.

On your keyboard they're clustered together, but you're probably thinking, Why not comma, period, and slash? There is reason to the madness. **J**, **K**, and **L** were chosen because they're directly below **I** and **O**. **I** and **O** are used to mark the In and Out points on clips and in sequences. They are probably the most commonly used keys on the editing keyboard. Hence **J**, **K**, and **L**, positioned conveniently for the fingers of your right hand with the **I** and **O** keys directly above them.

You can view your video at other speeds. You can play your clip fast forward by repeatedly hitting the **L** key. The more times you hit **L**, the faster the clip will play. Similarly, hitting the **J** key a few times will make the clip play backwards at high speed.

✏️*Tip*

Shortcut Help: If trying to remember all the keyboard shortcuts is shorting out your brain, you can get color-coded special keyboards with keys that display the shortcuts. A great tool I find is Loren Miller's KeyGuide™. No FCE editor should be without one. He makes them for a number of applications as well as FCE. You can find out more about them and order them from http://www.neotrondesign.com.

To play a clip one frame at a time, tap the **Right** arrow key. To play it slowly, hold down the key. To play slowly backwards, hold down the **Left** arrow key. Pressing **K** and **L** together will give you slow forward, and **K** and **J** together, slow backwards. To go back to the previous edit—the cut prior to the point where you are currently—use the **Up** arrow key. To go to the next edit event, use the **Down** arrow key. To go to the beginning of the clip, press the **Home** key; to go to the end press the **End** key.

Table 1.1   Some Principal Keyboard Shortcuts

Play	L
Pause	K
Play backwards	J
Fast forward	Repeat L
Slow forward	L + K
Fast backwards	Repeat J
Slow backwards	J + K
Go to previous edit	Up Arrow
Go to next edit	Down Arrow
Go to beginning	Home
Go to end	End
Mark the In point	I
Mark the Out point	O
Go to In point	Shift-I
Go to Out point	Shift-O
Play Around Current Point	\
Play from In point to Out point	Shift-\
Match Frame	F
Mark Clip	X
Add Marker	M

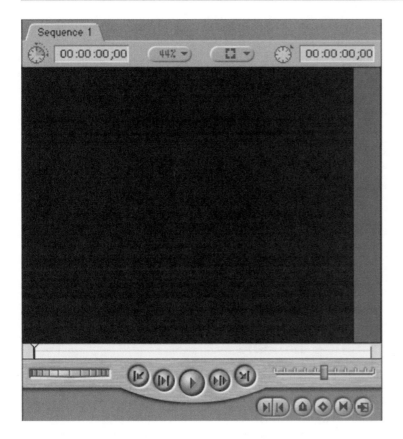

1.35 The Canvas Window

This is just the surface of the **Viewer**. We'll be visiting it again and again in the lessons to come, especially the tabbed windows behind the video window.

Exploring the Canvas

You'll probably first notice that the **Canvas** window (Figure 1.35) is similar to the **Viewer**.

Most controls are duplicated. Some have been placed in mirrored positions, such as the cluster in the lower right corner, which mirrors the cluster in the lower left of the **Viewer**. The **Shuttle** and the **Jog** are also in mirrored positions in **Canvas**, but they function the same.

The time displays at the top function the same as in the **Viewer**. The two popup menus in the top center are the same also.

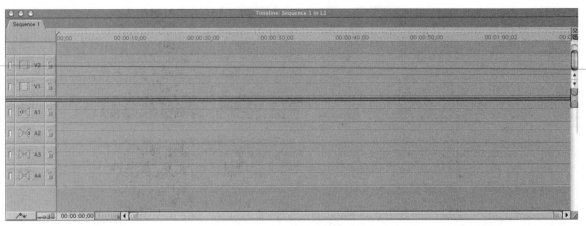

1.36 The Timeline Window

The **Canvas** is missing the **Recent** and **Generators** popups, but there are hidden features in the **Canvas** window that we'll look at in later lessons.

Timeline Window

Let's look at the **Timeline** window, which, being empty at this stage, isn't much to look at (Figure 1.36).

It's made up of tracks. Above the horizontal central double bar are the video tracks with the **Filmstrip** icon at the head. One of the icons will be yellow, indicating the targeted track. We'll talk about targeting more in later lessons. It's used to determine which tracks a piece of video or audio will be edited onto. FCE defaults to two video tracks visible, **V1** and **V2**. You can change this in **Preferences**, which we'll look at in the next lesson. An FCE sequence can have up to 99 tracks of video and 99 tracks of audio.

Table 1.2   Shortcuts

Viewer	Command-1
Canvas	Command-2
Timeline	Command-3
Browser	Command-4
Toggle between Viewer and Canvas	Q

Tip

Shortcuts: There are simple keyboard shortcuts to select each of FCE's windows. The principal windows are shown in Table 1.2.

Below the horizontal bar are the audio tracks with the **Loud-speaker** icons. There are four showing. **A1** and **A2** are targeted, awaiting a stereo pair of audio clips. **A3** and **A4** are ready for additional sound tracks. You can untarget a track by clicking the yellow icon. Retarget it by clicking it again. Most of the controls

1.37 Timeline Buttons

for the **Timeline** windows are along the bottom and the left edge of the window.

The two little buttons in the lower left corner of the **Timeline** window change the window display (Figure 1.37). The first from the left displays **Clip Overlays**, which allow you to adjust the clip's audio levels and video opacity. The button on the right sets the track height. There are four settings of track height. Choose whichever is comfortable for you and your monitor's resolution.

Next to these buttons is the **Current Time Display**. That's not the time on your watch; it's where you are in your sequence. Like all time displays in Final Cut Express, it's addressable. Click in it to type a new number, or add and subtract a value, just as you did in the **Viewer**. When you change the time in the current time display, the playhead immediately jumps to that time.

The slider next to the **Time Display** lets you change the horizontal scale at which your clips are displayed in the **Timeline** window. Drag the clip *Damine.mov* from the **Browser** into the **Timeline**. You don't have to be very precise, just drop it anywhere. It's a pretty long clip, so use the slider to adjust the scale of the **Timeline**.

The **Track Mover** tool lets you change the proportions of the video and audio panels, by moving the **Static Display Line** (Figure 1.38). This can also be split to show different sections of the video and audio panels simultaneously, which can be very useful when you're working with multiple tracks of video or audio. By pulling the tabs on the right edge, you can pull the **Static Display Line** apart (Figure 1.39). Much like word-processing software, this lets you keep a number of tracks displayed, while scrolling through the rest of the tracks independently.

In the upper right corner of the **Timeline** window are two tiny icons that tell you whether **Snapping** and **Linked Selection** are turned on (Figure 1.40).

If **Snapping** is on, the playhead, clips, and anything you move in the **Timeline** will want to butt up against each other as if they had magnetic attraction (Figure 1.40).

Turn on **Linked Selection** if you want the sound and the picture together when you grab a sync clip. With **Linked Selection** on,

1.38 Track Mover and Static Display Line Closed

1.39 Track Mover and Static Display Line Split

1.40 Left: Snapping and Linked Selection On
Right: Snapping and Linked Selection Off

they'll move in unison. With it off, the two elements can be moved separately. I recommend leaving **Linked Selection** on at all times, bypassing it only when necessary.

Summary

So ends Lesson 1. We've covered a lot of ground, made sure our system is properly set up, started up the software, and seen just the tip of the iceberg that lies under its deep waters. Spend some time clicking around in the Final Cut Express windows. You can't hurt anything. And remember to try the **Control** key to bring up shortcut menus.

In the next lesson you'll to learn how to set up your preferences and how to get your own material into the Final Cut Express edit suite.

Lesson 2

Getting Material into Final Cut Express

Digital video editing is divided into three phases:

- Getting your material into the computer
- Editing it, which is the fun part
- Getting it back out of your computer

This lesson is about the first part, getting your material into your computer. First you have to set up your application correctly. In Final Cut Express, as in most video editing programs, that means setting up your preferences—lots of preferences and choices for video and audio.

After setting preferences, we'll go into capturing your media. These fundamentals are absolutely necessary for Final Cut Express to function properly. Set it up right, get your material into your project properly, and you're halfway home. You cannot overestimate how important this is. Many preferences can be set in the Final Cut interface. In every OS X application, **Preferences** are now under the **ApplicationName** menu.

Setting Up a New Project

Let's begin by creating a new project.

1. Start by double-clicking the **Final Cut Express** icon in the *Applications* folder. Or better yet, if you've created a **Dock** alias for FCE, simply click on the icon in the **Dock**.

FCE will launch the last project that was open. If a previous project does open up, close the **Browser**, which will close the project.

2. Go up to **File>New>New Project** (**Command-E**).

Yes, it's **Command-E**, not the more customary **Command-N**, which is used to create a new sequence.

You get a new project called **Untitled Project** with the empty sequence in the **Browser** called *Sequence 1*.

Because FCE uses your project name to create folders inside designated folders such as the *Capture Scratch* folder, it's a good idea to give your project a name right away. At this stage you can't save the project because there's nothing to save. However, you can use **Save Project As** to save it with a name. FCE will use that name to create files in designated places on your hard drive.

3. Save the project inside your *Users* folder. FCE, like most OS X applications, defaults to saving in your *Documents* folder, which isn't a bad place to save your projects if you are the only one who needs to have access to them.

4. Go up to the **Final Cut Express** menu and select **Preferences** (**Option-Q**).

As soon as you open **Preferences**, you see the pane in Figure 2.1.

General Preferences

This is the **General Preferences** panel. In Final Cut Express, there are two separate places to set preferences:

- One for user preferences, which sets up how you want to work with the application
- Another specifically for audio/video preferences called **Easy Setup**, which deals with how you get your material in and out of your computer.

Preferences

General | Timeline Options | External Editors | Scratch Disks

Levels of Undo:	10 actions
List Recent Clips:	10 entries
Multi-Frame Trim Size:	5 frames
☑ Sync Adjust Movies Over:	5 minutes
Real-time Audio Mixing:	8 tracks
Audio Playback Quality:	Low

☑ Show ToolTips
☑ Warn if visibility change deletes render file
☑ Report dropped frames during playback
☑ Abort capture on dropped frames
☑ Abort capture on timecode break
☐ Prompt for settings on New Sequence
☑ Bring all windows to the front on activation

Still/Freeze Duration:	00:00:10:00
Preview Pre-roll:	00:00:05:00
Preview Post-roll:	00:00:02:00

☑ Autosave Vault

Save a copy every:	30 minutes
Keep at most:	40 copies per project
Maximum of:	25 projects

Thumbnail Cache (Disk):	8192 K
Thumbnail Cache (RAM):	512 K
RT Still Cache (RAM):	25 MB

Cancel   OK

2.1 General Preferences Panel

The **User Preferences** may seem daunting, made up of four tabbed windows, each full of potential booby traps. We'll work through it, starting with **General**, the first window. Fortunately, most of the items here can be left at their default setting.

Levels of Undo defaults to 10 actions, which seems to me a pretty good number. You can make the number of actions up to 32, but the higher you make it, the slower your system will get. The application will have to keep more stored in memory, making its performance sluggish. On a fast computer with plenty of RAM, I'd set it up to 32.

For **List of Recent Clips**, 10 seems like a good number also. This is the number of clips retained for the popup at the bottom of the Viewer (Figure 2.2). Again, a higher number means slower performance. The limit is 20.

Multi-Frame Trim Size sets the number of frames that slip in the **Trim** window. Five is the default. I prefer two. Pick what suits you. We'll look at items like multi-frame trimming in closer detail in later lessons.

Sync Adjust Movies Over allows you to let the application make sync adjustments for long DV clips. This was included in the original version of Final Cut Pro because of problems with early model Canon DV cameras, specifically the XL1, Eluras, and Opturas. It's still here in FCE because some cameras are still having similar problems, mainly that their sampling rates are not precisely 48,000 or 32,000 samples per second.

2.2 Recent Clips in Viewer Popup

It's almost impossible for a camera, a mechanical device, to be that precise. What's remarkable is that most DV cameras are extraordinarily accurate and will maintain sync for over an hour of play time down to a quarter of a frame. Still, the **Sync Adjust** is there, just in case. It defaults to being checked on with five minutes. It's probably best to leave this on. If you are having sync problems, you can switch it off and reimport your material. **Sync Adjust** only affects your clips on import, not on capture. With the cameras mentioned, you definitely must have it on. Switch it off if you are working with clips with timecode breaks. TC breaks will adversely affect the synchronization adjustment and will throw your material badly out of sync.

Real-time Audio Mixing determines how many tracks the application will try to play back in real time before it requires rendering. This is no guarantee that it will be able to do it, but it will try. The default is fine.

The default setting for the **Audio Playback Quality** popup menu is **Low**. It's fine to work in **Low**; it will allow a greater number of real-time tracks for playback. When you're outputting to tape, exporting, or doing an audio mixdown, these are automatically done at **High** quality. You don't need to reset this.

Still Image Duration sets the length of imported single-frame graphics and freeze frames made in FCE. You can change them once they're in FCE, but they'll appear at this length in the **Browser**. The default setting of 10 seconds seems long to me, so I set it to five seconds, a reasonable length for most stills or graphics from applications like Photoshop. Just type in the time you want. If you're doing training or other videos that require many full-screen graphics, leaving it at 10 seconds might be better for you. Though stills and freeze frames have a default duration of 10 seconds, they're actually two minutes and 10 seconds long when they're imported. The duration can be changed to any length you want. You have to set the maximum duration for the still inside the **Browser** before it is placed inside a sequence. After that, the still cannot be extended beyond its designated duration unless you use the **Fit to Fill** edit function, which we'll see in the next lesson. It can be made shorter, but not longer. There is also a sequence time limit of four hours that you cannot exceed.

In the previous lesson we talked about playing around the current time. If you hit the **Play Around** button or use the keyboard shortcut \, playback will begin a defined amount of time before the playhead and play for a defined amount of time past it. You define those times here. The default **Preview Pre-roll** is five seconds, a traditional pre-roll time for VTR machines. The default **Preview Post-roll** is two seconds. Five seconds for a pre-roll always feels long to me, so I set it down to two seconds. I leave the post-roll at two seconds. Play with it and see what feels right for you.

Thumbnail Cache (Disk) and **Thumbnail Cache (RAM)** values are relatively small. I'd keep at the default values of 8,192k and 512k, unless you like to work in the **Browser** with lots of bins in Icon view or like to keep thumbnails open in List view. If you do, you may want to raise these values from the default. Make sure you have extra RAM available. Some people make these numbers quite high, 30MB or more. I don't use icons much, so I leave it low.

RT Still Cache (RAM) will only be visible if you have a real-time capable machine. The default value of 25MB should be sufficient for most purposes. If you're working with very large still images at very high resolution you might want to raise this to 40 or 50MB, if you have available RAM.

On the right side of this window is a list of checkboxes. The default for the first five is checked on, and I leave them that way.

It's probably wise to leave **Abort capture on dropped frames** checked on. You may find that FCE is giving dropped frame warnings immediately when a capture begins. If this is happening, you might try switching this feature off and seeing if you can capture your material cleanly. Also, if it aborts 55 minutes into a one-hour capture, you've lost everything and have to start all over again.

The next setting is **Abort capture on timecode break**. This can be a bit of a nuisance. If you are having trouble capturing, you might want to switch off the two **Abort** settings. There have been instances where they have upset captures.

Prompt for Settings on New Sequence is self-explanatory. Leave it off once you've established your sequence presets.

Pen Tools Can Edit Locked Item Overlay should definitely be left off, I feel. It's easy enough to unlock a track to edit and then relock it, but making adjustments to locked tracks can be dangerous.

Bring all windows to the front on activation is useful. OS X has a feature that allows you to have windows from different applications in the foreground, overlapping each other. If this preference isn't checked on, if you're in another application and click on the **Timeline** to switch to FCE, only the **Timeline** window would come to the fore. Generally you don't want only one window, hence the need for this preference, which I would advise leaving on.

FCE has an *Autosave Vault.* Autosaving saves your project incrementally with a date-and-time stamp. This section in the lower right corner of the **General Preferences** panel is where you assign how often you want the project saved, how many copies to keep, and how many projects you want to be held. Saving a project to disk can take a moment or two. The larger the project gets, the greater the number of clips and sequences, and the longer the save will take. So interrupting your work flow by setting the **Save a copy** box too small might be counterproductive.

2.3 Restore Project Dialog

I find the default of 30 minutes a good number. You probably won't lose too much if the application does crash, plus you'll save a couple of days worth of work in the vault. If you make the save time to quick—say 10 minutes or less—you may want to increase the copies per project that's saved. The saved files can be called up from the *Autosave Vault* from the **File** menu by selecting **Restore Project.** You'll be given a dialog that offers you a list of time stamped copies of that project (Figure 2.4).

You can save up to 100 copies of each project, with a maximum of 100 projects. It works on a first-in/first-out basis. The oldest project saved is dumped into the **Trash** as new autosaves are added. Because it's not deleted from your hard drive, you can still retrieve an autosaved project from the **Trash** if you haven't emptied it.

2.4 Restore Project Warning

When you restore a project, the application first gives you the warning in Figure 2.4. The project then opens with its autosave vault name, something like *PrefsProject_01-29-03_0331*, which is the project name followed by a date and time stamp. After you restore a project I would recommend that you immediately do a **Save Project As** and revert to your old project name, replacing last saved project. Otherwise the *Autosave Vault* will start saving projects with the new date and time-stamped project name.

You can also use **Revert Project**, which as in other applications will take you back to the last saved state. Note that neither

Preferences

General | Timeline Options | External Editors | Scratch Disks

Default Number of Tracks:

Track Size: Medium

Thumbnail Display: Name Plus Thumbnail

2 Video   4 Audio

☐ Show Keyframe Overlays
☐ Show Audio Waveforms

Cancel   OK

2.5   Timeline Options Window

Restore nor **Revert** will bring back arrangements. These are in your preferences and will not be restored.

That's it for the first window of **Preferences,** the easy part. Open up the next tab, **Timeline Options** (Figure 2.5).

Timeline Options

Timeline Options is where you define your personal preferences for your sequence timeline layout. You can set:

- The track size
- The default number of tracks a new **Timeline** opens with
- The style the tracks are displayed in: **Name, Name Plus Thumbnail,** or **Filmstrip** (Figures 2.6–2.8).

🐾Note_____
Remember: Using **Filmstrip** will require considerably more system overhead and a larger **Thumbnail Cache** size.

| Dance1 | Dance2 | Dance3 | Stairs1 | Stairs2 | Temple1 | Temple2 |

2.6   Name Style

2.7   Name Plus Thumbnail Style

2.8   Filmstrip Style

Preferences

General Timeline Options External Editors Scratch Disks

External Editor Applications:

Still Image Files (Clear) (Set...) Jaguar/Applications/Adobe Photoshop 7/Adobe Photoshop 7

Video Files (Clear) (Set...) Jaguar/Applications/QuickTime Player

Audio Files (Clear) (Set...) Jaguar/Applications/Peak™ DV 3.0/Peak™ DV 3

(Cancel) (OK)

2.9   External Editors Tab

I leave the two checkboxes off (**Show Keyframe Overlays** and **Show Audio Waveforms**). They're more conveniently toggled on and off in the **Timeline** as needed.

All these settings in **Timeline Options** only affect any new sequences you create. Existing sequences will not be affected by these changes. To change the **Timeline Options** of an existing sequence you'll have to open the sequence and use **Sequence>Settings** (**Command-zero**) and change them there.

External Editors

Next in Final Cut Express' **Preferences** is the **External Editors** tab. Here you can define which applications are use to work on different types of files outside of FCE (Figure 2.9).

This allows you to launch an application to alter a clip in either the **Browser** or the **Timeline**. Select a clip and hold down the **Control** key for the shortcut menu choice **Open in Editor** (Figure 2.10).

Open 'Dance3'
Open in Editor
Duration (00:00:16:14)..
Properties...

2.10   Open in Editor

This will launch the application that you specify in this preferences panel. After you edit the clip—such as a still image in Photoshop—those changes will be reflected in FCE.

You can set **External Editors** for stills, video, and for audio. Be aware, though, that if you set the QuickTime Player as your editor for video files and choose **Peak DV** as your editor for audio files, then if you select **External Editor** for the audio portion of a sync sound clip, FCE will open the QuickTime Player, not Peak DV. FCE thinks of the audio track as part of a single video clip and so uses the QT Player. Single audio files, even if the creator type is QuickTime, will still open with the separate audio editor, such as Peak DV.

Scratch Disks

Next in the tabbed window is **Scratch Disks** (Figure 2.13). This is the most important of the four **Preferences** panels.

The *Waveform Cache*, the *Thumbnail Cache* and *Autosave Vault* all default to the drive or partition that you set when you first launched the application. These should all be set to the user's *Documents* folder, which is why you should accept the default location when you first start the application. These small files should not be on the media drive where they will cause drive fragmentation because they are constantly being dumped and rewritten.

Minimum Allowable Free Space On Scratch Disks defaults to 10MB. Many people feel that the hard drive will fragment heavily and slow down at this level. Some go so far as to say that you should leave 25% of your drive free. For large drives, this seems a bit excessive. I leave it at about 100MB and have not had problems. If you have a large single partition above 50GB, perhaps you could set this number to 1G.

Unless you have a particular reason, you should leave **Limit capture/export segment size to** unchecked. This feature limits the size of segments FCE can capture or export. There isn't any particular reason to limit it.

The **Limit Capture Now To** box makes it easier to use **Capture Now** by improving the application's performance. Without it, FCE would check the available hard drive space before it started **Capture Now**. This could take a long time while the application rummaged through your assigned drives. This box allows you to limit the amount of space FCE will search for. It will stop

Note

Changes in Photoshop: Sometimes changes made to a file in Photoshop, particularly to the layer structure and opacity, will cause the file to appear to be offline, bringing up the dialog in Figure 2.11. Select **Reconnect** and navigate to the PS file on your hard drive. If the dialog does not come up and the file still appears to be offline, select it in the **Browser**, and from the shortcut menu choose **Reconnect Media** (Figure 2.12). If that still doesn't work, just go back to the **Finder** and drag it back into your **Browser**.

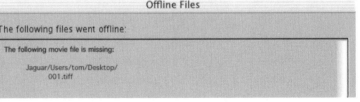

2.11 Reconnect Dialog

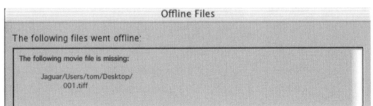

2.12 Shortcut Menu>Reconnect Media

2.13   Scratch Disks Preferences
        Panel

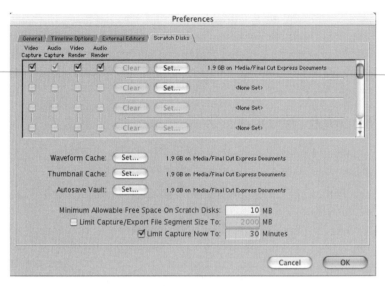

searching either when it runs out of drive space or reaches the limit you designate. The default is 30 minutes, or about 6G of file space at DV settings. FCE can search through this space quickly. If you're planning on capturing whole 60-minute tapes, you might want to uncheck this box.

Let's get back to the main body of the **Scratch Disks** window. Here you assign scratch disks for your captured material and for your render files. Normally you set your project's video, audio, and render files in the same location.

By default, FCE assigns separate render folders for audio and video. When you click the **Set** button, a navigation window allows you to select the location for these files. Usually I go to the drive I want to use for a project and select it (Figure 2.14).

Selecting the drive will create folders called *Capture Scratch*, *Render Files*, and *Audio Render Files* (Figure 2.15). The next time you want to set a scratch disk, do not select the *Capture Scratch*

NTSC vs. PAL

NTSC, which some wags say stands for Never Twice the Same Color, is actually the now-defunct National Television Standards Committee, which established the format used by television broadcasting in the United States. All of North America and Japan use this format as well. Europe and most of the rest of the world use PAL, for Phase Alternating Lines, which refers to the way color is handled. PAL uses a frame rate of 25fps. NTSC has a standard frame rate fixed at 29.97fps, not as many think a more manageable 30fps.

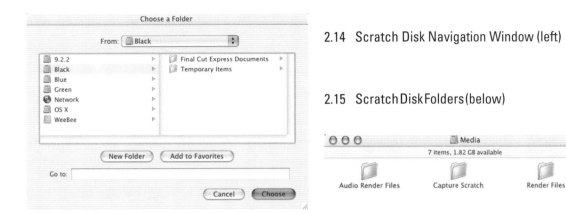

2.14   Scratch Disk Navigation Window (left)

2.15   Scratch Disk Folders (below)

folder; simply select the drive or partition. Selecting the folder rather than the drive will just make another *Capture Scratch* folder inside the current one. *Render Files* contains the video renders; *Audio,* the audio renders. As you capture your video material, it is stored in *Capture Scratch*.

If you have more than one hard drive or partition, you can set multiple locations in the **Scratch Disks Preferences** window. In FCE you can set up to 12 drives or partitions. The application automatically switches from one partition to another as they fill.

Easy Setup

From the **Final Cut Express** menu, select **Easy Setup,** or use the keyboard shortcut **Control-Q.** When you open **Easy Setup,** it brings up the panel in Figure 2.16.

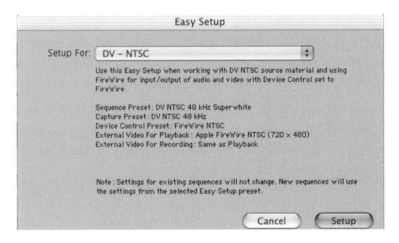

2.16   Easy Setup Panel

DV – NTSC
DV – NTSC 32 kHz – FW Basic
DV – NTSC 32 kHz Anamorphic
DV – NTSC 32 kHz FW Basic Anamorphic
DV – NTSC 32kHz
DV – NTSC 48 kHz – FW Basic
DV – NTSC 48 kHz Anamorphic
DV – NTSC 48 kHz FW Basic Anamorphic
DV – NTSC 48kHz – DV Converter
DV – PAL
DV – PAL 32 kHz
DV – PAL 32 kHz – FW Basic
DV – PAL 32 kHz Anamorphic
DV – PAL 32 kHz FW Basic Anamorphic
DV – PAL 48 kHz – FW Basic
DV – PAL 48 kHz Anamorphic
DV – PAL 48 kHz FW Basic Anamorphic
DV – PAL 48KHz – DV Converter

2.17   Easy Setup Popup

Note the description in the panel for the default setting of **DV NTSC**, based on standard DV with an audio sampling rate of 48kHz. From the popup you can select any of the 18 setups available, nine for NTSC and nine for PAL (Figure 2.17).

The trick to **Easy Setup** is to base it on the specifications used in your camera. If you're working with an audio sampling rate of 32kHz, choose one of those presets. If you work in **Anamorphic**, sometimes called widescreen or 16:9, choose one of those settings. If your camera or deck needs to use **FireWire Basic** instead of the standard **FireWire**, choose that. Check the Apple Final Cut Express web site's qualification page at http://www.apple.com/finalcutexpress/qualification.html.

Generally Canon and Panasonic cameras need FireWire Basic while Sony devices work with standard FireWire, also called iLink and IEEE1394. You should check with your camcorder manual to see its specifications. If you are using a DV convertor box to capture from analog material, choose one of the **DV Convertor** options. This is for use with a noncontrollable device, a device that will not provide the machine with any timecode, which is what it's looking for when it captures DV material.

What is anamorphic anyway?

Anamorphic is a 16:9 widescreen video. Though they have not caught on much yet in the United States, widescreen televisions are fairly common throughout Japan. Consequently, Japanese manufacturers have added this capability to many DV camcorders. The camera squeezes the pixels anamorphically (so that everything looks squashed, as if it's tall and narrow) to fit into a 4:3 frame and then unsqueezes them for playback on a widescreen TV.

The problem is that many people want to do 16:9 but don't have the equipment to do it properly. To monitor it, you need a widescreen monitor or one can switch between 4:3 and 16:9. FCE will output the correct 16:9 display if the presets are correct, but you won't see it correctly without the right monitor. You will not see a letterboxed version. Some fairly expensive decks will take a 16:9 image and output it as letterboxed 4:3. You can also place your 16:9 material in a 4:3 sequence and force it to render out the whole piece. You'll then have letterboxed 4:3.

Most DV camcorders will flag 16:9 material as such. They will read this regardless of whether you use the 16:9 setup. If you are shooting true 16:9 with an anamorphic lens, the correct setup will force FCE to treat it as widescreen material, even though it doesn't get the DV flag from the camera. So be careful. Don't select **Anamorphic** when your material is not 16:9, though it can be undone in the clip's **Item Properties** panel.

![Sequence Settings panel]

2.18 Sequence Settings Panel

The settings you choose here are for both your capturing and your sequences. The two need to match. Be careful that you don't use one setting to capture and then later change the settings for other material. Any sequences you create after changing the settings will reflect the new settings and will not work properly with material captured using the original settings.

Sequence Settings

Sequences use the same settings as those created for capturing. There may be instances in which you want to change the sequence settings, for instance, if you want to create a letterbox output for material that was captured in anamorphic.

To do this, create a new sequence (**Command-N**) and open it. With the **Timeline** window active, select the menu **Sequence>Settings,** or use the keyboard shortcut **Command-0** (zero). This will bring up the panel in Figure 2.18. It looks very much like the **Timeline Options** panel we saw in **Preferences,** except for the button in the lower left corner marked **Load Presets.** This will bring up a familiar-looking list of eight presets, four for NTSC and four for PAL (Figure 2.19). The list is shorter than the **Easy Setup** popup because there are no options for FireWire capture at this stage.

Capture

So now you've set up your preferences, and you're ready to get your video material into your computer. To begin, go to

☞ Tip_____

Mixing Settings: Do not try to mix settings. If you shot your video in 32kHz, do not think that by capturing in 48kHz your material will become 48kHz. All that will happen will be that your audio is liable to drift out of sync.

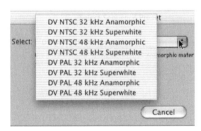

2.19 Sequence Presets

Preferences Folder

If you have problems with FCE, one of the first remedies anyone will suggest is to trash your *Preferences* file. If there is a problem with your system, it's often your preferences that are corrupt. It's easy enough to back up the prefs file. Go into your *User Home* folder, **Command-Option-H** from the **Finder**. Go to your *Library*, choose *Preferences*, and find the folder called *Final Cut User Data* (Figure 2.20).

2.20 Final Cut Express User Data Folders

Custom Settings   Final Cut Express 1.0 Prefs   Final Cut Express MOA Cache   Plugins

Inside you can find four items, including two folders, *Custom Settings* and *Plugins*.

The other items should be your *Final Cut Express 1.0 Prefs* and *Final Cut Express MOA Cache*. If you do need to trash your preferences, the only files you should remove are *Express 1.0 Prefs* and *Final Cut MOA Cache*. You should also delete the *com.apple.finalcutexpress.plist* file from the *Preferences* folder. It's a good idea to back up the two files in the *Final Cut Express User Data* folder.

With these backed up and safe, whenever you do need to trash your preferences, simply replace them with your saved set. Do this with the application closed.

File>Capture (Command-8). This brings up the **Capture** window (Figure 2.21).

The window is divided in two. On the left is a **Viewer** like the standard FCE **Viewer,** but this is a viewer for your tape deck or camera. The control buttons—**J, K, L, I,** and **O** keys and spacebar—work exactly the same as in the FCE **Viewer** except that they control your deck through the FireWire cable.

2.21 Capture Window

The **Timecode** in the upper right of the **Viewer** portion of the **Capture** window is your current timecode on your tape, and the **Duration** on the upper left is the duration you set with your In and Out points as you mark the tape (Figure 2.22). Notice the displays at the top of the window that tell you how much available drive space you have on the designated scratch disk and how many minutes of video you can store on it.

In addition to your keyboard shortcuts for **Mark In** and **Mark Out**, you also have buttons and timecode displays at the bottom of the viewer for these functions (Figure 2.23).

The two inner buttons mark the In and Out points, **In** on the left, **Out** on the right. The timecode on the left is the In point, and the timecode on the right is the Out point. Of the buttons on the far outside, the left one will take the tape deck to the assigned In point, and the far right one to the assigned Out point.

On the right of the **Capture Viewer** window is **Logging** window (Figure 2.24).

At the top of the **Logging** window is the Logging Bin name (Figure 2.25). The button on the far right will add a bin to the **Browser** and designate it the logging bin. Clicking the button again will add a new bin inside the previously designated bin. Using the button to the left, right next to name, will take the logging bin up one level. If you click it enough times it will go right up to the **Browser** level. There is however no button to take you back down through the hierarchy. Making a Logging Bin means that any captured material will be added directly to that designated bin. The bin appears in the **Browser** with the icon in Figure 2.26 or in List view with the icon in Figure 2.27.

You can also select a Logging Bin directly in the **Browser** with a shortcut menu. **Control**-click on a bin, and from the shortcut menu choose **Set Logging Bin** (Figure 2.28).

☞ Tip

Capture Size: The size of the Capture window is determined by your window arrangement. If you want a large display for the Capture window, set your arrangement to **Standard** before you start up Capture. If you want a smaller screen on your computer monitor, set the arrangement to **Wide** before you launch the capture window.

2.22 Time Displays in the Capture Window

2.23 Capture Window Controls

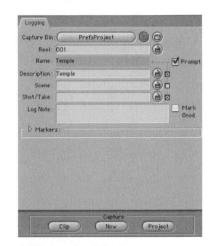

2.24 Logging Window

2.25 Logging Bin Name

2.26   Logging Bin Icon

2.27   Logging Bin Icon in List View

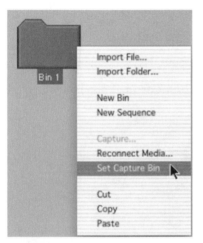

2.28   Set Logging Bin in Shortcut
Menu

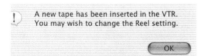

2.29   Reel Change Warning

2.30   Reel Number Entry

One critical piece of information in the **Logging** panel is the **Reel** name or number. It is extremely important that reel numbers be properly assigned. Each reel should have a separate number. The number should be written on the tape, and that number should be put in the **Logging** window. This number is actually attached to the QuickTime file when it's captured and is important for FCE being able to recapture material should you ever need to. This is so important that when the application is in Capture mode, it will autodetect that the reel in your camera or deck has been ejected and a new reel inserted and will put up the warning message in Figure 2.29.

The reel number can be entered in the panel in Figure 2.30. The little clapperboard to the right can be clicked to increment the number.

In the **Logging** window you can enter information about your clips before you capture them. You can give them names based on **Description**, **Scene** and **Shot/Take** number, or other entry. You probably want to keep these as short as you can. They can be combined through the **Prompt** checkboxes, next to the tiny clapperboard icons, into creating a name for the clip (Figure 2.31). You can't actually enter a name for the clip in the **Name** area of the **Logging** window.

Below the **Naming** portion of the window is a box that you can twirl open with a disclosure triangle. This box allows you to add and name markers (Figure 2.32). We'll look at markers more closely in later lessons, but here markers are a way of letting you add more information about a clip, keyed to a specific point somewhere inside the material. Once the clip has been captured, markers will appear as pink ticks in the **Timeline**. They can also be accessed from the **Browser**, as we'll see in the next lesson.

Strategies for Capturing

There are basically three strategies for capturing DV material, and you choose the one you want to use with the buttons at the bottom of the **Logging** window (Figure 2.33). The options you have are:

- Now
- Clip
- Project

Capture Now

This is the simplest way to work, but it gives you least control. It also requires that your material is properly shot without timecode breaks. These can cause havoc with any capture, particularly a **Now** capture.

Capturing large chunks of video with **Now** is a common work strategy. To use **Now,** you simply put the deck in play and click the **Now** button. A **Capture** screen comes up and begins recording as soon as it's checked your drives and found a video signal from your camera or deck.

If you are working with a noncontrollable device using the **DV Convertor** preset, **Now** is the only capture choice available to you. I would recommend that, if at all possible, you dub your analog material to DV tape and then use the tape—properly reel numbered, of course—as your master. Dubbing allows you to easily access the material again if you ever need to recapture.

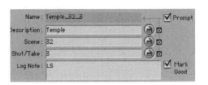

2.31 Naming Prompts

2.32 Marker Window

FCE records the clip on your designated scratch disk until one of four events occur:

- It runs out of hard drive space.
- It hits your preference time limit.
- It aborts because of timecode break or dropped frames as set in your preferences.
- You hit the **Escape** key and stop the process.

If the capture stops because of the time limit, the deck also stops. The message in Figure 2.34 appears on the computer screen.

After your capture is complete, the video appears as a clip called *Untitled 0000* inside the **Browser** or designated logging bin (Figure 2.35), unless you named the clip prior to capturing. Whenever a clip is captured, it is saved inside the *Capture Scratch* folder on the drive you selected in your **Preferences**. Inside *Capture Scratch* there will be a folder with the project's name, one folder for each project.

Inside that folder is where your captured material is stored. Your clip will be in that project's folder with the same name *Untitled 0000*, or the name you gave it. It's probably a good idea to name

2.33 Capture Buttons

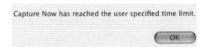

2.34 Capture Now Time Limit Message

2.35 Untitled Clip in Browser

2.36 Named Clip in Browser

✎ Note_____

Monitoring: When capturing, audio should be monitored through external speakers connected to the camcorder or deck you're playing back from. You will not be able to hear the sound through the computer's speaker during logging or capturing. See the section on "Monitors" and "Speakers" in the previous lesson on pages 4 and 5.

2.37 Clip Naming Window

the clip before you hit the **Now** button, then it will appear in the **Browser** and in your *Capture Scratch* folder with the name you assigned (Figure 2.36). If you capture a clip using **Now** and you decide you don't want to use it, you'll have to go into your *Capture Scratch* folder, dig it out, and throw it into the **Trash** to get it off your hard drive and retrieve that drive space.

Using **Capture Now**, you can bring all your video material into your computer for editing into smaller subclips rather than using your deck to select clips.

FCE has a wonderful tool for those working in DV with the **Capture Now** option. This is the ability to automatically mark up shot changes with **DV Start/Stop Shot Detection**. We'll look at it on page 67 in Lesson 3.

Clip

Another option in the **Capture** window is the **Clip** button. This requires that you enter **In** and **Out** points for where you want the capture to begin and where it should end. Using the **Clip** method you mark up the section of video you want to capture and then press the **Clip** button. This is a controlled form of **Capture Now**.

1. Mark an In point near the beginning of the reel and then an Out point near the end.

2. Click **Clip** and you will get a dialog box asking to confirm the name (Figure 2.37). If you didn't name the clip in the **Logging** window, you'll have to enter one now. Notice the little clapperboard to the right of the name box. This lets you increment the name numerically.

3. Click the **OK** button and let the deck and the computer do its thing.

4. If you enter a clip name that already exists in the project's scratch folder, you'll get the dialog box in Figure 2.38 asking you to rename the clip, skip capture, or abort it.

If the clip is not active in your project, or mistakenly got captured into the scratch folder, you'll also get an option to **Overwrite** the existing clip.

You will first get a large black window at first and at the bottom information about what's happening, such as in Figure 2.39, which shows that the deck is cueing, the clip that's being captured, the duration and how much more to capture off that reel.

When capture begins, you'll see the image in the **Capture** window and the display in the bottom will change to the **Now Capturing** message in Figure 2.40, which gives the clip and duration.

Do not be dismayed that the quality of the video in the **Capture** window seems poor and stuttering. A computer monitor cannot display a full-screen interlaced image with full motion at full resolution during capture.

Once the clip is captured, it will appear in its own **Viewer** (Figure 2.41), and the **Clip** icon will be seen in the **Browser** (Figure 2.42). It's already saved in your *Capture Scratch* folder.

5. Just close the **Viewer** and you're ready to capture your next clip.

After you've captured your material, you are ready to edit. Close the **Capture** window before you start, however. You should not try to play video while **Capture** is open. So shut it down before you begin editing.

Once you've captured your material, you'll notice that it appears in the **Browser** in List view as a clip with a duration but with no In or Out points defined. **Capture** only sets the media limit, and FCE assumes you will want to edit the material further, so no In or Out points are designated. The clip has the *de facto* In and Out points marked by the limits of the media; they're simply not displayed in the **Browser** in the **In** and **Out** columns.

Project Capture

Project capture is designed to let you recapture material for old projects to reconstruct them. To do this, reopen the project. If the material is not available, you will get the **Reconnect** dialog box we saw at the beginning of the previous lesson (Figure 2.43). Click the **OK** button and let the project open.

All the media will probably appear offline, with the **Browser** displaying clips with red slash marks through them (Figure 2.44) and the words *Media Offline* across a glaringly red **Canvas** (Figure 2.45).

You could at this point simply evoke the **Capture** window and press the **Project** button. This will bring up the dialog box in Figure 2.46.

2.38 Duplicate Clip Name Warning

2.39 Cueing Source Material

2.40 Now Capturing

2.41 Clip Viewer

2.42 Clip in Browser

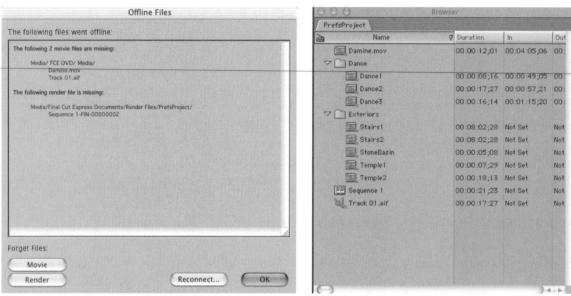

2.43 Reconnect Window

2.44 Browser with Offline Clips

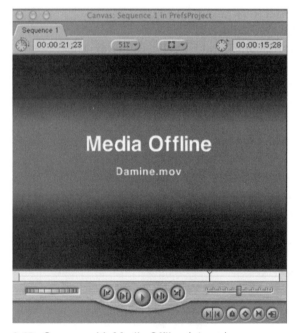

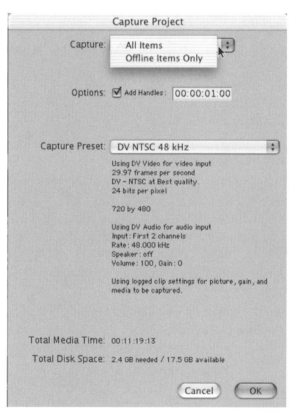

2.45 Canvas with Media Offline (above)

2.46 Capture Project Window (right)

```
                    Insert Reel
001 – 00:02:32:04 – 5 clips – READY
002 – 00:04:42:24 – 2 clips – READY
003 – 00:01:19:09 – 3 clips – READY
005 – 00:02:11:07 – 6 clips – READY




Ready for capture.

 Show Details...              Cancel    Continue
```

2.47 Insert Reel Window

Normally the popup at the top would only display **All Items,** but should some of the clips be available to you while others are offline, then you'll get the choice of either picking **All Items** or **Offline Items Only.**

Notice the box that allows you to **Add Handles.** This will set the computer to capture a designated amount of material beyond the In and Out points defined in your clips. You can select any of the available **Capture Presets,** and the window will display what your selected settings are. At the bottom you get an indication of the hard drive requirements for **Total Media Time** and **Total Disk Space.** Check that you have enough drive space for the capture. Also look closely at the media time to make sure it looks about right, that you're capturing all the media you need but not too much.

When you click **OK,** you'll get a window telling you what tapes will be required for the project capture and how much will be captured off each tape (Figure 2.47). Load the first reel and click **Continue.** FCE will prompt you whenever a reel change is required.

If you capture with handles, the clips will come into the **Browser** with your designated In and Out points marked already, not the usual **Not Set** indication, and if you open the clip into the **Viewer,** you'll see that there is the extra media beyond the marked In and Out points.

It's important to understand the way project capture works. It works best if you've captured your material using the Clip method—that is, selected the portions of the video you want to use, and captured them as separate clips. After you've edited your project, and you want to rebuild it at a later date, reopen your project file. Delete everything except the sequence or clips you want to recapture, start up the **Capture** window, and click the **Project** button. The application will now only recapture those clips that it needs to reconstitute your sequence. It will not capture any of the clips that you didn't use and that you deleted from your project.

If you captured whole reels of tape or in large chunks, FCE will want to recapture all the pieces that use even a very small portion of your clips. So if you originally captured a 60-minute reel, and use only 10 seconds of it, the application will still want to capture the entire 60 minutes just to get that 10 seconds you need to reconstitute your sequence.

Recapturing only works on the DV material for your project. When a project is complete, you should separately back up imported audio and graphics files. You should also be aware that tracks recorded using the **Voice Over** tool are not recapturable as they have no useful timecode. It's a good idea to build an **Import** bin that contains audio files, still images, graphics files, as well as your voice over tracks. The **Source** column will let you find the file path to where the media like stills and voice overs are stored. These should be backed up separately if you want to recreate the project at a later time. It may be simplest to burn this data material onto a CD or DVD for storage.

Summary

With these two lessons, you have just about completed step one of the three steps of digital nonlinear editing. You have set up your system, moved your video material from the recording medium into the computer, imported some material—music or still images, perhaps—captured other material, maybe consolidated your video. Having all the elements you need in your computer, you're now ready to begin the second part: editing, the fun part.

Timecode Breaks

Timecode breaks or control track breaks have been the bane of video editors since tape machines were invented. Many editors have cursed many a cameraperson for failing to keep good TC on the tapes. This cursing has not stopped with the widespread use of nonlinear editing systems. Tapes are still being brought into edit rooms with breaks or discontinuities in timecode. These days, most consumer and pro-sumer cameras are designed to generate frame-accurate timecode, and that's the way tape should be delivered. FireWire uses the TC recorded on tape when the video was shot to find your clips and control the deck during capture. This timecode information is passed on to the application and remains with the clip throughout the editing process. It's important to understand what happens in the camera while you're shooting.

There are a number of ways to ensure that there are no breaks in your DV TC. The simplest way, which I recommend for beginners and students in particular, is to prestripe your tapes, that is, record black and timecode on your tape before you shoot. You can do this in any camera or VCR: put the device in VCR mode and press the record button. With some cameras you might have to do it in camera mode; just put a lens cap on it or point it at a wall. Now whenever you shoot, your tape will have TC written on it. The camera will then read the TC and start writing from whatever it reads. No breaks.

If you don't want to prestripe the tape, you then just have to be careful when you shoot. After you shut off the camera to change batteries or play back your tape to review what you shot, for instance, not sim-ply stop it after a shot, it's a good idea to back up the tape just a second to get back into the area of time-coded material. This is why it's always a good idea when shooting to let the camera run for a few moments after the action you're shooting is complete, before you stop the recording. That way you will have that moment or two of unnecessary material to back up into.

Any timecode break is liable to cause a sudden loss of AV sync when you capture across it. So if you do have a tape with TC breaks in it, one of the simplest ways to get around the problem is to dub the tape. By dubbing it from one deck or one camera to another, the video and audio portion of the tape is actually cloned exactly as it was on the original, while at the same time, the recording deck is creating new, unbroken timecode.

Aside from shooting carefully, or prestriping the tape, another way around the problem is to use the **Clip** to capture material between the timecode breaks. You can also log your clips, changing the reel name with each timecode break.

Lesson 3

Cutting Up Those Shots

There is no right way to edit a scene or a sequence or even a whole film or video; there are only bad ways, good ways, and better ways. Final Cut Express has a number of different ways, usually three or four, to do most of the editing functions. You can edit directly in the **Timeline** with the mouse, in the **Viewer** with buttons or shortcuts, and for precision in the **Trim Edit** window with various tools, buttons, and shortcuts.

In this lesson we're going to look at some video and edit it. I'm going to give you a number of different ways of working with it and a few different ways to cut it up—I call them Slice and Dice.

Loading the Lesson

1. Start by loading the DVD that came with this book into your DVD drive. Open the DVD.

This is a hybrid DVD and will probably start up your DVD player when you mount the disk, but if you double-click on the DVD itself you will find a folder called *FCE DVD-ROM Contents*. Inside that folder are a number of other folders. You'll see two folders, one called *Media* and another called *Projects*. Inside

Media is a QuickTime file and other material, and inside *Projects* are numbered lesson folders.

2.   To start, if you have not already done so, drag the folder called *Media* onto your media drive.

This may take a while. It contains the video material used in this book. When you begin any lesson that needs material from the DVD, first you should drag the *Media* folder onto your computer's media drive. The DV clips included there will play much better and more smoothly from your high-speed drive than from any DVD drive.

3.   When that's finished, drag the folder *Lesson 3* from the *Projects* folder on the DVD onto the system hard drive of your computer. You should probably place it in the *Shared* folder inside your system's *Users* folder or in the your *Documents* folder.

4.   Eject the DVD from the drive.

5.   Open the *Lesson 3* folder now on your system hard drive.

Inside you'll find two FCE project files called *L3 and L3a*.

6.   Open *L3* by double-clicking it, which will launch the Final Cut Express application.

The project is empty except for one sequence that is also blank.

Setting the Scratch Disk

Before you do anything else, check your scratch disk. It a good practice when you're starting a new project or opening a project you haven't worked on in a while to assign the *Scratch Disk* and the *Autosave Vault*.

1.   Go to the **Final Cut Express** menu. Select **Preferences** (**Option-Q**) and click on the **Scratch Disks** tab (Figure 3.1).

2.   To set the scratch disk, click on the top **Set** button and select to your media hard drive as the *Scratch Disk*.

Selecting the media drive for your scratch disk will create inside it folders called *Audio Renders Files*, *Capture Scratch*, and *Render Files*.

Importing the Movie

1.   Use **File>Import** (**Command-I**) to import the *Damine.mov* file from the folder inside the *Media* folder on your hard drive.

3.1   Scratch Disks Preferences

Or you can drag the clip directly from the *Media* folder into your **Browser.**

2. After it's imported, double-click the *Damine.mov* in your **Browser** to open it in a **Viewer.**

You'll notice in the upper left corner the duration of the clip shows 8:02;28. This is the material we're going to cut up in these lessons. This is the master clip.

Slice and Dice

We have basically two strategies for cutting up a long stretch of video such as this, which might be from the capture of a reel of tape.

1. The first is to create short clips while leaving the whole material intact in each clip. I call this the Slice method.

2. The second is to make subclips, which divide the master clip into shorter sections, each only the length of the selection. We'll call this the Dice or Subclip method.

They both have advantages and disadvantages. It's important to understand the distinction between different types of clips:

- The source media is the actual digital material on your hard drive. The master clip, *Damine.mov* in this case, is the clip in your **Browser** that points directly to the media on your hard drive. It contains every frame of the source media. Figure 3.2 shows the master clip opened into the **Viewer**. Notice the duration in the upper left.

- A sliced clip is the same as the master clip it's taken from, except that a start point and an end point are defined for a particular shot. Figure 3.3 shows a sliced clip in the **Viewer**. Notice that only a small piece of the clip is defined in the **Scrubber Bar**. The duration is now only about $18^1/2$ seconds.

- In a diced clip, not only are the start and end points defined, but also the media that the clip can use is limited. The clip does not have all the media available that's in the original. Figure 3.4 shows the same clip made into a sub-clip. Again, the duration is just that of the single shot.

We'll look at this more closely later in the lesson on page 65, but first let's start with slicing.

Slice 1

Let's look at one of the three methods of slicing up your material.

1. Make a new bin in the **Browser** from the **File** menu: **File> New>Bin**, or more easily with the keyboard command **Com-mand-B**.

2. Name the new bin **Clips**.

3. Now double-click *Damine.mov* to open it in the **Viewer**.

In this method, you can work either in the **Viewer** or in the **Time-line**. We'll start in the **Viewer** by looking at the material, selecting the pieces we want, and marking them with In and Out points.

4. Play the clip in the **Viewer** and stop when you get to the shot of a stone water basin with a bronze dragon's head spout. (It's the third shot in, at 17;15.)

5. Use the **Left** and **Right** arrow keys to find the first frame of this shot and press **I** to mark the In point.

6. Play the clip and find the end of that shot. It's fairly short, about five seconds.

7. When you've found the end, press **O** for Out point. After you set the Out point, the duration in the upper left of the **Viewer** should 5:08.

8. Grab the picture in the **Viewer**, drag it into the **Browser**, and drop it on the **Clips** bin.

Edit Points

A note on the place where edit points occur. The shot change between edits actually takes place between the frames. That is, you see one frame, and the next frame you see is the first frame of a different shot. So when you're marking In and Out points, you should know where the shot change is actually taking place. If you mark the In point for a frame that you're looking at in the **Viewer**, that will be the first frame of the new clip. The edit will take place in the space before that frame. If you mark the frame you're looking at as an Out point, that will be the last frame in the clip, and the edit will take place after that frame.

3.2   Master Clip Opened in Viewer

3.3   Sliced Clip in Viewer (upper right)

3.4   Subclip in Viewer

You've now made a new clip in the **Browser.** You need to rename this clip something appropriate.

9. Twirl open **Clips** if you're in List view, or double-click it to open the bin into its own window.

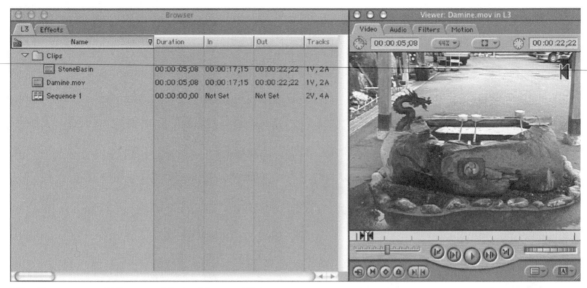

3.5   Browser and Viewer with the Master Clip

10. Double-click on the name *Damine.mov*, which will highlight it and open a renaming box. Type in a new name, *StoneBasin*.

At this stage the **Browser** in List view and the **Viewer** should look something like Figure 3.5. I am using the **Window** arrangement called **Wide**.

✎ Note_____

Renaming Clips: You can rename your clips anything you want, move them around to various bins, place bins within bins, and arrange your material any way you like, but be aware that the underlying media that remains on your hard drive is unchanged in any way. Most importantly, its name is not changed. So if you ever need to reconnect the media or recapture it, FCE will always want to do it under its original naming convention and not change it to anything you do in the **Browser**.

Let's push on.

1. Double-click again on *Damine.mov* in the **Browser**.

You'll notice it still has In and Out points marked into **Viewer**, those points you marked for the clip that became *StoneBasin*.

2. Hit **Shift-O**, which, if you're not already there, will take you to the Out point you marked for *StoneBasin*.

3. As we just did with the shot *StoneBasin*, use the technique of marking In and Out points to cut out a few more shots from *Damine.mov*.

4. As you mark them, drag each into the **Clips** bin, naming the clip appropriately.

Now you're building up a collection of shots that you can edit together in any order you want. This is the first Slice method in the **Viewer.**

Slice 2

The second Slice method is in the **Timeline.** This is where you really are slicing with a digital razor blade.

1. First open *Damine.mov* from the **Browser** into the **Viewer.**

It will probably have an In and Out point marked. We need to clear those.

2. **Control**-click on the **Scrubber Bar** at the bottom of the **Viewer** to evoke a shortcut menu.

3. Select **Clear In and Out.** This will—surprise, surprise—clear the In and Out points (Figure 3.6).

4. If it's not already open, open the empty **Timeline** by double-clicking on *Sequence 1* in the **Browser.**

5. Drag *Damine.mov* into it, dropping the clip on **V1.**

When you place a clip in the **Timeline,** the playhead automatically jumps to the end of the clip, ready for you to place another clip in position. In this case, we don't want to do that.

6. Click in the **Timeline** window to make it active (or use **Command-3**), and then press the **Home** key to take you back to the beginning of the **Timeline.**

7. Press the spacebar to play *Damine.mov.* The video plays in the **Canvas.**

8. Again use the spacebar to stop and the **Left** and **Right** arrow keys to find the start of the shot of the stone basin.

9. Make sure **Snapping** is turned on. Check the indicator in the upper right corner of the **Timeline** window. We saw this at the section on the **Timeline** in Lesson 1 on page 29. Toggle it on and off with the **N** key.

✎ *Tip*
Clearing from the Browser: If you've opened a clip from the **Browser** and want to clear its In and Out points, you can use the keyboard shortcut **Option-X.** You can use this way to clear In and Out points in the **Timeline** also. You can't, however, clear the In and Out from a clip that's been opened from the **Timeline.**

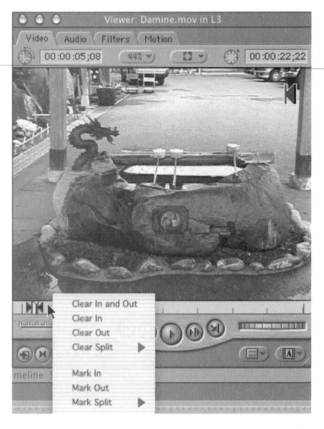

3.6 Viewer Scrubber Bar Shortcut Menu (left)

3.7 Blade Tool in the Timeline (below)

✎ Tip
Keyboard Shortcut: In addition to using the **Blade** tool, you can simply move the playhead to where you want to make the cut and hit the keyboard shortcut **Control-V.** This will cut the clip right at the playhead.

10. Select the **Blade** tool from the **Tools** palette and move it along the **Timeline** to the **Playhead** line. As you move along the clip in the **Timeline,** your cursor will show the **Blade** tool, rather than the **Selector** (Figure 3.7). Notice the dark triangles at the top and bottom of the playhead line indicating that the cursor is at the playhead.

11. Click with the **Blade** tool to cut the clip at the playhead.

This will cut the video and audio on the clip as though you were cutting it with a knife or a razor blade, which is what used to be used to cut film and audio tape, and even videotape when it was first edited. What you are doing is the digital metaphor for the same process.

12. Go to the end of the shot, using the **Left** and **Right Arrow** keys to find the first fame of the next shot.

13. Click the **Blade** tool again or use the keyboard shortcut **Control-V.**

Let's make a second bin for these clips.

1. Click in the **Browser** to make it active or use **Command-4**.

2. Use **Command-B** to create a new bin and name the bin **New-Clips**.

3. Grab the cut clip from the **Timeline** and drag it into **New-Clips**. Again rename the clip *StoneBasin*.

4. In the **Timeline** window, click on the piece that you've cut from the master clip. This will highlight the edited section.

5. Press **Delete**. This will remove the clip from the timeline, but it will also leave a gap in the timeline. So let's undo that using **Command-Z**. If you ever need to redo, use **Command-Y**.

The undo will make the shot reappear in the hole in the timeline. Instead of simply deleting it, we will do what's called a *ripple delete*.

1. Select the clip, hold down the **Shift** key, and hit **Delete**.

In addition to removing the clip, the ripple delete also pulls up all the other material in *Damine.mov*, shortening the timeline.

2. Use the spacebar and the arrow keys to find some more shots. With **Control-V** or the **Blade** tool, cut up the material and drag the shots into the **NewClips** bin. Continue to use ripple delete to remove material as you move it into the bin in the **Browser**.

Immediately after the stone basin clip, you'll find a shot of a temple. The shot begins looking toward a canopied bell in the foreground with a stand of pines and late afternoon sun shining through them. The shot then pans right from the trees to the temple. The camera is set to auto-iris, and as the shot pans, it darkens so that the temple is hardly visible. Immediately afterwards, the shot repeats itself, this time properly exposed.

3. Select the darker, poorer shot, and cut it up with the keyboard shortcuts. Now instead of dragging it into the **New-Clips** bin to be saved, ripple delete it to remove it from the sequence.

Working like this, you can quickly cut material into shots. You can use this process to weed out the bad shots, removing the chaff from the wheat, as it were.

Edit Points Redux

We talked about where the cut takes place when you're editing, that the In point cuts the space before the frame you're looking at, and the Out point cuts after the frame you're looking at. The **Razor Blade** always cuts on the gap in front of the frame you're seeing in the **Canvas**. So to get the last frame of *StoneBasin* in the Slice method, you have to be looking at the first frame of the shot after it. If you do **Control-V** on the last frame of the basin shot, the next shot will have one frame of the stone basin at its head.

👉 *Tip*

Switching Cursors: The letter **B** will call up the **Blade** tool. The letter **A** is the shortcut that will return you to the **Selection** tool. (Think *A* for arrow.) Of course, with the cursor in **Blade** mode, you cannot select a clip. Trying to select a clip will cut it. So to do ripple deletes, you would need to switch back and forth between the **Blade** and the **Selector.** You can do this quickly using **A** and **B**. Or you can leave your cursor in **Blade** mode, and instead of clicking to select a clip, hold down the **Control** key when the cursor is above the clip you want to remove. Holding down the **Control** key will change the cursor from the **Blade** to the shortcut menu. Mousing down will open the menu, and from the menu you can select the function **Ripple Delete**. Neat, isn't it?

Slice 3

With the Slice 2 method, you're cutting the pieces you want to keep and moving them into the **Browser.** Let's look at another method that works almost exclusively in the **Timeline.** Here we'll simply cut away the pieces we don't want to use and leave behind in the **Timeline** the shots that contain the good material.

1. Undo your ripple delete of the dark shot.

2. Undo the edit at the end of the shot. Use **Command-Z** as many times as necessary to get back to where the dark shot is still unedited in the sequence.

3. With the playhead parked at the beginning of the dark temple shot in the **Timeline,** press the **I** key to enter an In point in the **Timeline** window.

4. Play forward until you find the end of the shot.

5. Again use the **Left** and **Right** arrow keys to find the last frame of the dark shot, *not* the first frame of the next shot as you did in Slice 2.

6. Press the **O** key to enter an Out point in the **Timeline,** which should look like Figure 3.8.

7. Now hit **Shift-Delete** to execute a ripple delete to remove that section of the video.

3.8   In and Out Point Marked in the Timeline Window

🦎 *Note*

Important: It is critical that you have nothing selected in the sequence when you use this technique. Anything that is selected—clip, audio, title, anything—will be ripple deleted instead of the marked In and Out section. The simplest way to avoid this is to press **Command-D** for **Drop** or **Deselect All.** This drops anything that's been selected. A good habit to get into before you execute this technique is to always make the **Timeline** the active window and press **Command-D,** or if you really like the menus, **Edit>Deselect All,** the opposite of **Command-A, Select All.**

This method is a fast and efficient way to cut material quickly. You end up with the shots you want to keep in the **Timeline**. Simply pull them into the bins in which you want to store them and rename. I'd use this method for working on something like a news story, where fast turnaround and quick cutting is necessary, and you're not concerned with storage, organization, or logging your material carefully.

Slicing, whether in the **Viewer** or the **Timeline**, has the advantage of quickly and easily accessing all your material while still cutting it up into shots for editing. It has a couple of disadvantages:

- The problem of not being able to scrub easily in the **Viewer** when the shot is very long
- The problem of transitions

Dice

I call it dicing because, as you'll see, we're making clips, which, though the same size as the clips in the Slice method, are more finely honed so that only the clip's defined duration remains with each clip.

1. Once again, open *Damine.mov* in the **Browser** into the **Viewer** and remove any marked In or Out points with **Option-X**.

2. Create a new bin in the **Browser** and name it **Clips2**.

3. Go back in the **Viewer** to that now-familiar shot toward the beginning of the stone basin. Mark up the In and Out points as you did in the first Slice method.

4. Now instead of just dragging the clip into the **Browser**, go to the **Modify** menu and select **Make Subclip** (Figure 3.9), or use the keyboard shortcut **Command-U**.

Command-U creates a subclip that automatically appears in the **Browser** with the same name as the clip it was taken from and with the name highlighted. In this case it will be *Damine.mov* subclip.

5. Before we do anything else, rename it *StoneBasin*, and let's drag the new subclip into **Clips2**.

⟍ Note

Browser and Timeline Clips: This is a good point to explain a bit about the relationship between the clips in the **Browser** and the clips in the Timeline. Quite simply, there is no relationship—no direct, linked relationship, anyway. They are separate, distinct items. They may be copies of each other, but they are separate clips that share the same media. So in the first Slice method, when you mark up the master clip with In and Out points, you are marking one clip and making copies of it in the **Clips bin**. When you drag the master clip from the **Browser** and place it in a **Timeline**, you are placing a copy of the master clip. So when you razor blade and ripple delete the clip in the Timeline, you are not in any way affecting the master clip that remains untouched in your **Browser**.

3.9   Modify>Make Subclip

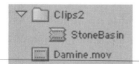

3.11 Subclip in Bin

This is the subclip method of cutting up a long clip. Notice the different icon created for subclips, indicating that they are torn out of another clip (Figure 3.11). When the **Browser** is in Icon view, subclips and ordinary clips are indistinguishable. It would have been nice if the torn edges indicator carried over.

👉 Tip_____

Subclipping without Switching Bins: If you want to place all the subclips from a master shot in one bin, move the master into the bin first, and then whenever you create the subclip, it will appear in the same bin. When you're done, you can move the master clip out of the bin.

Match Framing

It's sometimes important to find the master clip material from which either a sliced clip, or more importantly a diced subclip, is extracted. In the Slice method, you have the master clip to hand in every clip you make, but in the subclip, the original material is probably hidden in your **Browser**. Fortunately, Final Cut provides a simple, efficient method to find your place in the original material. If you open the subclip in the **Viewer**, all you have to do is press **Shift-F**, which match-frames you back to the original material. In other words, Final Cut immediately loads into the **Viewer** the original master clip parked at exactly the same frame that you were looking at in the subclip. It can be an extremely useful tool.

Though it doesn't have its own separate QuickTime file, the subclip is treated as a separate piece of media, even though in reality it's not. Though the subclip is only a portion of the piece of media on your hard drive called *Damine.mov*, it's treated in FCE as a complete, self-contained piece of media. The advantage to working in the subclip method is that it's easy to scrub the clip, running the mouse along the length of the media.

If you need to access more of the media within that subclip, select **Remove Subclip Limits** from the **Modify** menu. When you do this, the clip, if it's in the **Viewer,** will suddenly disappear, and a slug will be loaded in its place. I'm not sure why the application does that. If you again open that clip after the subclip limits are removed, the clip will revert to its whole length, without In or Out points.

You can also remove subclip limits from a shot or a whole bin of shots directly in the **Browser.** Just select the bin and pull down **Remove Subclip Limits** from the **Modify** menu. All the subclips will revert to full-length clips.

👉 Tip_____
Keeping Ins and Outs: If you want subclips to retain their In and Out points after the subclip limits are removed, you need to set In and Out points for them. The simplest way is to drag them into a sequence first. Dragging the subclips into a timeline will immediately define In and Out points for the clips. If you then **Remove Subclip Limits**, the clips will behave as sliced clips, their Ins and Outs defined, but the whole lengths of the media available on either side.

DV Start/Stop Detection

DV Start/Stop Detection is probably the best way to work with your material in FCE. The way this works in Final Cut Express is it uses the start/stop information from your camera to create markers on your video. Once the markers are set, they can be used to either slice or dice the master clip. Here's how it works.

1. Bring your long clip of DV material, either captured with the Clip method or with **Now**, into FCE.

2. Select the clip or clips.

3. From the **Mark** menu, select **DV Start/Stop Detection**.

You will immediately see the FCE scanning monitor (Figure 3.12) scan multiple clips at once. It can handle even whole bins. It produces clips with markers at each camera start/stop.

These markers can actually be turned into subclip segments. They appear in the **Browser** as a clip with markers (Figure 3.13). Note that **DV Start/Stop Detection** will only work on clips in the **Browser** or **Viewer**. It will not work on a clip in the **Timeline**.

You'll see that there are now markers for each shot change. You'll also notice that the In point for each segment is defined, but that

✎ Note
DV & Clock: DV Start/Stop Detection only works if you've set the clock in your camera. What's being detected is the time difference between the end of one clip and the beginning of the next. No clock, no time difference.

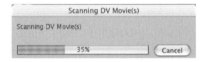

3.12 Scanning DV Movie(s)

Segment 5

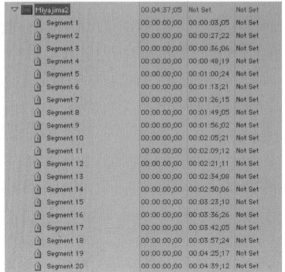

3.13 Segmented Clip in Browser (left)

3.14 Master Clips with Segments in Viewer (right)

neither duration nor Out point are. If you double-click on the clip itself, it opens in the **Viewer** with all its segments (Figure 3.14).

If you double-click on one of the segment markers in the **Browser**, the segment will open in the **Viewer** as if it were a subclip. You only see the limits of the media as the segment defines them. You can either drag it into a **Timeline**, or you can drag the segment back into the **Browser** or into a bin, rename it, and treat it just like any other subclip.

3.15 Mark to Markers

In addition to making markers in segments, FCE has the ability to make each segment of a marked-up clip not only into a subclip, but also into a separate clip of its own. Simply place the playhead anywhere between two markers, and press the keyboard shortcut **Control-A**. This is called **Mark to Markers** and will immediately mark and In and Out point on the nearest markers on either side of the playhead (Figure 3.15).

You can also do this by selecting **Mark to Markers** from the **Mark** menu. (Though note that as of this writing, the menu selection is sometimes dimmed when working in the **Viewer**, while the keyboard shortcut still functions.) **Mark to Markers** will slice your clip, marking the In and Out points and leaving the entire length of the material intact. You can now drag the marked shot into a bin to be stored and renamed.

Organizing the Clips

Once you've got your material diced up, you should spend some time getting it put away so that you can find it again. There are no firm rules about this, and I find each project tends to dictate its own organizational structure. Usually I begin with one bin that holds all the master shots. These are usually pretty big chunks of video: 10, 20, 30 minutes, usually not smaller. From the master shots, clips are separated out into bins. Keeping the master shots has the advantage that you can go back to the material in bulk to look through it again. As the project nears completion, I like to do this to see if I overlooked or discarded anything, which can be useful in light of the way the material gets cut together.

The separate bins can be organized in a variety of ways. Narrative projects tend to have material broken down in scene bins, with sub-bins for different types of shots or characters, depending on how complex the scene is. Documentary projects tend to break the material down into subject matter: a bin for all the forest shots, another for logging scenes, another for road work, another for weather, another for all the interviews, another for sound, another for narration tracks, another for music, another for graphics. As I said, there are no hard and fast rules on how material is organized.

The real trick is to break down your material into enough bins so that your material is organized, but not so many bins that it becomes difficult to find material. As you move clips into bins, add notes—lots of them. The more information you include on the clips, the easier it will be to find them.

Cutting up your shots and organizing them into bins is critical to working efficiently, particularly for long-form work, projects longer than 20 minutes or so. The longer the project, the more tapes you have, the more sequences, the more complex everything becomes. Having your material well organized is crucial. Fortunately FCE provides ways to help you.

Principally you have bins, and bins within bins. The **Browser** also gives you:

- **Comment** fields
- **Log Notes**
- A **Good** check mark

Do not overlook or hurry through the note-taking and data-entering process. All editors have their own ways of organizing material, loading information into the computer, and keeping it consistent. However you do it, it opens up to you one of computer-based editing's great boons, the computer's ability to search through huge amounts of data almost instantly. But you have to enter the information first. You can enter it either directly in the **Browser** fields, or by **Control**-clicking the clip and selecting **Item Properties**. The information can be entered in the tabbed **Logging Info** panel (Figure 3.16).

➤ *Tip*_____
Subclip Conversion: Another way to turn all the segments from a **DV Start/Stop** clip into subclips is to drag a marquee around markers in the **Browser**. Then press **Command-U**. Or you can select the markers you want and drag them into a bin. Either hitting **Command-U** or dragging the clips into a bin will copy each of the segments and turn them into subclips.

3.16 Logging Info Panel

> **Note**_____
> **Other Memory:** All these tools are a great help to editors, but nothing helps an editor in long form more than a good visual and aural memory. Simply being able to remember material over perhaps hundreds of tapes is a real gift, but even without this talent, looking closely at all your material, making good notes, and having a decent search engine will go a long way toward making your life a lot easier.

What is entered here also appears in the **Browser** columns and will be searchable with FCE's search engine. You can access a clip's **Item Properties** directly from the **Viewer** with the keyboard shortcut **Command-9**. I find the simplest way to enter information for clips is in the **Browser** as I make and rename subclips (Figure 3.17).

Final Cut has an excellent search tool, which is why adding the notes is so important. Let's take a look at it.

1. Begin by opening the project called *L3a* from the *Lesson 3* folder on your hard drive.

2. To search for something in any project, use the same keyboard shortcut as the **Finder: Command-F.**

3. This brings up the **Find** window (Figure 3.18). The first popup lets you search:

    - The open project
    - All open projects
    - The *Effects* folder

It searches anything tabbed into the **Browser.**

The second popup selects **All Media** or a choice of **Used** or **Unused Media,** while the third popup lets you replace or add to existing results. The two popups at the bottom define parameters. The left one sets where it's going to look (Figure 3.19).

👉 *Tip*

Using Find to Keep Track: Because FCE doesn't keep track of shots that are taken from the **Browser** and put in a sequence, the **Find** window is one way to do this. By selecting the **Unused** popup, you can find the material. You can then use the check mark in the **Good** column to marked the unused clips. Unfortunately, **Find** only searches media, not subclips, so if any part of a piece of media is used, even one subclip, then all the subclips based on the same media are considered used.

Unless you have pretty good idea where the information is—for instance, if you're looking for a specific type of file—just leave it on the default **Any Column.** The right popup lets you limit the

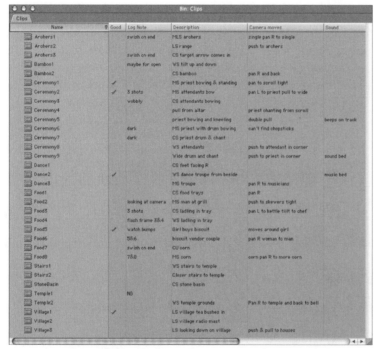

3.17   Browser Logging Info

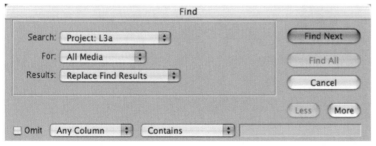

3.18   Find Dialog

Any Column
Name
Duration
In
Out
Type
Comment 3
Comment 4
Length
Capture
Source
Tracks
Good (Y/N)
Log Note
Audio
Frame Size
Compressor
Aud Rate
Aud Format
Reverse Alpha (Y/N)
Anamorphic (Y/N)
Scene
Shot/Take
Reel
Comment 1
Comment 2
Offline (Y/N)

3.19   Search Parameters

search parameters to speed up the process by limiting the number of results (Figure 3.20).

Let's do a search in project *L3a*. In the entry box at the bottom right of the **Find** window, type in *drum*.

If you press the **Find All button** rather than the default **Find Next**, the requested clips appear in a new **Browser** window (Figure 3.21).

Note the two buttons at the bottom, which let you:

- Show a selected item in the regular **Browser** bins

- Remove selected items from project

An important point to understand about this **Finder** is that all the items it locates are directly related to the items in the **Browser**. Unlike FCE's usual behavior where clips in sequences and bins can be copies of each other, here the found clips are directly linked to the clips in the **Browser**. Highlight a clip here, and it's

Starts With
Contains
Equals
Ends With
Less Than
Greater Than

3.20 Search Options

3.21 Finder Results

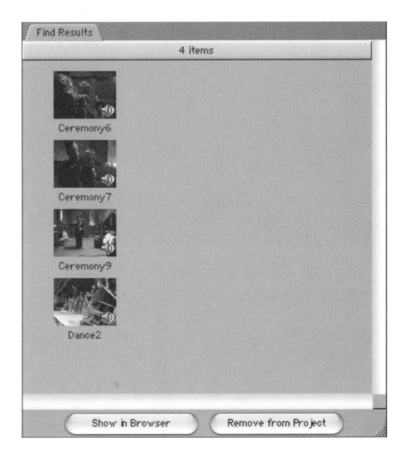

highlighted in the **Browser**. Delete a clip here and it's deleted from the **Browser**.

Look Before You Cut

However you work your video into clips or subclips, what you're really doing is looking through your material. What you should watch for is relationships, shots that can easily be cut together. Getting familiar with the material is an important part of the editing process, learning what you have to work with and looking for cutting points.

While looking through the material in the **Timeline**, some editors even like to roughly cut up the shots into sequences as they sort through the pictures. As they come to groups of shots that work together, some editors put them together in sequences.

Spend a little time going over *Damine.mov*. Slice it up and drag the clips into the bins, or dice it up into subclips and drag them into bins. It won't take that long, and you'll find you work faster and faster as you get familiar with the tools and using the keyboard. You'll be able to slice and dice these shots fairly quickly. It's a short reel, about eight minutes long. In project *L3a* the shots have been cut up into subclips and are inside the bin called **Clips**.

You can have multiple sequences open at the same time. Timelines normally tab together into one **Timeline** window, but you can pull the timelines apart so that you have two sequences open on the screen at the same time. You can simply pull shots from one sequence into another. By doing this, you're actually copying the shot from one sequence into the new sequence.

One way some editors like to work is to build storyboards in bins. Working in Large or Medium Icon mode, you can:

- Trim and set the clips
- Set the Poster frame
- Arrange the layout order of the shots in the **Browser**.

It's a fast, easy way to move shot order around, to try different arrangements and sequences. Though you can't play the clips back as a sequence, you can make a quick arrangement of shots. Then marquee through the shots and drag them into the **Timeline** (Figure 3.22).

The shots will appear in the sequence in the order they are in the bin. Notice the shots in the **Timeline** in Figure 3.22 follow the bin

Tip
Other Searches: The search engine isn't only for finding shots. You can search for anything in FCE. You might want to find a filter or a transition. You can search for those as well.

3.22 Storyboarded Bin and Shots in the Timeline

order as they are laid out, left to right, top to bottom. Be careful with the row heights: clips that are placed higher up in the bin will appear earlier.

Summary

In this lesson we've covered slicing and dicing clips as well as organizing our material so that we can work efficiently. In the next lesson we'll look at editing sequences, moving your clips into the **Timeline** and trimming them with some advanced editing tools.

Lesson 4

Editing Basics: Building Your Sequence

Now that you've got your material into Final Cut Express and sliced and/or diced it up, we're ready to begin putting it all together.

Loading the Lesson

As in the previous lesson, start by loading the DVD into your DVD drive. When you begin any lesson that needs material from the DVD, you should first drag the needed media elements onto the media drive of your computer. The sound and video clips included there will play much better and more smoothly from your computer's high-speed media drive than from any DVD drive. For this lesson you'll also need the folders called *Media* (if you haven't dragged it over already) and *Lesson 4*, which is inside the *Projects* folder on the DVD.

1. Drag *Lesson 4* onto your internal system drive. Again, probably the best place for it is in the *Shared* folder in the *Users* folder or in your *Documents* folder.

You have to have both folders because this lesson's project file is in the *Lesson 4* folder, while the media, which will again be

4.1   Offline Files Dialog Box

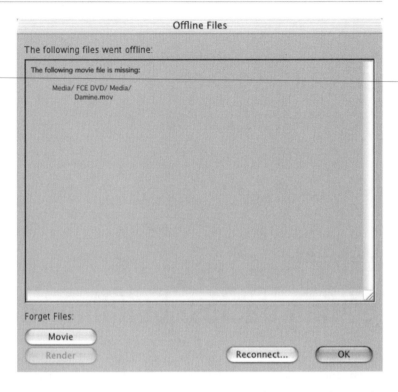

Damine.mov together with a short audio file, are in the *Media* folder.

2. Before opening anything, eject the DVD from your computer.

3. Now open the *Lesson 4* folder on your hard drive and double-click the project file, *L4*, to launch the application.

When the project finishes loading, you'll be greeted with the dialog box in Figure 4.1.

4. Do *not* press **Enter** or click **OK**. Instead click on the **Reconnect** button.

Do not click the **Movie** button underneath **Forget Files** either, because the application will do exactly that: forget that it needs the media. After you click **Reconnect**, you will get the **Reconnect Options** dialog box in Figure 4.2.

The computer will now search through your hard drives looking for *Damine.mov*. When the file is found, you'll get a dialog box that looks similar to the one in Figure 4.3.

5. If this is the correct file on your media drive, click the **Select** button.

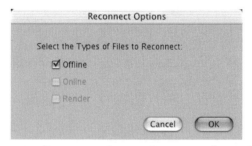

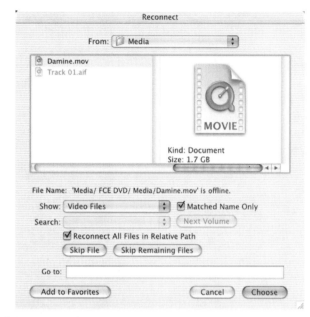

4.2   Reconnect Options Dialog Box (above)

4.3   Reconnect Selection Box (right)

Final Cut will now reconnect all the material for the project. Then you're ready to go. If it does not and asks to reconnect the clips, simply point them to the same file *Damine.mov*. *Track 01.aif* should be pointed to the file of that name in the *Media* folder.

Setting up the Project

The project you'll be working on is inside the *Lesson 4* folder and is called *L4*. Should the project ever get corrupted, you can always retrieve a fresh copy off your DVD. Double-click *L4* to open the project or launch the application if it's not already started up.

Inside the **Browser** of your copy of *L4*, you'll see three sequences:

- *Sequence 1*
- *Food*
- *Slip & Slide*

Sequence 1 is empty. We'll look at *Food Sequence* in a moment and *Slip & Slide* later in the lesson. In the **Browser** there is also the master clip, *Damine.mov*, together with a bin called **Clips**. Open the **Clips** bin and you'll see the shots from *Damine.mov* diced into subclips.

Though subclips normally appear without In points and Out points set, I've marked Ins and Outs at the beginning and end of each subclip. The advantage this gives you is that you can order the subclips in reel order based on their timecode In point, rather than their alphabetical order. So if you look at **Clips** in List view (**View>Browser Items>as List**) and click on the column header **In**, the clips will arrange themselves in timecode order.

Working with the Clips

I'd like to focus on one particular section of the video in this lesson: the food material. Take a quick look at *Food Sequence*. This is where we're going. To begin, let's look at where we're coming from, the material we have to work with.

1. Open the empty *Sequence 1* and double-click on the clip in the **Clips** bin called *Food1*, which will bring it into the **Viewer**.

The shot is 4;09 long, four seconds and nine frames.

2. Play the shot, or scrub it until you find the point just before the camera starts to pan from left to right across the trays of food. Mark an In point here.

3. Let the pan play through, give it a beat, and then stop.

4. Enter an Out point.

This will probably make the shot just over three seconds long.

Try it a few times until you get the pacing of the movement down. You might find that the more times you try it, the more you're shaving off the shot. Perhaps you'll feel the front needs to be shortened as well. Instead of beginning right at the start of the shot, enter an In point just before the camera pans right. When you have it the way you want it, you're ready to move it into the **Timeline**.

There are essentially three ways to get material from the **Viewer** to the **Timeline**:

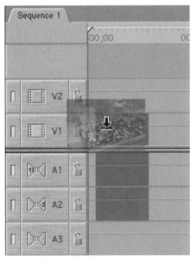

4.4 Dragging into the Timeline

- Simply drag it there. Grab the image from the **Viewer** and pull it directly into the **Timeline**, dropping it onto **V1** as shown in Figure 4.4.

- The second way is to drag the clip from the **Viewer** to the **Canvas,** and the visual dialog box, called the Canvas Edit Overlay (see Figure 4.5) immediately appears. Drop the clip on **Overwrite.**

- The third method is to use **Overwrite's** keyboard shortcut, **F10.**

Which way you execute the edit is a question of personal preference. Many people prefer to drag to the **Timeline.** It can be easy when you're unpracticed to drop the clip into the wrong track or to do an **Insert** instead of an **Overwrite** when you drag to the **Timeline.** I prefer the accuracy and exactness of dragging to **Overwrite.** This seems to work well on a PowerBook where there is no separate mouse and the **F** keys are awkward to use. On a full-sized keyboard, though, the speed of using shortcuts is hard to beat.

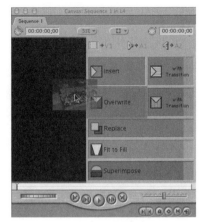

4.5 Canvas Edit Overlay (CEO)

✎ Note

Dropped Frames: One of the most common causes of dropped frames, especially for new users of FCE, is that their viewing window is not fit to the video. If you look at your DV video in a small frame while the material is set to full size, you're expecting the computer to display only portion of the video while playing it back. If this doesn't produce dropped frames on playback, it will at the very least show as stuttering video on your computer monitor. You can always tell if the image is too large for the viewing window when you see scroll bars on the sides, as in Figure 4.6. To correct this, simply select **Fit to Window** from the **Viewer Size** popup or the keyboard shortcut **Shift-Z. Shift-Z** is also used in the **Timeline** to fit the contents into the window.

4.6 Fit to Window

Overwrite

Let's look at the **Canvas Edit Overlay (CEO)**(Figure 4.5). It offers seven different editing options. The most commonly used is the **Overwrite** command.

1. Drag the clip from the **Viewer** until the box marked **Overwrite** highlights.

2. Drop the clip.

It will overwrite whatever is in the timeline beginning at the point at which the playhead is parked.

4.7 Target Track Indicators

☞ *Tip*

Target Tracks: When you drag a clip onto the **CEO**, you'll notice the target tracks at the top of the display (Figure 4.7). Your clip will be placed on these tracks. The indicators serve as a handy last warning before you execute the edit.

This is a three-point edit. In a three-point edit you're defining three elements required to execute the edit function:

- Where you want the clip to start
- Where you want the clip to end
- Where you want to place the clip

The three points are most commonly defined by:

- Marking In and Out points in the **Viewer.**

- Using the playhead as the marker for the In point in the **Timeline.**

So that we can look at the functionality offered in the **CEO**, let's quickly drag a few shots into the **Timeline** to see how they work.

☜ Note

Overwrite Constraint: Note that though you can drag a clip directly from the **Browser** to the **CEO, F10** does not overwrite directly from the **Browser. F10** only works when overwriting from the **Viewer.** If the **Viewer** is closed, **F10** will simply put in a slug, a long section of black with a stereo audio track.

1. If you haven't already done it, drag *Food1* from the **Viewer** and drop it on **Overwrite.**

2. Select clips *Food2* and *Food3* in the **Browser** and drag them directly to the **Overwrite** box in the **CEO.**

The clips will appear in the **Timeline** following *Food1* in their bin order. Note that every time you place a clip in the **Timeline**, the playhead automatically leaps to end of the clip, ready for the next edit event, and the **Canvas** displays the last frame of the sequence (Figure 4.8).

Insert

If **Overwrite** is the most commonly used of the **CEO** features, then the next most used must be **Insert.** This is where an NLE system shows its power.

1. Move the playhead to the edit between *Food1* and *Food2*.

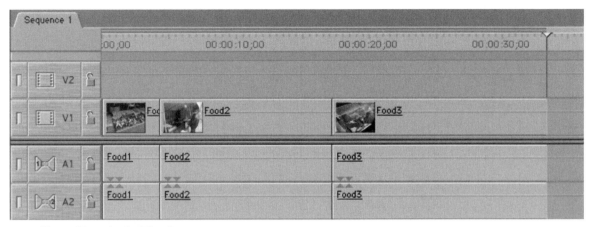

4.8   Three Shots in the Timeline

As you move the playhead onto the edit point, it should snap strongly to the join and display on the tracks the marks in Figure 4.9. If you don't see the snap marks, **Snapping** is turned off.

2.   Press the **N** key. Try it several times, toggling the **Snapping** function on and off.

👉 *Tip*

Select an Edit: A useful keyboard shortcut is the **V** key, which selects the nearest edit point and moves the playhead to it.

4.9   Snap Markings

The Magic Frame

If the playhead moves to the end of the last clip in a sequence, the **Canvas** displays the last frame of the clip with a blue bar down the right side. This is the Magic Frame, because the playhead is actually sitting on the next frame of video—the blank, empty frame—but the display shows the previous frame. Try it.

1.   Go to the end of the sequence, and you'll see the last frame of the video.

2.   Now move the last clip in sequence away from the others, leaving a gap in the **Timeline**.

3.   Use the **Up** key to go to the end of the shot before the gap. Here you don't see the last frame of the video, but at the end you see the first frame of black, the empty space. This is important to remember that the playhead is always sitting at the start of the video frame, despite what the Magic Frame shows you.

4.   Move the clips back together when you're done.

4.10 The Insert Edit

The **N** key may become one of your most often-used keys in Final Cut Express. You'll find as you work with the application that you'll be constantly changing from one mode to the other.

Now with snapping on, you should have the playhead parked between the clips.

3. Grab *Food5* directly from the **Browser** and drag it to the **Canvas**, calling up the **CEO**.

4. Drop it on **Overwrite** to see what happens.

Food5 wipes out all of *Food2* and some of *Food3*.

5. Quickly undo that with **Command-Z**.

6. This time, instead of dragging *Food5* onto **Overwrite**, drag it onto **Insert**.

Immediately the **Timeline** rearranges itself. *Food5* drops into the **Timeline**, appears between *Food1* and *Food2*, and pushes everything farther down in the **Timeline**, as shown in Figure 4.10.

Insert will move everything down the track regardless of a clip's position. So if you insert into the middle of the clip, the clip will be cut, and everything on all the tracks will be pushed out of the way. This applies to all tracks, including music or narration, which you may not want to cut.

Track locks are useful in these circumstances. For instance, to prevent an insert from slicing into a music track, lock the track or tracks. All the other tracks will move, but the locked tracks will remain stationary.

Let's try this and see what happens.

1. Undo the insert edit that you did when moving *Food5* into the **Timeline**.

2. In the **Browser** is an audio track called *Track 01.aif*. Grab the icon and drag it directly into the **Timeline** and place it on tracks **A3** and **A4**. It's a stereo pair of music.

3. Execute the **Insert** edit with *Food5*. Immediately you'll notice that not only is the video being inserted into the sequence, but the music track is actually being cut with the insert.

4. Undo that edit with **Command-Z**.

5. Just click on the track locks (Figure 4.11) at the head of each track. (Remember to lock or unlock both tracks of a stereo pair.)

6. Redo the **Insert** edit, and you'll see that though the video moves to accommodate the clip, the music track now does not.

7. Before we go any further, let's undo the insert edit and remove the audio on **A3** and **A4**, bringing the **Timeline** back to just three clips, *Food1*, *Food2*, and *Food3*.

You can also use **Control** key and the shortcut menu to do a ripple delete (Figure 4.12), or ripple delete with **Shift-Delete**.

4.11 Track Locks

Alternative Overwrite and Insert

Overwrite and **Insert** are the primary functions in the **CEO**, but let's look at another way to do them.

Drag *Food5* directly from the **Browser** to the **Timeline**. As you drag it onto the edit point between *Food1* and *Food2*, a little arrow appears, indicating how the edit will be performed. If the arrow is pointing downward as in Figure 4.13, the edit will overwrite. If the little arrow is pointing to the right as in Figure 4.14, you will be doing an insert, which will push the material out of the way. Notice as you do this how the two-up display in the **Canvas** changes. In Figure 4.15 the video is being overwritten, beginning at the end of *Food1* and wiping out all of *Food2* and most of *Food3*. In Figure 4.16 the shot is being inserted between *Food1* and *Food2*.

You'll notice also as you work in the application that in addition to the arrow indicators, the clip colors change. In **Overwrite**, the track color changes to the highlighted brown color. In **Insert**, the track simply has an outline box.

The point at which the arrows switch from **Overwrite** to **Insert** is indicated by the faint line running horizontally through the clip about a third of the way from the top. If the clip is in the upper third, the edit will be an **Insert**. If it's in the lower two-thirds, the edit will be an **Overwrite**. It's the faint horizontal line you see running through the clips in Figures 4.13 and 4.14.

4.12 Shortcut Menu Ripple Delete

4.13 Overwrite Arrow

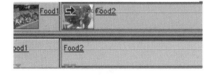

4.14 Insert Arrow

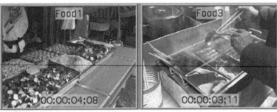

4.15 Overwrite Two-Up Canvas Display   4.16 Insert Two-Up Canvas Display

Replace

We'll skip **Overwrite with Transition** and **Insert with Transition** for the next lesson and look at:

- **Replace**
- **Fit to Fill**
- **Superimpose**

Replace is remarkably sophisticated in the way it works. It will replace a clip in the **Timeline** with another clip either from the **Viewer** or dragged from the **Browser** to the CEO. The trick to understanding how **Replace** works is to understand that it works precisely from the point at which the playhead is positioned.

Let's do a **Replace** edit.

1. Start with your base three shots in the **Timeline**, *Food1, Food2,* and *Food3.*

2. Place the playhead at the edit point between *Food1* and *Food2* so that we're at the beginning of *Food2.*

3. Open *Food5* into the **Viewer** and make sure the playhead there is close to the beginning of the clip.

4. Drag it into **Replace** in the **Canvas**. *Food5* will immediately replace *Food2* in the **Timeline**.

The **Viewer** and the **Canvas** will show the same frame because Final Cut has taken the frame that was in the **Viewer** and placed in exactly the same frame position as the shot it's replacing in the **Timeline**. It's extended the shot forward and backward from that point to exactly fill the duration of the shot it's replacing.

Take a look at the clips in Figure 4.17.

The clip in the **Timeline**, *Food2*, has the playhead parked toward the end of the shot. I want to replace it with the clip *Food5*. In the **Viewer** *Food5* is near the beginning of the shot. The current position of the playhead in *Food5* is indicated. I won't be able to

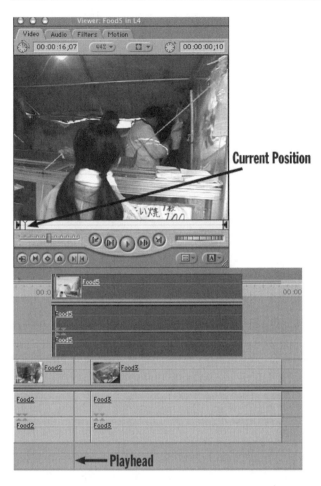

Current Position

Playhead

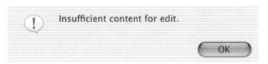

4.17 One Clip Trying to Replace Another (left)

4.18 Insufficient Content Message (below)

> ⚠ Insufficient content for edit.
>
> OK

replace *Food2* with *Food5* even though the new clip is much longer than the clip it's replacing. Why? Because FCE calculates the **Replace** edit from the position of the playhead. There just aren't enough frames in front of the current position of the playhead in *Food5* in the **Viewer** to replace all the frames in front of the current position of the playhead in *Food2* in the sequence.

If you tried to do a **Replace** edit to *Food5* in place of *Food2* in the **Timeline** you'd get the error message in Figure 4.18.

👍 *Tip*_____

Alternative Replace: Another way to do a replace function is to use **Overwrite** after first defining the limits of the shot you want to replace. That's easy to do in FCE. With the playhead parked over the shot, press the **X** key. This sets In and Out points on the timeline that are exactly the length of the clip, as in Figure 4.19. If you now do an overwrite edit, it will effectively replace the shot in the **Timeline**.

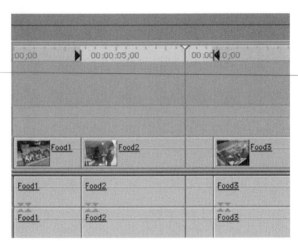

4.19 Ins and Outs in the Timeline   4.20 Slow Motion Clip in the Timeline

Fit to Fill

Fit to Fill functions similarly to **Replace** except that it's never hampered by lack of media. **Fit to Fill** simply adjusts the speed of the clip to match the area it needs to occupy. This it a great tool for putting in still images or titles that you want to be a specific length. Because they aren't real video, Final Cut will produce the images very quickly and accurately. It's a little more problematic when using it with video where it raises some serious problems.

1. Open the clip *Food7* in the **Viewer**.

You can see by the duration in the upper left corner of the **Viewer** that *Food7* is quite a bit shorter than *Food5*.

2. With the playhead parked over the middle of *Food5* in the **Timeline**, hit the **X** key to mark an In and Out point in the **Timeline**.

3. Drag the clip from the **Viewer** and drop it on the **Fit to Fill** box, or use the keyboard shortcut **Shift-F11**.

The clip will immediately drop into the **Timeline**, and unless it is exactly the same size as the clip it's replacing, a red line will appear at the top of the **Timeline**. The red line indicates that the section of the **Timeline** needs to be rendered. This section needs to be rendered because of the speed change to *Food7*, which is now in slow motion to accommodate the **Fit to Fill** edit. The clip in the timeline also shows the speed change, in this case, 47% of real speed (Figure 4.20).

But that's not quite true. Let's check the speed.

4. Select the clip in the **Timeline** and hit **Command-J**, which calls up the **Speed** dialog box (Figure 4.21).

In this case the speed is 47.45%.

5. Close the dialog box, select the clip in the **Timeline**, and press **Command-R** for render.

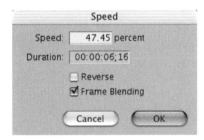

4.21   Speed Dialog Box

You will quickly get the progress bar in Figure 4.22, showing you how long it will take to render. Will there be time for a bathroom break? Maybe we could fit lunch in.

When you play back the render, you'll probably notice that the sound is also slomoed in addition to the picture. This may be an interesting effect on some occasions, but it certainly calls attention to itself and can be distracting for the audience.

4.22   Render Progress Bar

Modify>Speed (**Command-J**) is where all clip speed changes are made. It is unfortunately not possible to ramp speed up or down so that it accelerates and decelerates.

4.23 Superimposed Clip

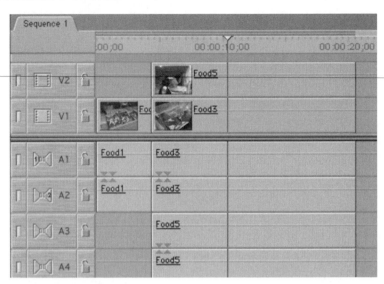

Superimpose

Superimpose is used primarily to place titles on the track above the video. It again works a bit like **Replace**. The clip you're super-imposing takes its duration from the clip you're placing it above. Simply drag the clip on **Superimpose** and it will be placed above the clip that the playhead is sitting on.

Let's ripple delete the middle shot of the three in the **Timeline** so that we're left with only *Food1* and *Food3*.

1. Place the playhead somewhere over the middle of the *Food3*.

2. Drag *Food5* from the **Browser** to the **Canvas** and drop it on the **Superimpose** box, or use the keyboard shortcut **F12**.

The clip appears in the **Timeline** above the clip on the target track, *Food2* in this case, as in Figure 4.23. Notice where the audio track has gone onto **A3** and **A4**, the tracks below the target track.

Let's Start Editing

Now that we've gone through the principal means of going from **Viewer** to **Canvas**, let's edit in the **Timeline** itself, trimming and adjusting the clips. We'll edit together a quickly paced sequence of shots.

I like to begin by looking at the material I'm going to use for the sequence. The simplest way to do this is to lay everything out in shot order in the sequence.

1. Use **Command-A** in the **Timeline** and then **Delete** to remove everything you have there.

Whenever you delete everything in the **Timeline**, the playhead will move to the beginning.

2. Set the **Browser** to In point list order by clicking on the **In** column.

3. Select the clips *Food1* through *Food8*, drag them onto the **Canvas**, and drop them on **Overwrite**.

4. Click on the **Timeline** window and press the **Home** key.

You're ready to start viewing. We're looking for movement and shots that can be cut together. Once I've looked at the clips in reel order, I then start looking at the clips individually, cutting them down to size and rearranging them.

Making a Sequence

Rather than working on the clips in the **Timeline**, let's start afresh with the first clip.

1. Again, delete everything in the **Timeline**.

2. Double-click on *Food1* in the **Browser** to open it into the **Viewer**.

3. Scrub through to the point where the camera starts moving from left to right.

4. Find the beginning of the movement and mark the In point.

5. Now find the end of the movement and mark the Out point. We can leave the shots a little loose at this stage.

6. After you've marked the In and Out points, drag the clip to **Overwrite** or press **F10**.

I'm not sure which part of the second shot, *Food2*, I'll use at this stage. I'll probably use something, so I'll cut a long piece.

1. Open *Food2* into the **Viewer** and take the shot from just before the zoom starts and let it run almost to the end, including the part with the hands turning the skewers.

2. Again **Overwrite** to the **Timeline**.

✎ Note_____

Different In Point: If you want to superimpose at some point other than right over a clip you can do this by entering an In point in the Timeline. Go to the **Canvas** or the **Timeline** window and press the I key to mark an In point (Figure 4.24). This will be the In point for the next edit, and when you drag the clip from **Viewer** to **Canvas** to **Superimpose**, the clip will drop at the marked In point and not at the playhead's current position.

4.24 In Point Mark in the Timeline

Food3 is a little more complex. I want to use more than one part of the shot.

1.   Start by marking the In at the beginning of the shot.

2.   ~~Mark the Out just before the small pull back.~~

3.   **Overwrite.**

By putting the shot in the **Timeline**, I made a copy of the shot that's currently loaded in the **Viewer**. So now I can simply set new Ins and Outs for the clip that's still in the **Viewer** without affecting what I've already done to the shot in the sequence.

1.   Set a new In point in the **Viewer** just before the pan left begins.

2.   Let the shot carry over to the steaming kettle, until about the 8;15 mark.

3.   Add that to the **Timeline.**

4.   Take a third section from that clip, from just before the camera tilts up until shortly before the shot ends and add that to the **Timeline.**

Food4 is a very short shot, but it might fit nicely before the close-up of the steaming tray.

1.   Position the **Timeline** playhead between *Food2* and *Food3* in sequence.

2.   Open *Food4* into the **Viewer** by double-clicking on it in the **Browser.**

3.   Drag the clip to **Insert** or use the shortcut **F9.**

Let's look at *Food5*. It's the most human part of the material, the little girl at the food stall. My thought is to use it as bookends: the little girl at the beginning of the sequence and at the end.

1.   Make the first part of the shot one clip, basically until after she hands the vendor her money.

2.   Make sure the playhead is at the start of the **Timeline,** then drag to **Insert.**

3.   Make the second part of *Food5* begin shortly before the vendor reaches for the biscuit and let it go until just before the end.

4.   Move the playhead to the end of the **Timeline.**

5.   Drag the second half of *Food5* from the **Viewer** to **Overwrite,** or use **F10.**

We want *Food6* to go just before the last shot.

1. Open up *Food6* in the **Viewer** and play it.

2. Set the In point near the beginning.

3. Set the Out point after the move with the biscuits, around 3;05.

4. In the **Timeline**, the playhead is probably at the end of the material. Use the **Up** arrow to move backwards one edit.

5. Now drag the clip from **Viewer** to **Insert**, or use **F9**.

After looking at *Food7* again, I decided to drop it from the scene altogether. I want a short piece of *Food8* before the last shot.

1. Take the piece of the movement of the pan right of the steaming corn to the tray of roasted corn.

2. Insert it before the last shot, as in the previous steps.

Editing the Sequence

The total duration of this little sequence should be roughly about 35 seconds, depending on how tightly you cut the shots. Looking through it, it's obvious it needs to be tightened up as well as have the order rearranged.

Swap Edit

Let's begin by pulling *Food8* from the end of the sequence and placing it as the second shot. This is called a *swap* edit.

1. Grab the shot and start to pull it along the timeline.

2. After you've started the movement, hold down the **Option** key.

Don't press the **Option** key until after you've started to move the clip while you're already in mouse-down mode. As you move, a downward hooked arrow appears on the clip (Figure 4.25).

3. When you get to the edit point between the first and second shot in the sequence, drop the clip.

If you look at the **Timeline**, you'll see that you've done an insert edit as well as a ripple delete. You've removed the clip from one point on the timeline, placed it somewhere else in the timeline, and pushed everything out of the way to make room for it. This is a great hidden tool. I use it often. Also notice the **–00:26:02** in

> ✏ *Tip*_____
>
> **Timecode Location:** To go to a specific timecode point in either the **Canvas**, the **Viewer**, or the **Timeline**, simply tap out the number on your keypad (in the case of working with *Food6*, type in **305**) and press **Enter**. The playhead will immediately move to that point.

4.25 Swap Edit Arrow

4.26 Overwrite Arrow when Dragging (above)

4.27 Insert Arrow when Dragging (above right)

4.28 Close Gap Shortcut Menu (lower right)

Figure 4.25. This shows how far in the sequence you've moved the clip: 26 seconds and two frames from its original position.

> **Note**
>
> **Swap Edit Limit:** The Swap Edit function that lets you move clips will only work on one clip at a time. Unfortunately, you can't grab a couple of clips or a small section of clips and do the same thing. It also works best if you have **Snapping** turned on to avoid slicing off a little bit of shot by accident.

Once you've done this, you'll discover something unfortunate. Now we have two shots one after the other that pan from left to right. Sometimes it works—not very often. In this instance I think it looks dumb. Let's put *Food4* and the first *Food3* clip right after *Food8*. However, if you select both clips with a marquee drag and then drag them along the **Timeline**, you'll get the downward **Overwrite** arrow as in Figure 4.26. So don't do that.

1. If you hold down the **Option** key while dragging the two clips as you did earlier, you'll get the **Insert** edit arrow in Figure 4.27. Drag the two clips *Food4* and *Food3* to the edit point between the second and third shots that are now in the sequence, between *Food8* and *Food1*.

Unlike moving a single clip, however, your **Option**-drag insert edit will not ripple delete as it did earlier. It will leave a hole in the sequence.

2. Hold down the **Control** key and click on the empty space.

3. Then select **Close Gap** as in Figure 4.28.

👉 *Tip*_____

Gaps and Syncing: FCE defines a gap as a space in the **Timeline** that extends across all tracks. So if you have a music track on **A3** and **A4**, for instance, FCE will not see the space between the shots on the video tracks as a gap. This is where the ability to lock tracks really helps. If you lock those music tracks, you can then close the gap. Or use **Option**-lock to lock all other tracks, and again you can close the gap.

Besides the shortcut menu, there are two other ways to close a gap in the track:

• With the playhead over the gap, hit **Control-G**.

• Click on it to select the gap and then hit the **Delete** key.

There is another way to do this operation besides **Option**-dragging the group of clips.

1.   Select the clips.

2.   Cut them with **Shift-X** instead of **Command-X**.

Shift-X performs a ripple delete instead of a simple lift edit that leaves a gap in the track. This not only cuts the clips out of the timeline, but also closes the gap the missing clips created. Not only that, more importantly, it copies the clips into the clipboard, just like a word processor would.

3.   Now go to wherever you want to place the clips and use **Shift-V**, which will paste the clips as an insert edit. **Command-V** would also paste, but as an overwrite edit.

Let's look through the sequence again. It's getting better, but there are still a few edits I don't like and quite a few shots that need trimming. We'll get to trimming in a moment, but let's rearrange a few more shots.

In the first shot, I like the way the camera moves around the girl at the beginning, and I like the way she hands over her money with her fingers splayed out. I don't care for the hesitation in the middle.

1.   Double-click on the first shot in the sequence to bring it into the **Viewer**.

2.   Scrub or play the shot until you find the point just after the camera finishes moving around the girl, about 2;16.

3.   Press the **F** key.

This is the **Match Frame** key. It immediately moves the playhead in the **Timeline** to the frame that corresponds to the one on the **Viewer**, and displays the matching frame in the **Canvas**. It also makes the **Canvas** the active window so you can immediately use

4.29 Food Sequence Beginning

Control-V to slice the clip in the sequence. There are now two halves to the first shot in the sequence.

4. Open the second half in the **Viewer**. Find the point just before the vendor reaches his hand out for the money, about 3;15.

5. Repeat the process: Hit **F** and **Control-V**. You have now isolated the section you want to cut out.

6. Ripple delete it either by **Control**-clicking to call up the shortcut menu or by selecting it and hitting **Shift-Delete**.

The **F** key is a very useful tool as a means of finding your place in the **Timeline**.

In the previous lesson, I showed you a simpler technique that would work well here. Undo all these steps that cut a section out of *Food5*, and we'll do the edit entirely in the **Timeline** window.

1. Start by making sure nothing is selected in the **Timeline** (**Command-D**).

2. Go to the head of the sequence and start to play it, stopping again just after the first camera move around the girl.

3. Press **I** to enter an In point in the **Timeline**, around 1;10.

4. Play until just before the vendor reaches for the money. Scrub the playhead if it's easier; use the **J**, **K**, and **L** keys or the **Left** and **Right** arrow keys.

5. With the playhead at about 3;00, press **O** to enter an Out point in the Timeline.

6. Now do a ripple delete. Press **Shift-Delete** to remove that short section of the shot.

Obviously the sequence now has a jump cut. So let's take the third shot in the sequence, the shot of the corn, *Food8*, and do a swap edit. Drag with **Option** to drop *Food8* between the two halves of *Food5* at the beginning of the sequence. The beginning of the **Timeline** should look like Figure 4.29.

As you go through the sequence, you'll see another jump cut between two parts of *Food3*. The camera pans right from the cooking tray to the steaming kettle and then in a separate shot

> **Tip**
> **Moving the Playhead:** Shift-Left or Right arrow will move the playhead forward or backward in one-second increments.

tilts up from the kettle to the cook. I would remove the first of these shots, taking out the pan. I've seen that cooking tray already, but the kettle and the chef are new.

The arrangement is almost right, but there is a problem with the very last shot that I don't care for. Just after the vendor puts the biscuit in the bag, the camera jiggles. I'd like to remove this. So let's do this in the **Timeline**.

1. Scrub or play through *Food5*, the last shot in the sequence, to the frame when the biscuit just disappears into the bag behind the counter.

2. Use **I** to mark the In point in the **Timeline**.

Right after this the camera is jostled.

3. Move further down to where the vendor is about to reach forward with the bag, as his hands separate. This is about midway through *Food5*.

4. Mark the Out point with the **O** key and ripple delete the middle portion.

Now we have the same problem we had in the first shot.

This time we're going to move *Food3* from its earlier position. This is the shot of the tilt from kettle to cook.

5. Drag and then add the **Option** key before you drop it between the two halves of *Food5* that you just split.

Jump Cuts

The sequence as we've laid it out so far has the most obvious form of jump cut, which is any abrupt edit that jars the viewer. This is generally considered a *faux pas*. The most common cause is placing side-by-side shots, such as the two halves of *Food5*, that are very similar, but not the same. You get this disconcerting little jump, as if you blacked out for a fraction of a second. It suddenly pulls the viewers out from the content of the video as they say to themselves, or perhaps even out loud, "What was that?" You can also get a jump cut if you put together two very different shots, such as the shot of a long street with the small figure of a person in the distance, cutting to a tight closeup. It's disorienting because the viewer has no reference that the close-up belongs to the person seen in the far distance in the previous shot. These are jump cuts. The general rule is to avoid them if you can. Or use them so often that it becomes your style. Then it's art.

If you look through the sequence, you'll see that the shots are in the order we want, but we still need to tighten it up, trimming the shots to make them faster paced.

✌ Tip

4.30 Scaling Slider and Tabbed Slider

Timeline Scaling: You can change the scale of the **Timeline** to zoom in and out with the tabbed slider at the bottom of the window. Pulling either end of the tab will change the scale of the **Timeline** window. At the bottom left is a little slider that will adjust the scale (Figure 4.30).

My personal favorite is to use the keyboard shortcuts **Option-=** (think **Option- +**) to zoom in and **Option--** (that's **Option-minus**) to zoom out. What's nice about using the keyboard shortcuts is that it leaves the playhead centered in the **Timeline** as you zoom in and out. Just be careful a clip isn't selected in the **Timeline** because the scaling will then take place around that rather than around the playhead. You can use **Command-+** and **Command--** to scale in other windows, but **Option-+** and – will always scale the **Timeline** regardless of what's the active window.

The Trim Tools

4.31 The Tools

The trim tools—**Roll** and **Ripple, Slip** and **Slide**—are among the tools shown in Figure 4.31. The trim tools themselves are clustered in the fourth and fifth buttons.

The first two trim tools, **Ripple** and **Roll**, change the duration of clips, while the second two, **Slip** and **Slide**, leave the clip duration intact.

A *ripple* edit moves an edit point up and down the timeline by pushing or pulling all the material on the track, shortening or lengthening the whole sequence. In a ripple edit, only one clip changes duration, getting longer or shorter. Everything else that comes after it in the track adjusts to accommodate it. In Figure 4.32 the edit is rippled to the left, and everything after moves left to accompany it, just as in a ripple delete.

A *roll* edit moves an edit point up and down the timeline between two adjacent shots. Only those two shots have their durations changed. While one gets longer, the adjacent shot gets shorter to accommodate it. The overall length of the track remains unchanged. In Figure 4.33 the edit point itself can be moved either left or right.

A *slip* edit changes the In and Out points of a single clip. The duration of the clip remains the same, and all the clips around it

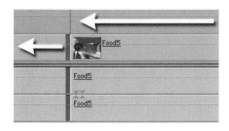 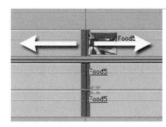

4.32 Ripple Edit Left (far left)

4.33 Roll Edit Directions
          (immediate left)

remain the same. Only the In and Out of the slipped clip change. If more frames are added on the front, the same amount are cut off the end, and vice versa, if some are added to the end, an equal amount are taken off the beginning. In Figure 4.34 the contents of the shot change by changing In and Out points, but neither its position in the **Timeline** nor either of the adjacent shots are affected.

A *slide* edit moves a clip forward or backward along the timeline. The clip itself, its duration and In and Out points remain unchanged. Only its position on the timeline, earlier or later, shortens and lengthens the adjacent shots as it slides up and down the track. In Figure 4.35 the shot *Food6* can slide up and down the timeline. The shot itself doesn't change, only the two adjacent shots.

The Ripple Tool

We're first going to work with the **Ripple** tool. Press the fourth button and extend the popout to select the tool as in Figure 4.36. You can also call it up by pressing **RR**; that's the **R** key twice.

Let's use it on some of the shots we want to work on. Start with the edit between shots *Food4* and *Food3*. Take the tool and place

4.34 Slip Edit Direction

4.35 Slide Edit Directions

4.36 The Ripple Tool

4.37 Ripple Tool Right

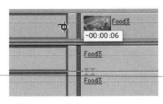

4.38 Ripple Tool Left

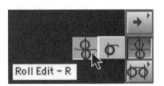

4.39 The Roll Tool

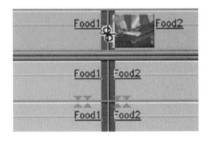

4.40 The Roll Tool in the Timeline

it near the edit. Notice it changes direction as you move it across the edit as in Figures 4.37 and 4.38.

When the tool is on the right side it will ripple the second shot; when it's on the left side, it will ripple the first shot.

In this case, we want to ripple the second shot. The edit almost works, but it can perhaps be a little improved by tightening up. The hesitation at the beginning of *Food3* looks awkward. You can ripple right in the timeline. As you grab the clip, you will get a small two-up display in the **Canvas**.

A word of caution about rippling. If you're working with material that's cut to narration or music, rippling will easily upset the timing of the sequence, as it's pulling and pushing the entire track and its sync sound. So what's working for you at this moment in the edit may be ruining something else further down the timeline. In these cases, the **Roll** tool may work better for you.

The Roll Tool

The **Roll** tool is also under the fourth button in the **Tools** as in Figure 4.39. It can be evoked with the **R** key. It works similarly to **Ripple** and can be used in the **Timeline** as in Figure 4.40.

The **Roll** tool acts on both shots, extending one shot while shortening the other. While the **Ripple** tool changes the entire length of the sequence by moving everything up and down the line, the **Roll** tool only affects the two adjacent shots.

Using **Roll** and **Ripple**, tighten up some of the shots in the sequence. I rippled the zoom into the skewers in *Food2* until all you see are the hands turning over the sticks on the grill.

The Slip Tool

Let's look at **Slip** and **Slide** next. These work in the **Timeline** and the **Viewer** and do pretty much what their names imply. **Slip** is one of my favorite tools, though I'm not very keen on the display

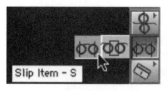
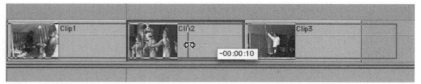

4.41 The Slip Tool   4.42 The Slip Tool in the Timeline

in Final Cut Express. You can select the **Slip** tool from the fifth button in the **Tools**, as shown in Figure 4.41, or call it with the **S** key.

I've created the *Slip & Slide Sequence* to help explain these two tools. Open the sequence by double-clicking it in the **Browser.** Use the **Slip** tool to grab the middle clip in the sequence. Move the clip from side to side, and you'll see the display in Figure 4.42. What you're doing is slipping the media for the clip up and down its length. The overall duration of the clip remains unchanged but the section of media for that duration is adjusted.

The **Canvas** again shows you a two-up display. This is showing you the first and the last frames of the video. The shot in the sequence begins at 3;00 and ends at 5;00, a two-second shot. By slipping the clip 10 frames as we see in the figures, the shot will now start at 3;10 and end at 5;10, keeping the same duration. It starts later so it will end later. If the shot slipped in the other direction it would start earlier in time, but also end earlier.

The two-up display will help you from slipping the clip too far into some unwanted material. If you're working in the Slice mode we discussed in the last lesson, you can see if you're slipping into the next shot.

It is also possible to slip in the **Viewer**, which can be especially beneficial when you're adjusting a clip before you bring it into the **Timeline.**

1. To slip in the **Viewer,** double-click the clip to load it into the **Viewer.**

2. Hold down the **Shift** key as you grab either the In point or the Out point and drag. This way you will drag both points together and maintain a constant duration (Figure 4.43).

This is *slipping,* and what you see in the display (Figure 4.43) is the start frame in the **Viewer** and the end frame in the **Canvas.** It doesn't matter which end you grab to pull; the display is always the same: start in the **Viewer,** end in the **Canvas.**

☆ Tip
Ripple and Roll Shortcuts: You can also use the **Ripple** and **Roll** tools incrementally with keyboard shortcuts in the **Timeline**. Select the edit point by moving the playhead over it and pressing the **V** key. Now, by using the **U** key, you can toggle through **Ripple Right**, **Ripple Left**, and **Roll**. Whichever edit you have selected, you can now move incremental with the less-than bracket < and the greater-than bracket >. (Actually, it's the comma and period, but most people think of it as < and >.) Each tap will move the edit one frame left or right in the direction the bracket is pointed. **Shift-<** and **Shift->** will move the edit whatever duration you have set for **Multi-Frame Trimming** in your **General Preferences**. This also works if you select a clip in the **Timeline** and choose either the **Slip** or **Slide** tools.

4.43 Slipping in the Viewer with the Canvas Display

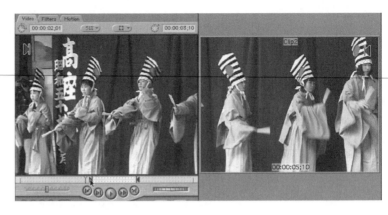

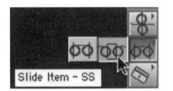

Slide Item - SS

4.44 The Slide Tool

The Slide Tool

Let's look at the last trimming tool, the **Slide** tool, also in the fifth **Tools** button (Figure 4.44). The **Slide** tool can be brought out with **SS** (S twice).

Like the **Slip** tool, it also works only in the **Timeline**. The **Slide** tool doesn't change anything in the clip you're working on; it simply grabs the clip and pulls it forward or backward along the timeline, wiping out material on one side, extending the material on the other side, as shown in Figure 4.45.

Notice that you're not only moving the clip, you're also affecting the two adjacent clips, which is why they're highlighted with boxes.

The **Canvas** display (Figure 4.46) is unlike other two-up displays. You don't see the clip you're moving at all. What's displayed are the two adjacent shots:

- On the left, the end of the shot in front of the one you're moving
- On the right, the beginning of the shot after the one you're moving

In these figures, by moving *Clip2* earlier in time, the first shot *Clip1* is being shortened by 10 frames, while the last shot *Clip3* is being lengthened by 10 frames.

4.45 The Slide Tool in the Timeline

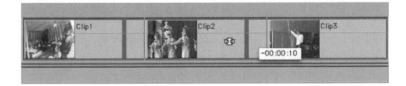

4.46 The Slide Tool Canvas Display

You are limited in how far you can slide a clip by the amount of media available in the adjacent shots. If you move to the end of the available media, the film sprocket overlay will appear in the two-up display.

Look at your finished sequence. It should look something like the sequence called *Food* in the **Browser**. I still wouldn't be very happy with the piece, principally because the audio is so abrupt and choppy, marking each cut. Work would need to be done to smooth out the sound, perhaps extend sound from a single clip, or add some constant underlying sound from somewhere else. But that's for another lesson.

How Long is Long Enough?

A static shot, either close-up or medium shot, needs to be on the screen a much shorter time than a long shot in which the audience is following a movement. A shot that has been seen before, a repeat, can be on the screen quite briefly for the audience to get the information. Though there is no hard and fast rule, generally shots without dialog remain on the screen no more than six to eight seconds on television with its small screen. In feature films shots can be held for quite a bit longer because the viewer's eye has a lot more traveling to do to take in the full scope of the image. This is probably why movies seem much slower on the television screen than they do in the theater. While a close-up can be on the screen quite briefly, a long shot will often contain a great deal of information and needs to be held longer so that your viewer has time for his or her eye to rove around it. A moving shot, such as a pan, you can often hold longer because the audience is basically looking at two shots, one at the beginning and the other at the end. If the movement is well shown—a fairly brisk move, no more than about five seconds—you can also cut it quite tightly. All you need to show is a brief glimpse of the static shot, the movement, and then cut out as soon as the camera settles at the end of the move.

Summary

In this lesson you've learned how to use the **Canvas** editing tools:

- Overwrite
- Insert
- Fit to Fill
- Replace
- Superimpose

You've learned how to use the various sequence editing tools:

- **Roll** and **Ripple**
- **Slip** and **Slide**

When you want to smooth out cuts or to change between scenes, you might want to use transitions. That's what we're going to look at in the next lesson: lots and lots of transitions, how they work, and how to use them.

Lesson 5

Adding Transitions

Transitions can add life to a sequence, ease a difficult edit into something smoother, or give you a way to mark a change of time or place. The traditional grammar of film that audiences still accept is that dissolves denote small changes, while a fade to black followed by a fade from black mark a greater passage of time. With the introduction of digital effects, any imaginable movement or contortion of the image to replace one with another quickly became possible—and were quickly applied everywhere, seemingly randomly, to every possible edit. They can be hideously inappropriate, garish, and ugly. But to each his own taste. Transitions can be used effectively, or they can look terribly hackneyed. Final Cut Express gives you the option to do either or anything in between. Let's look at the transitions FCE has to offer. There are quite a few of them, 77 to be exact, though there is quite a bit of redundancy in the transitions. Some people seem to think that just because Apple put all those transitions in there you have to use them all. Remember most movies only use cuts and the occasional dissolve. Most television programs are just cuts only with a fade in at the beginning and a fade out at the commercial breaks.

Loading the Lesson

Let's begin by loading the material you need on the hard drive of your computer.

1. Open the hybrid DVD. From the folder called *FCE DVD-ROM Contents,* drag the *Media* folder from the DVD to your hard drive, if you don't already have it on your media drive. Again, this contains the media for the project.

2. You may also want to drag the folder called *Transitions* from the DVD onto your media drive. This contains samples of each of the 77 transitions available in Final Cut Express.

3. Also drag onto your system drive from the DVD *Projects* folder the folder called *Lesson 5.* Put it in the *Shared* folder inside *Users* or in your *Documents* folder.

4. Eject the DVD and open the *Lesson 5* folder on your hard drive.

5. Double-click the project file, *L5,* to launch FCE.

6. Once again, go through the reconnect process as in the previous "Loading the Lesson" on page 75 in Lesson 4. You will first get the **Offline Files** window. Click the **Reconnect** button.

Inside your copy of the project *L5* you'll find in the Browser:

- An empty sequence called *Sequence 1*
- The master clip *Damine.mov*
- A still image called *Gradient.pct,* which we'll use later
- The bin called **Clips**

To see the basic settings for each of the 77 FCE transitions, use **File>Import>Folder** to bring into the application the *Transitions* folder you copied onto your hard drive. The folder contains bins with all the transitions grouped in the same fashion they are in the application.

Last time we worked with the food clips. This time we'll be working with a different section of the master clip. When you open the **Clips** bin, you'll see the shots from *Damine.mov* diced into subclips so that each clip is self-contained, as in the previous lesson.

Applying Transitions

Next let's look at the transitions themselves. In the **Browser,** usually behind the **Project** window, is a tab called **Effects.** If you open it, you see a window with a group of folders—sorry, bins—as in Figure 5.1. You'll notice more than transitions in this window. For the moment, we're going to concentrate on the *Video Transitions* bin.

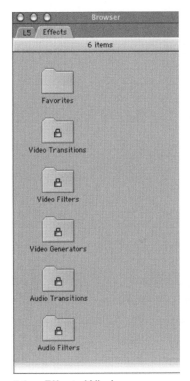

5.1   Effects Window

5.2   Video Transitions Window

This window does not maintain strict interface standards: for some reason, the **Name** column does not force alphanumeric ordering. The order is created internally in FCE, and the first bin is **Favorites**. You can park your special transitions and effects here. It's probably empty now.

Double-click on *Video Transitions* to open the bin. It should look like Figure 5.2. The **Video Transitions** window shows yet more bins, and these bins contain a total of 77 video transitions. I'd be very surprised if any one has actually ever used them all in earnest on real projects, not just playing with them to try them out. The

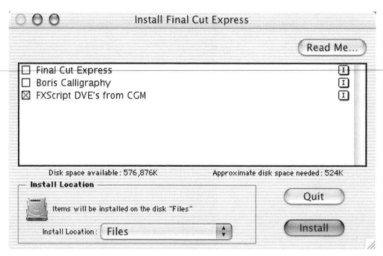

5.3   Installing FXScript DVE's

Transitions bin in your **Browser** contains previews of each of the transitions available in FCE. We're going to try some of them out in this lesson, but before we get into using the transitions, first let's see how the **Favorites** bin works.

Favorite Transitions

Open the *Dissolves* folder, which holds seven different types of dissolves. Who would have thought there were so many ways to do a dissolve?

1. Grab the most commonly used transition in video or film, the **Cross Dissolve**, and drag and drop the transition over to the **Favorites** bin.

2. Open **Favorites** and switch it to **List** view as in Figure 5.4. Remember **Shift-H** will toggle through the views.

3. In **List** view you can change the duration of the transition to your favorite length. Other transitions that have different parameters like borders and adjustable shapes can also be saved here in favorite configurations.

🐾 Note

Missing DVE's: If your Video Transitions bin is missing the **FXScript DVE's** bin, you will need to go back to your install CD and load it. Quit the application first. Load the FCE install CD and run the FCE installer. When you get to the **Software Selection** window, uncheck the **Final Cut Express** checkbox, but do check the **FXScript DVE's from CGM** box and click the **Continue** button (Figure 5.3). This will load the FXScript DVE's into the appropriate folder of your system.

👍 Tip

Real-time Transitions: Whenever a transition's name appears in bold in either the *Video Transitions* folder or in a menu, that indicates that the transition can be played back in real-time. These transitions only appear like this if your system is capable of real-time preview.

You may notice that the transition in the **Favorites** bin is a duplicate. The usual behavior when moving items from one bin to another is that the item is relocated. But when moving an element to **Favorites,** a copy is created. You can put any transitions, video or audio; any effect; or even a generator into **Favorites.** You can rename the transition or effect anything you want.

🐾 Note

Saving Favorites: It's important to note that Favorites are saved as part of your preferences. If you trash your Preferences file, your Favorites go with it. There is a simple solution to this. Drag the Favorites bin from the Effects panel and place it in your Browser. This is a copy of the Favorites bin in Effects, and will remain with the project, even if the prefs are trashed. I keep a *Favorites* project and in it a bin with my favorite effects and filters, sometimes in stacks in separate folders. Whenever I want to access these effects, I open the project and drag the whole folder into the new project. I add new effects to it and occasionally I burn the project onto a CD as a backup.

The default transition in Final Cut Express is the **Cross Dissolve** with a default duration of one second. There are a number of ways to apply a transition in Final Cut Express:

- Drag the transition from the **Effects** panel of the **Browser,** and drop it on an edit point.
- Select the edit point. (Remember, **V** will select the nearest edit point.)Then use the **Effects>Video Transitions** menu and select one.
- Select the edit point, and apply the default transition with the keyboard shortcut **Command-T.**
- Select the edit point, and by **Control**-clicking on the edit point, call up the default transition from the shortcut menu (Figure 5.5)

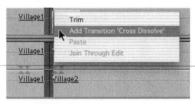

5.5 Transition Shortcut Menu

5.6 Transition Error

5.7 Insufficient Content

5.8 Film Sprocket Overlay in the Viewer

There are a couple of other ways that we skipped in the last lesson, using the two items in the **Canvas Edit Overlay:**

- **Insert with Transition**
- **Overwrite with Transition**

The default transition will appear in your sequence when you select **Insert with Transition** (**Shift-F9**) or **Overwrite with Transition** (**Shift-F10.**)

Checking the Media

1. Let's begin by opening up *Sequence 1*.
2. Next select the three clips at the bottom of the **Clips** bin called *Village* and drag them directly to the sequence. It might be helpful to use **Shift-Z** (**Fit to Window**) if the clips appear too small in the **Timeline.**

Remember these are all subclips, and so each shot you just placed in the timeline contains the full extent of the media for that clip on the hard drive. Or at least Final Cut Express thinks so.

Let's try putting a transition onto the sequence we've laid out.

3. Grab the **Cross Dissolve** transition from either the **Dissolve** bin or from **Favorites** and drag it onto the edit point between *Village1* and *Village2*.

You see that this isn't possible because you get the transition drag icon with a small **X**, as shown in Figure 5.6. If you try to perform the edit by using the keyboard shortcut **Command-T** you'll get the error message in Figure 5.7. Why is this happening? The answer is simple. There isn't enough media in either clip to perform the transition. The shots must overlap; frames from both shots must appear on the screen simultaneously. For a one-second transition, both shots have to have one second of media that overlaps with the other shot.

1. Double-click *Village 1* in the **Timeline** to open it into the **Viewer.**
2. Go to the end of the shot. Use **Shift-O** to take you to the Out point.

If **Overlays** are switched on in the **View** popup as they normally are, you'll see the telltale film sprocket hole indicator on the right edge of the frame (Figure 5.8).

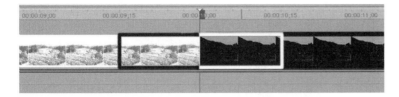

This overlay tells you that you're right at the end of the available media for that shot. There needs to be extra media available to create the overlap for the transition, as shown in Figure 5.9.

The pale shot on the left has to overlap the dark shot on the right by half the length of the transition, and vice versa. If that media does not exist, you can't do the transition. FCE always assumes as a default that the transition takes place centered around the marked edit point, not that it ends at the edit point. Therefore, to execute the default one-second transition, you need at least half a second, 15 frames, of available media after the Out point on the outgoing shot, and 15 frames in front of the In point of the incoming shot. In this case there is nothing, hence the error messages when you try to execute the transition. Unless you think of it ahead of time—and many times you don't—you'll have to deal with it when you're fine-tuning your edit. Often you'd rather not deal with transitions while you're laying out your sequence, leaving them until you've laid out the shot order.

If you know you have extra media in the original clip, you can always go back to extend the media. If this option is available, it's easy to do in FCE. Select **Remove Subclip Limits** from the **Modify** menu.

However, in this case, extending the media will push it into another shot, producing a flash frame during the transition, something to be avoided. This is one of the benefits of subclipping. To be able to put in transitions, we'll have to trim the Out point on *Village1* and the In point of *Village2*. We could do this just by dragging the ends of the shots to make them shorter, but that would leave a hole in the **Timeline**. Instead, we'll use the **Ripple** tool to shorten the shots.

1. Select the **Ripple** tool from the **Tools** palette, or use the keyboard shortcut **RR**.
2. With the **Ripple** tool, click just to the left of the edit point between *Village 1* and *Village2,* as in Figure 5.10.

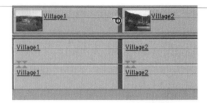

5.10 Ripple Tool in the Timeline

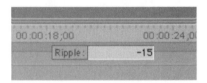

5.11 Ripple Value in the Timeline

3. With **Ripple** active, type in *–15* for 15 frames. Notice the display that appears in the middle of the **Timeline** window (Figure 5.11). Press the **Enter** key.

We know this is the navigation shortcut for going backward half a second. Because we're in the **Ripple** tool, we're rippling it backwards one-half second.

4. Next click on the right side of the edit point at the start of *Village2*.

5. This time type **+15** and press **Enter** to ripple the edit point half a second.

We've now rippled *Village2's* In point by half a second, half a second off the end of the first shot, half a second off the beginning of the second.

Over these three shots laid in the **Timeline**, if I ripple the Ins and Outs on both edits in the **Timeline**, taking 15 frames off the end and the beginning of each shot, I reduce the overall duration by two seconds. This will substantially change the timing of my sequence. If you plan to use transitions between shots, it's best to allow for the extra material within the shot before you lay it in the **Timeline**.

6. Once you've rippled the two edits, go the edit point in the sequence between *Village1* and *Village2* and apply the transition.

If you drag a transition from the **Transitions** bin to an edit point, it does not need to be dragged only to the center line. It can also be dragged to the out clip so that the transition ends at the edit point (the A side), or to the in clip so the transition begins at the start of the clip (the B side). This can only be done, of course, if there is sufficient material for this type of transition. If you only have video available for the transition overlap on one side of the edit, you should not try to execute the transition from the menu or with **Command-T**. These will always execute the default centered on transition edit. If one of the shots does not have enough material to do the transition, you'll get a one-frame transition. Just be careful, because it may seem that a transition has been entered into your sequence when there really isn't anything there of value.

If you double-click on the transition itself in the **Timeline**, it will open into the **Viewer**. This is the **Transition Editor**, which we'll

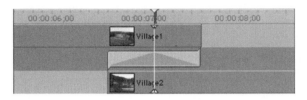

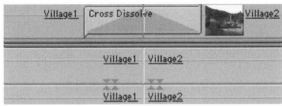

5.12 Clips Overlapping in the Transition Editor

5.13 Center on Edit Transition

look at in detail in a moment. Here you can see how the video overlaps and why extra material—handles—are needed on either end of the transition to create the effect (Figure 5.12).

Once it's in the **Timeline**, the transition displays in one of three ways, depending on how it was placed. Figure 5.13 shows the center position; the other two appear as in Figures 5.14 and 5.15.

Making the transition to start or end on edit is useful if you only have media available on one side of the edit point, if you have a title or other clip on a track without any material adjacent to it, and of course at the beginning or end of your program.

Notice the sloping line indicators showing the type of alignment in each case, and also note that the two latter transitions can only be half-second dissolves. When the sequence was rippled by 15 frames on each side of the edit point, only enough media was made available for a center-aligned transition. If the transition is to end on the edit point, the incoming shot has to be extended a whole second underneath the outgoing shot to accommodate it. Similarly, if you wanted to start the transition on the edit point, the outgoing shot has to extend one second into the incoming shot, one second beyond the start of the edit point. If we made these changes, then we could also easily change the type of transition alignment with a control shortcut menu on the transition in the **Timeline** (Figure 5.16).

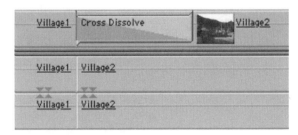

5.14 End on Edit Transition

5.15 Start on Edit Transition

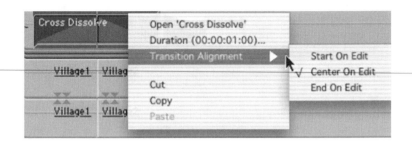

Using the Canvas Edit Overlay

Let's back up a bit to see a better way to do this.

1. Delete everything in the **Timeline**.

2. Open *Village1* from the **Browser** into the **Viewer**.

Because this will be the first shot in the timeline, I won't need to shorten the front of the clip.

3. Hit the **End** key to take you to the end of the shot.

4. Type *–1.* (minus one period) and enter. This will move the playhead back one second.

5. Press **O** to enter the Out point and drag to the **CEO Overwrite** box, or press **F10** to overwrite it into the **Timeline**.

6. Open *Village2* in the **Viewer** from the **Browser**. This clip we should shorten on both ends.

7. Go to the beginning of the clip. Type *+1.* and enter an In point.

8. Then go to the end of the clip and enter an Out point one second before the end (type *–1.* and press **O**).

9. Drag *Village2* from the **Viewer** to **Overwrite with Transition** as in Figure 5.17—not to **Overwrite**. Or press **Shift-F10**.

The clip immediately drops into the **Timeline** after the first clip. The default transition has been added at the beginning of the clip, as well as a default audio crossfade. Adding the audio crossfade is a bonus that enhances the edit and helps to smooth the transition (Figure 5.18). If you use the shortcut menu to create a transition in the **Timeline**, this also will add the audio crossfade.

Rendering

In adding your transition to your sequence, you may have encountered the need for rendering for the first time. After you've

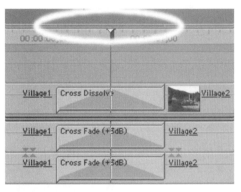

5.18 Transition with Audio Cross Fade

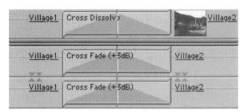

5.17 Overwrite with Transition

5.19 Render Indicator

entered a transition, you'll see that the narrow bar at the top of the **Timeline** has changed color from the normal mid-gray. It will have changed to red or green, depending on your system capabilities. If you are working with a system with no real-time capabilities, then a bright red line will appear over the transition, indicating that a portion of the sequence needs to be rendered (Figure 5.19).

I've circled the red bar because the grayscale image doesn't show it clearly. If your system were capable of real-time transitions, this bar would appear green. All other transitions will need to be rendered.

Rendering means that the application has to create media for which none exists. Most of the two shots are on your hard drive, but not for the 30 frames that make up this one-second cross dissolve, during which one shot is changing into the other. The material of one shot mixed together with another is not on your hard drive. All you've done is give the computer instructions to create that media. If you try to play across that part of the timeline with a non–real-time system, the **Canvas** will momentarily display the message in Figure 5.20.

5.20 Unrendered Warning

Real-time Preview

FCE's real time can only be seen in the **Canvas** and only when the external viewing is switched off. It will not send a real-time DV signal out the FireWire cable. So you have a choice: either monitor through FireWire but not in real time, or monitor on your desktop screen.

So if you think you have real-time capabilities and you're still seeing a red line in your sequence, it's probably because you have **External Viewing** turned on. You can switch it off from the **View** menu, by going right down at the bottom to the **Video submenu**. Here you can select either **Real-Time** or **FireWire**. Fortunately there is a keyboard shortcut that will quickly toggle this on and off: **Command-F12.**

Remember, this is real-time preview only. As soon as you revert to viewing your video externally or you want to output your material to tape, all those items that were in real time on your desktop a moment ago now have to be rendered out.

Aside from the real-time effects, there are also the so-called **Proxy Effects**. These effects have a yellow rather than red or green render bar. A **Proxy Effect** is one that plays in real time but only as an approximation of the full effect; some of its controls and features will not be included in real time. There are many ways to render out these various effects. Unfortunately, Apple has made this process far more complex than is necessary. The various render commands are shown in Table 5.1.

Sequence	Effects	Window
Render All		⌥R
Render Selection		⌘R
Mixdown Audio		⌥⌘R
Render RT Effects		⌃R
Render Proxy Effects		⌥⌘P

5.21 Sequence>Render

There are many ways to render out these various effects. The various render commands are shown in Table 5.1. The displays in the **Sequence** menu (Figure 5.21) change depending on the conditions in the **Timeline**. The key shortcuts to remember are **Option-R** to **Render All** and **Command-R** to **Render Selection** or **Render In to Out.**

Table 5.1   Render Commands

Render All	Option-R	Render Real Time Effects	Control-R
Render Selection	Command-R	Render Proxy Effects	Command-Option-R
Render In to Out	Command-R (yes, the same shortcut)	Mixdown Audio	Command-Option-R (yes, it's the same)
Render nonRT Effects	Command-R (one more time)		

👉 Tip_____

Playing the Red: By using **Option-P**, you can still play through a red transition without leaving the sequence, albeit not in real time, but in slow motion. This is a good way to see if the transition will play smoothly, if there are any unforeseen flash frames or other unpleasant hiccups in the effect. The faster your system, the faster it will play through the transition. More complex effects that we will see later will only play slowly, even on the fastest computers, without hardware assistance. What's good is that FCE caches the playback, so that the first time you play back using **Option-P**, it might take quite a while, but the next time the playback will be considerably faster. This only applies to using **Option-P**. Regular play with the spacebar will still produce the unrendered message. You can also scrub through a transition by switching *Snapping* off and mousing down in the *Timeline Ruler*, slowly moving the playhead through the transition area.

Render Management

Render files are stored by FCE in the *Audio Render Files* folder and the *Render Files* folder of your designated scratch disk. The renders are stored in separate folders based on the project name, one folder for each project. FCE keeps track of the renders required for the output of each sequence. It keeps all the renders it generates for each session, so while you're working you can step back through those 32 levels of undo and not lose your renders. As you keep rendering and changing and re-rendering, FCE holds onto all those renders it creates while the application is open. At the end of the session, however, when you quit the application, it dumps any render files it no longer needs to play back any of the sequences in the project. It will hold onto any renders it needs for play back. All these render files will start to pile up after a while. If you delete a project, its render files won't go with it. They'll just sit on your hard drive in the folder with the projects name.

It's a good idea to weed out the old files in your render folders, video more importantly than audio because the files are much larger. Sometimes it might be as simple as discarding an old project folder, throwing out all the renders associated with it. Sometimes, for long-form projects that go on for a long time, managing your render files requires you to go in and dig out these old files. The simplest way to do this is to open up the *Render Files* folder for that project and switch the window to List view as in Figure 5.22. List view will show you not only the file names, which are pretty meaningless, but also the date modified. By clicking on the **Date Modified** column, you can sort the renders by when they where created, giving you a clue about which ones

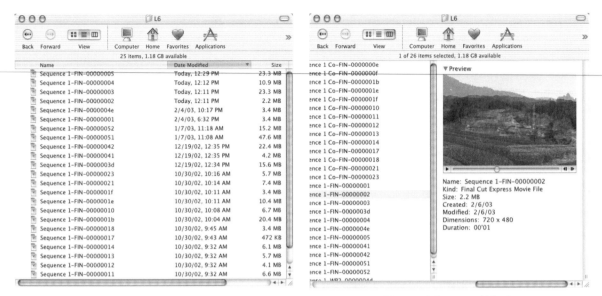

5.22 Render Files in List View

5.23 Render Files and Preview Window

are worth keeping and which aren't. If you're uncertain, just select the render file while in List view and then switch to Column view, where you can use the preview window to actually look at the little QuickTime file that the render generates (Figure 5.23). Move the files you think don't need into the trash and then run the project. If the project needs some of the render files you'll get the **Reconnect** dialog box. That will give you a chance to move back into the *Render Files* folder the missing items.

Controlling Transitions

Once you've played back your transition with **Option-P** a couple of times, or rendered it out and looked at it, you may discover that it isn't quite the way you'd want it to be. You may want to shorten or lengthen it or shift the actual edit point. Assuming you have material available for this, it is easiest to do in the **Timeline** itself. To change the duration of the transition, simply grab one end of it and pull, as in Figure 5.24. It's a good idea to switch **Snapping** off before you do this, because it's easy to snap the transition down to nothing. As you pull the transition, a little window displays the amount of change as well as the new duration of the transition. If you have an audio crossfade as well as a transition, that will also change with your action. While you're dragging the transition end, you'll get the two-up display in the **Canvas** that shows you the frames at the edit point (Figure 5.25).

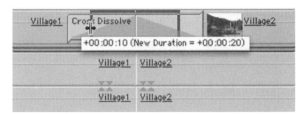

5.24 Shortening Transition in the Timeline

5.25 Two-Up Display in Canvas

You can also change the edit point in the center of the transition. Simply move the **Selector** to the center of the edit, and it will immediately change to the **Roll** tool, allowing you to move the edit point, together with the transition along the **Timeline**, left and right as desired (Figure 5.26). You can also ripple either shot, but to do that you have to call up the **Ripple** tool (RR) and then pull either shot left or right, shortening or lengthening the sequence while not affecting the transition (Figure 5.27). Again, the two-up display in the Canvas will show you the frames you're working on.

Transition Editor

Final Cut gives you another way to control the transition and fine tune it. This is done in the **Transition Editor** (Figure 5.28), which we saw briefly earlier.

Double-click on the transition itself in the **Timeline** window to evoke the **Transition Editor**. It opens in the **Viewer**. The **Viewer** displays the transition as a separate track between the two video tracks on which the clips sit.

The **Transition Editor** allows you to control the transition. Some of them, such as **Swing** in Figure 5.28, have quite a few controls. At the top in the center is a small group of buttons that let you position where the transition will occur. The transition will be

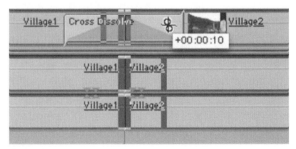

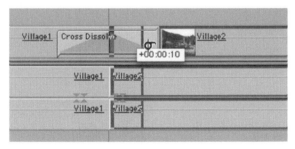

5.26 Rolling the Transition Edit Point

5.27 Rippling the Transition Edit Point

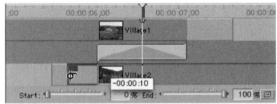

5.28 Swing Transition Editor

5.29 Rippling Clip in Transition Editor

placed in the default centered position between the two clips, shown by the middle button. Using the left button moves the transition so that it begins at the edit point. The right button in moves the transition so that it ends at the edit point.

The primary purpose of the **Transition Editor** is to access the controls some transitions offer you. Here you can also fine tune the effect, to shorten or lengthen it as needed. As in the **Timeline**, you can do this by dragging either end of the transition. The **Canvas** displays the end and start frames for the two shots.

By grabbing the center of the transition, you evoke the **Roll** tool, which allows you to drag the transition forward and backward along the clips, provided there is available media.

You can also ripple edit either the end of either outgoing or incoming clip by pulling it (Figure 5.29). You don't have to call up the **Ripple** tool. Simply by moving the cursor into position, it will change to the appropriate tool. As with all ripple edits, you are changing the duration of the tracks involved and may be pulling the alignment of clips on different tracks out of kilter.

Notice the two sliders in the **Transition Editor,** one for **Start** and the other for **End,** each with percentage boxes adjacent. The transition starts at 0% completed and ends at 100% completion. You can adjust these sliders so that the **Cross Dissolve** will pop in at more than zero to start or suddenly finish before the transition reaches completion. In **Cross Dissolve** this produces a rather ugly effect. There is also a small arrow button to the right of the **End**

Note_____

Navigating the Transition Editor:
The **Grab Handle** in the upper right corner lets you pull a transition from the **Transition Editor** onto an edit point in the **Timeline**. This is useful if you've opened the editor directly from the **Transitions** bin. This is the only way you can grab it drag the transition. There is also a popup for recent clips in the **Transition Editor.**

slider. This will swap the effect for you, usually reversing the direction. Below that is a small circle with a red cross in it. This is the **Parameters Reset** button. This is useful for more complex transitions. Also note that the **Reset** button does not reset the **Start** and **End** sliders, nor the arrow, only the other parameters.

Using Transitions

Now that we know how to add and trim transitions, let's look at the transitions themselves. To change the transition:

- Drag the new transition from transitions folder in the **Effects** window and drop it on the existing transition in the timeline or

- Select the transition in the **Timeline** by clicking on it and then select a new choice from the **Effects>Video Transitions** menu.

I'm not going to go through each of the transitions, though I would like to highlight a couple because they will show you how the controls work in some of the other changeable transitions. To see all the transitions, look at the individual QuickTime movies in the *Transitions* folder on the DVD. Many of the transitions have lots of variables, such as colored borders and the direction in which a motion transition such as **Swing** occurs.

FXScript DVE's Page Peel

There are a number of FXScript DVE's Page Peels, but let's look at the main one to see how the controls work (Figure 5.30). Some of these controls are available in other transitions as well.

Page Peel is often overused, but sometimes it really is the right effect, especially for wedding videos. This is also the first introduction to FCE's **Well**.

Apply the transition and double-click on it to open it into the **Transition Editor** (Figure 5.31).

The **Direction** dial changes the angle at which the page peels back, while the **Rotate** controls how much the peel pivots as it turns under. With **Rotate** you can make it seem as though the page will peel in one direction, and then swing it around so that it turns back into another.

The **Radius** slider sets the tightness of the peel. The farther it moves to the left the tighter the arc becomes.

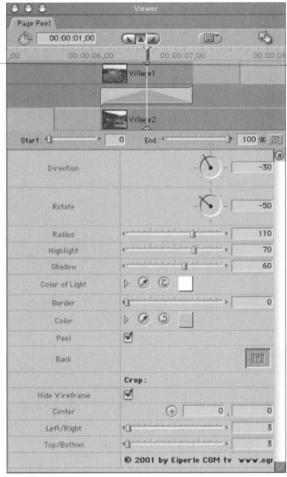

5.30 FXScript DVE's Page Peel

5.31 Page Peel Controls (right)

The **Highlight** slider sets how shiny the highlight on the back of the page appears, while the **Color of Light** swatch lets you put a colored gel over the light that creates the shine on the back of the image. The farther to the left you move the **Highlight** slider, the more muted the shine becomes. There is no control of the width of the highlight area.

The **Shadow** slider effectively controls the contrast between the shine and the backing image. With the slider pushed all the way to 100, you just get a black-and-white back, all black shadow with the **Highlight** on it.

The **Border** lets you add a colored edge to the image. The color is set by clicking in the swatch below it.

If you uncheck the **Peel** checkbox, the image will not only peel back, but also curl in on itself. With a tight **Radius** you'll get the image rolling up like it's a scroll.

The **Well** lets you use another image as part of an effect. In this case, the **Well** lets you map another image onto the back of the **Page Peel**. The default is to place the same image, flopped, on the back of the page, but you can use any image in your project.

To put a color on the back, use the **Video Generator** in the **Viewer** to create a color matte.

1. Open any clip into the **Viewer**. The **A** with the **Filmstrip** icon in the lower left corner evokes the **Generators** (Figure 5.32).

2. Select **Matte>Color**.

Set the color in the **Control** tab (Figure 5.33). Click on the swatch to access the system color picker (Figure 5.34). Note the swatch tray at the bottom which lets you move color selections from application to application, not only within FCE.

3. Switch back to the **Video** tab and drag the **Color Matte** from the **Viewer** into the **Browser**. That's a good place it for future use, if you want to use the same color for other effects.

4. Reopen the **Page Peel** transition from the **Timeline**, and pull the **Color Matte** from the **Browser**. Drop it into the **Well**, making it part of the transition.

5. You should leave **Hide Wireframe** checked on. Without it, a gray box is added to the frame during the transition.

The **Crop** sliders let you cut off any black fringing that appears on the edges of some digitized material. This is in the blanking area outside the television mask and not normally seen by the viewer, but when the image moves so that its edges become visible, then the few lines of black on the edge of the frame can be seen. For this reason, FXScript DVE's transitions have added this feature.

6. The tiny **Arrow** checkbox at the top toggles between peeling the page off, the default, and peeling the page on, an unusual variation.

🐭Note
Static Well: Unfortunately the **Well** won't track an image or change if a video clip is used. The **Well** simply uses the In point of the video clip as its map. In the case of **Page Peel**, there is no movement on the back-side of the page. Sorry.

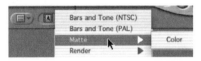

5.32 Generators Button

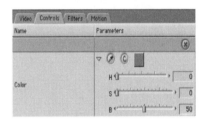

5.33 Color Matte Controls Tab

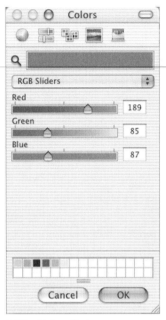

5.34   Color Picker

5.35   Softwipe Controls

Softwipe

Softwipe looks deceptively simple, but under its simplicity of control is disguised a huge amount of power. The power is in the **Method** popup under **Pattern**, coupled with the **Pattern Well** (Figure 5.35).

Let's first look at the default controls, which activate the soft-edged color bar that wipes one image off, replacing it with another. The **Softness** control at the top regulates how blurry the edges of the transition are where one image replaces another. The **Width** slider at the bottom sets the width of the color bar. Set **Width** to zero, and you get a soft-edge directional wipe with no color overlay. The **Direction** clock sets the angle at which the wipe moves. It's fully controllable, anywhere in the 360° circumference.

With the popup set to **Direction**, the **Center** point crosshairs have no effect, but if you switch the popup to **Radial**, you now get a soft-edged radial wipe. Now the **Center** point crosshairs controls where the radial generates. Click the **Crosshairs** button and then click in the **Canvas** where you want the wipe to originate (Figure 5.36).

Pattern is what makes **Softwipe** a crucial tool in Final Cut. In the project **Browser** is an image called *Gradient.pct*. If you open it up and take a look at it in the **Viewer**, you'll see that it's a complex, grayscale checkerboard pattern. This is the basis of patterning in

Softwipe or any gradient wipe. The image will be wiped on or off, based on the grayscale values of pattern image. The darkest parts of the pattern image will be where the incoming image will appear first, and the lightest parts will be where the image will appear last. In the gradient pattern we have, some of the outside boxes will appear first, while as the transition approaches mid-point as in Figure 5.37 the lower left to upper right diagonal of the image will still be from the outgoing shot. There is no end to the huge variety of patterns you can get to manipulate this control. If you don't like a pattern, simply replace it another.

To apply the pattern, drag it and drop it into the upper of the two **Pattern Wells**, the little icon with the filmstrip and the question mark (Figure 5.38).

The **Temporary Pattern Well** allows you to place a pattern or other image on the screen that's actually visible as the transition takes place. This will replace the **Color Width** if it's active.

There is a folder of *Softwipe Patterns* on the FCE installation CD that gives you 65 grayscale images. Copy these onto your computer to make them available to use with this transition. They are inside the *Extras* folder, inside *FXScript DVE's by CGM*. There is also a *Workshops/Tutorials* folder that's a useful resource for the CGM effects.

Softwipe is probably my favorite and most used transition, after a simple **Cross Dissolve**. I like it because it is so infinitely variable, and you can always find some way to make it look just a little different and just right for the effect.

Conclusion

If those aren't enough transitions for you, there are more third-party transitions, such as the Video Spice Rack from Pixelan http://www.pixelan.com.

That's it for transitions. Everybody has their favorites, I'm sure. Mine are fairly simple: mostly **Cross Dissolves** and **FXScript Softwipes**. Many I've never used. Many should probably never be used, and most you'll probably never see. Next we go on to advanced editing techniques and working with audio.

5.36 Softwipe Radial

5.37 Softwipe Pattern

5.38 The Well

Lesson 6

Advanced Editing: Using Sound

Film and video are primarily visual media. Oddly enough, though, the moment an edit occurs is often driven as much by the sound as by the picture. So let's take a look at editing sound in Final Cut Express. How sound is used, where it comes in, and how long it lasts are key to good editing. With few exceptions, sound almost never cuts with the picture. Sometimes the sound comes first and then the picture; sometimes the picture leads the sound. The principal reason video and audio are so often cut separately is that we see and hear quite differently. We see in cuts. I look from one person to another, from one object to another, from the keyboard to the monitor. Though my head turns or my eyes travel across the room, I really only see the objects I'm interested in looking at. We hear, on the other hand, in fades. I walk into a room, the door closes behind me, and the sound of the other room fades away. As a car approaches, the sound gets louder. Screams, gunshots, and doors slamming being exceptions, our aural perception is based on smooth transitions from one to another. Sounds, especially background sounds, generally need to overlap to smooth out the jarring abruptness of the hard cut.

Loading the Lesson

This is going to sound familiar, but it's worth repeating. Begin by loading the material you need on the media hard drive of your computer

1. If you don't already have it on your drive, drag the *Media* folder from the *FCE DVD-ROM Contents* folder for the book's DVD to your media drive

2. Open the *Projects* folder on the DVD and drag the *Lesson 6* folder into the *Shared* folder on your system hard drive or your *Documents* folder.

3. Eject the DVD, open the *Lesson 6* folder, and double-click the project file *L6* to launch the application

4. Once again, choose the **Reconnect** option to relink the media files when the **Offline Files** dialog appears

Setting up the Project

You'll find in the project's **Browser** an empty sequence called *Sequence 1* and a number of other sequences that we'll look at during this lesson. There is also the master clip *Damine.mov* and the folder called *Clips*, which contains the subclips pulled from the master

Viewing Your Material

In this lesson we're going to look at the religious ceremony at the heart of the Dengaku festival itself, *Ceremony1* through *Ceremony9*, in the **Clips** bin.

The Trim Edit Window

Before we get into editing this material, we should take a look at FCE's **Trim Edit** window, which is a powerful tool for precisely editing your material and looking at edit points.

1. You open the **Trim Edit** window by double-clicking on an edit point, or by moving the playhead to an edit point and using the menu **Sequence>Trim Edit** or the keyboard shortcut **Command-7**.

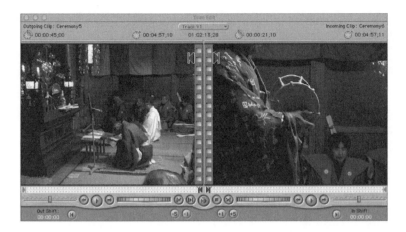

6.1 Trim Edit Window

2. Let's bring a couple of shots into the **Timeline**. Select *Ceremony5* and *Ceremony6* in the **Clips** bin and drag them directly to **Overwrite** in the **Canvas**.

3. Double-click on the edit point between the shots in the **Time-line**. This will call up the window in Figure 6.1.

Notice the sprocket hole indicators on the inner edges of the frames. This overlay indicates that the clips are at the limits of their media, but we can still ripple this edit just as we did in the previous lesson when we had to ripple the two shots to create room for a transition.

The green bars over the frames in the **Trim Edit** window indicate what mode you're in. When a green bar appears over both sides, as in Figure 6.2, you're in Roll edit mode. By clicking on one side or the other, you can either ripple the outgoing shot (as in Figure 6.3) or the incoming shot (as in Figure 6.4). To get back to Roll edit, click on the space between the two frames.

6.2 Roll Edit Indicator in Trim Edit

6.3 Ripple Left Indicator in Trim Edit

6.4 Ripple Right Indicator in Trim Edit

6.5 Roll Edit Indicator in the Timeline

6.6 Ripple Left Indicator in the Timeline

6.7 Ripple Right Indicator in the Timeline

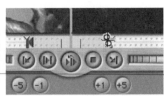

6.8 Roll Edit in Trim Edit

You can toggle between the **Ripple** and **Roll** tools in the **Trim Edit** window with the U key. The U key cycling between **Ripple Left, Ripple Right,** and the **Roll** tool is also reflected in the way the edit point is selected in the **Timeline** (Figures 6.5–6.7).

You can ripple and roll the edit points by dragging them in either window. When you're in Ripple mode, the cursor will change to the **Ripple** tool, and when you're in Roll mode, the cursor automatically becomes the **Roll** tool, as shown in Figure 6.8.

You can also use the little plus and minus buttons at the bottom of the window to make incremental edits on either side of the **Trim Edit** window. You can move the edit point by one or five frames at a time. The five-frame value can be changed anywhere from two to nine in the preferences in **Multi-Frame Trim Size.**

The spacebar serves an interesting function in the **Trim Edit** window. It acts in play-around loop mode. It will play around the edit point again and again so you can view it repeatedly.

There's a lot of useful timecode information at the top of the **Trim Edit** window. Notice that the **Trim Edit** window displays the master clip timecode at the top of each window, which is not the timecode you see when you open each subclip individually into the **Viewer.**

- The number to the far left is the duration of the outgoing shot, *Ceremony5* in this case (*A* in Figure 6.9).
- The next timecode number is the Out point of the outgoing shot (*B* in Figure 6.9).
- The center number under the track indicator is the current time in the sequence (*C* in Figure 6.9). Ignore the fact that it starts with one hour.
- The next number displayed is the duration of the incoming shot (*D* in Figure 6.9).
- On the far right of the window, the number is the current In point of the incoming shot, *Ceremony6* (*E* in Figure 6.9)

The Split Edit

A common method of editing is to first lay down the shots in scene order entirely as straight cuts. After you've laid the material out as cuts, you can begin applying transitions, as you did in the last chapter. But because audio and video so seldom cut in parallel in a finished video, you will have to offset video and audio.

When audio and video have separate In and Out points that aren't at the same time, the edit is called a split edit (Figure 6.10), J-cut (Figure 6.11), or L-cut (Figure 6.12). Whatever you call it, the effect is the same. There are many ways to create these edits, which I lump together as split edits.

In the Timeline

Many instructors tell you to perform these edits in the **Viewer,** but I think the **Viewer** is the least flexible place to create them. Let's set up a split edit inside the **Timeline.** It's a much more logical place to perform this type of work and very effective.

Delete whatever you have in your sequence and bring in *Ceremony2.* Just drag it straight to the **Canvas** to **Overwrite** from the **Clips** bin. Play through this shot in the **Timeline.** It starts out as a cutaway and then later pans across to the principal priest. You may notice that the priest's chanting begins before the camera reaches him. This will create a small problem for us that we'll quickly fix. The finished split edit can be seen in the **Browser** inside the *Split Edit Sequence.*

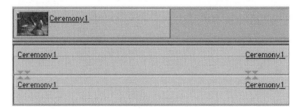

6.10 Split Edit (above)

6.11 J-cut (above right)

6.12 L-cut (right)

The Cutaway

Any editor will tell you that cutaways are the most useful shots. You can never have too many, and you never seem to have enough. No editor will ever complain that you have shot too many cutaways. A cutaway shot shows a subsidiary action or reaction that you can use to bridge an edit, like the shot of the interviewer nodding in response to an answer. The cutaway allows you to bridge a portion of the interviewee's answer where the person has stumbled over the words or has digressed into something pointless. A wide shot that shows the whole scene can often be used as a cutaway. Make note of these useful shots as you're watching your material.

Let's first cut out the pan to the priest reading.

1. Working in the **Timeline**, find the point just before the camera pans from right to left.

2. Use **Control-V** to cut the shot.

3. Play forward until you find the point where the camera settles on the priest reading from the scroll.

4. Again use **Control-V** and the **Ripple Delete** (keyboard shortcut: **Shift-Delete**) to remove the section of the shot that contains the pan.

5. Play across the edit you've created.

Split Edit Process

You'll see at once that the sound of the priest when he begins chanting has been cut off. This sounds quite ugly, but it's not a problem. It can be easily repaired with a split edit.

1. Hold down the **Option** key and click in the audio tracks on the edit point as in Figure 6.13 to select only the audio portion of the edit.

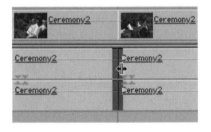

6.13 Selecting Audio Edit

It may be helpful if you turn on the audio waveform display in the **Timeline**. You can do this with the keyboard shortcut **Command-Option-W**.

2. Once the audio edit has been selected, hit **R** to call up the **Roll** tool.

3. Holding down the **Option** key, drag the audio edit point toward the head of the **Timeline**, well past where the chanting will begin (Figure 6.14). If **Snapping** is turned on, it may be helpful to toggle it off with the **N** key.

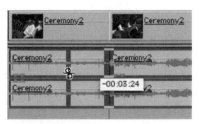

6.14 Dragging the Audio Roll Tool

🐾 *Note*
Toggling Linking: Option-clicking the audio (or video) edit point will only toggle off **Linked Selection**, if **Linked Selection** is turned on. If **Linked Selection** is off, **Option**-clicking the edit point will toggle it on.

Notice a small box appears that gives you a time duration change for the edit you are making. We know the chanting is just a second or so before the start of the edit, so drag back well past that. You're overshooting the point at which you want to make the edit. I find this makes it easier to find a good cut point than simply trying to edge it into place. The **Timeline** audio waveform display will make it easy to see where the chanting begins

4. Scrub the **Timeline** or play that portion of the **Timeline** around the voice entrance back and forth a few times.

5. Use the arrow keys to precisely find the point where the audio starts. Once you've found the spot, leave the playhead parked there.

6. Again use the **Option-Roll** edit on the audio edit point and pull it back to the voice in point. Now it would be helpful if you toggled **Snapping** on with the **N** key. The roll edit will snap right to the playhead as in Figure 6.15.

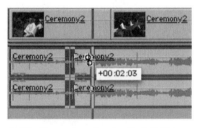

6.15 Dragging Audio Roll Edit to the Playhead

Now the sound should play smoothly, coming in while the acolytes are bowing and then continuing after the cut to the priest.

In this case the edit works quite smoothly because you're cutting within the same scene with basically the same audio ambience. However, this type of edit between scenes can create a jarring sound track. I often prefer to use a variation of this technique.

Alternative Method

Instead of doing the roll edit on the same inline audio track, I first move the audio down to an empty track so that the sound of the two shots overlap. This is easy to do.

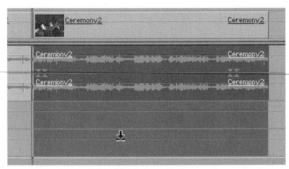

6.16 Dragging Audio to New Track   6.17 Out of Sync Audio

1. First undo the edits you've done so that you're back at the state of having a straight cut between the two pieces of *Ceremony2*, with the priest's voice cut off.

2. Before beginning the split edit, **Option**-click on the audio portion of the track. This selects it independently from the video portion, temporarily unlinking the selection.

3. Now drag the audio track down to an empty audio track. Do not hold down the **Option** key, or you'll duplicate rather than move the audio track. As you drag it downwards, hold down the **Shift** key to constrain the movement to the vertical axis (Figure 6.16).

☞ Tip
Moving Clips between Tracks: Another way to move those audio tracks onto the lower layers is simply to hold down the **Option** key and select the tracks. With the tracks selected, still holding down the **Option** key, tap the **Down** arrow key. Each time you tap the key, the tracks will move down one layer. You can use the arrow keys to move any clip up or down in the layers, provided there is room on the track for the clips.

If you don't hold down the **Shift** key, the sound can easily slip out of sync with the picture. If that happens, you'll see time indicators in the **Timeline** tracks (Figure 6.17) showing you how far out of sync the clips have slipped.

The time slippage shows in a red box. The minus number means that the audio is two frames ahead the picture. The plus number in the video indicates that the picture is two frames behind the sound.

Syncing: If the audio does slip out of sync, you can often get it back in sync with the *Undo* command, but if you can't undo it, the easiest way is to **Control**-click on the red box and choose **Move to Sync** from the shortcut menu (Figure 6.18).

You could also nudge the clip back into sync. **Option**-click on the audio to select the audio portion of the clip. If you just click on the audio, you'll select both video and audio even though they are out of sync. With only the audio selected, use the < or > keys to slide the clip forward or backwards.

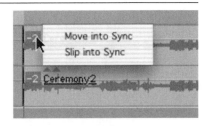

6.18 Move to Sync

With the audio now on a separate track, you can now use the basic arrow tool, the **Selector,** to drag the audio edit point.

4. Hold down the **Option** key before you grab the end of the audio and drag the sound under the audio of the previous shot as in Figure 6.19.

One nice thing about doing the audio overlap on a lower track is that you get a visual display of the edit point in the **Canvas** while you drag the audio, which can be a useful guide. You can also do this with an **Extend** edit.

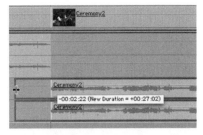

6.19 Option-Dragging Audio Edit to Overlap Sound

Extend Edit

Final Cut's **Extend Edit** is another nice way to perform a roll edit. It's a simple way to move an edit point, even one with a transition.

1. **Option**-click on the audio edit to select it.
2. Move the playhead in the **Timeline** to where you want the edit to move. Press **E** or select **Sequence>Extend Edit.**

If the selection is dimmed in the menu or you hear a system warning, it's because you don't have enough media to perform the **Extend Edit.** What's nice about **Extend Edit** is that, like **Roll,** you can do it to sync picture and sound or to audio and video separately.

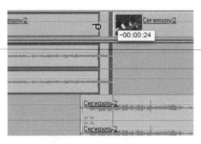

6.20　Rippling Video

6.21　Sync Link Broken after Ripple Edit

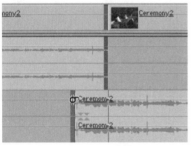

6.22　Selecting Empty Side of Audio Edit Point

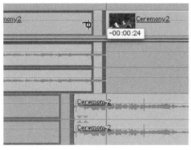

6.23　Rippling Split Edit with Empty Space

Removing Jiggle

Now that you've done the split edit, you may still have a little jiggle on the end of the first *Ceremony2* clip. A moment after the camera pans down the group of bowing men, just after it settles, it moves up and down a bit before beginning the pan that you've cut out. The simplest way to remove this bobble is to ripple the video.

1. Select the **Ripple** tool (**RR**) and place the cursor slightly to the left of the edit point, as shown in Figure 6.20.

As soon as you let go of the mouse, something bad happens, I'm afraid. I think Final Cut's behavior is unfortunate in this technique. It actually breaks the sync link on the second shot (Figure 6.21). This does not occur when the audio tracks are inline. But there is a way around this problem.

2. With the **Ripple** tool, click in the video portion to the left of the edit as before.

3. **Command**-click in the empty space right next to the audio on **A3** to select the space on the empty side of the edit (Figure 6.22).

Now if you do the ripple edit, the empty space will be rippled as well, pulling the sync-linked audio with it (Figure 6.23).

Editing in the Timeline is a quick and easy way to work. Many people like it because it keeps you flowing through your material without taking you away from the sequence of shots. There are two other methods of doing split edits:

- One in the **Trim Edit** window

- The other in the **Viewer**

In the Trim Edit Window

This is where I prefer to do split edits. It's simple to use, efficient, and gives you good control over the material.

So that you won't have to go back and make up the edit again, I've prepared the sequence *Pan Edit Sequence*. Before we open it, though, let's duplicate it.

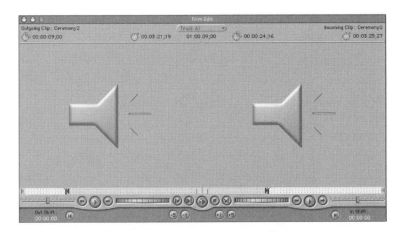

1. Select *Pan Edit Sequence* in the **Browser** and from the menus select **Edit>Duplicate** or use the keyboard shortcut **Option-D**.

2. Open up the duplicate you just created and look at the two halves of *Ceremony2* that are in the **Timeline.**

The pan has been cut out, but the audio of the chanting is still clipped, so you're ready to do the split edit.

3. **Option**-double-click on the audio track on the edit point between the two parts of *Ceremony2*

We have to **Option**-double-click because we want to open the audio separately without affecting the video edit point. You can also **Option**-click on the audio edit point to highlight the edit and then hit **Command-7**. Either way will open the **Trim Edit** window as shown in Figure 6.24. It would be really nice if actual waveform displays of the audio showed up here rather than simply the large speaker icons.

If you drop the sound tracks to **A3** and **A4** so that the audio will overlap as you did earlier, then **Option**-double-clicking on the end of the audio track will call up the **Trim Edit** window with black on the left and the speaker icon in the right window.

In either case, if you open the **Trim Edit** window with the standard **Selector** (Arrow) tool, the window defaults to working in Roll mode, which is what we want.

I like using the **Trim Edit** window for several reasons:

*   You have the playaround feature with the big **Play** button or the spacebar.
*   You can listen to the audio track by scrubbing it.

☞ *Tip*
Moving Slowly in Trim Window:
Unfortunately, the arrow keys will not move the playhead slowly in the **Trim Edit** window. You can though click and hold down the **Next Frame** or the **Previous Frame** buttons to move slowly forward and backward. You can also move forward slowly by holding down the **K** and **L** keys together. To move backwards slowly, hold down the **K** and **J** keys together. To go forward one frame, hold down the **K** key and tap **L**. Backwards one frame, tap **J**. Remember the spacebar here works to preview the edit point, which is very useful. And use the **U** key to toggle between the **Roll** tool and **Ripple First Shot** and **Ripple Second Shot**.

- You can use the **J**, **K**, and **L** keys to rock and roll the play-head.

- You can use the **I** or **O** keys to set In or Out points.

When you use these features, the Timeline will immediately update the track position, sliding the audio of the second half of the shot under the first.

4. Use the play keys or scrub the track in the right window to find the In point for the start of the priest's chanting.

5. Press **I** and the audio portion of the track with be rolled in the **Timeline**.

These tools are key to creating interesting and effective audio tracks in Final Cut. Learn them and get comfortable using them.

In the Viewer

6.25 Audio Panel

You can work in the **Viewer** similar to the way you work in the **Trim Edit** window, but in the **Viewer** you have even greater control because you can actually see the audio waveform displayed. You can edit with precision.

1. Start by undoing the audio trim you just did in the duplicate of the *Pan Edit Sequence*. You should be back to the two halves of *Ceremony2*

2. This time, **Option**-double-click on the audio portion of the second half of the shot. This will open the **Audio** panel in the **Viewer** (Figure 6.25). You can clearly see in the waveform where the chanting begins that's been cut off by the edit.

3. Scrub through the audio to find the beginning of the chanting, and position the playhead at the start of the sound.

4. Use **Command-+** to zoom in around the playhead to see the waveform in real detail.

5. Before you enter a new In point, switch to the **Roll** tool (**R**) and then enter **I** for in.

This will do the same as the **Trim Edit** window, the Timeline will update with the new edit point.

Backtiming

Let's look at how to control the video and lay it over picture so that the audio comes in first, a technique called backtiming.

Creating the Bed

To explain this concept, let's built a new sequence. My finished sequence *Drum Sequence* is in the **Browser.** You may want to look at it first. Or you may want to do the exercise and watch it later or not at all. Start by opening *Sequence 1* and deleting anything that you may still have in it. To begin the sequence, let's look at the shot *Ceremony7*. It's about 20 seconds long and shows a medium-close shot of a priest chanting and banging a drum. Obviously this shot is too long to play as it is. On the other hand, I do want to see the priest in a closeup at some point. Because this shot contains the music, I want to use it as the basis for the scene. This will be the key shot in the scene. It's often useful to establish the key shot first, and then build the rest of the scene around it. Using this shot allows me to create a continuous event, with a couple of added bonuses:

- I don't have to cut the music, though in this case its repetitive nature would make cutting fairly simple.

- When I come to the priest banging the drum, he will be in sync.

1. Double-click on *Ceremony7* in the **Browser** to open it in the **Viewer.**

2. Play the clip from the beginning.

It starts with the priest chanting. Then there is a response from the others. Around 11;05 the priest chants again. This is the point where we want to come to him.

We're going to create a split edit in the **Viewer** before we even move the clip into the **Timeline.**

3. At 11;05 in the **Viewer Scrubber Bar,** hold down the **Control** key, and from the shortcut menu, select **Mark Split>Video In** (Figure 6.26).
   Or use the keyboard shortcut **Control-I.**

4. Now play the clip until the priest finishes his chant, about 15;13.

5. Again use the **Control** key in the **Viewer Scrubber Bar,** but this time from the shortcut menu select **Mark Split>Video Out** (or **Control-O**)

The clip in **Viewer** should look something like Figure 6.27. Notice the way the split edit is displayed in the **Scrubber Bar,** In and Out points marked only in the upper portion of the bar.

6.26 Marking Split In Point (left)

6.27 Marked Split In and Out Points (below)

6. Drag *Ceremony7* to the **Canvas Edit Overlay,** to either **Insert** or **Overwrite,** so that it drops into the **Timeline** at the beginning of the sequence.

Filling in the Blanks

What we need to do next is fill in the blanks, the area at the beginning of the shot and at the end. To do this we'll use some of the other shots from the event. I used the close shot as the bed for the scene because audio/video synchronization is more critical in the closer view than in the long shot such as in *Ceremony9.* This shot starts wide and at the end pushes into a priest sitting in the corner. It would be a classic way to begin the scene, with a wide, establishing shot. The trick here is to use the sound of the bed with the picture of this shot, the problem being to match sync the two. FCE gives you some tools to do this. Markers are the most important.

Adding Markers

Markers can be used as visual references. Points can be placed:

- On a clip in the **Viewer**

- On a selected clip in the **Timeline**
- On the **Timeline** itself

We'll get back to editing the sequence in a moment, but let's look at the how to work with markers.

1. Open the master clip *Damine.mov* into the **Viewer** and press the spacebar.

2. As you play the clip, tap the **M** key.

Each time you hit **M**, a marker will be added to the clip. You don't have to add markers on the fly. You can add them with more precision by scrubbing or by using the arrow keys to find a frame before marking. You can move between markers easily with the keyboard shortcuts **Shift-M** to go to the next marker, or **Option-M** to go to the previous marker.

3. With the playhead on a marker, press **M** to call up the **Edit Marker** dialog window, where you can enter descriptive information and comments (Figure 6.28).

4. You change the start time. You can also change the duration, making an extended marker. You can delete the marker, or add comments and on-screen text. These are searchable in the **Timeline**, by the way.

The markers will actually appear over the media on the computer screen, at least while the clip isn't playing and the playhead is on the marker. This will only be seen if **Overlays** are turned on in the **View** popup of the **Viewer** or the **Canvas**.

If the marker is extended, the text will appear over all the frames the marker covers. If you add the comments to the markers before you make the subclips, the information will be carried over into the subclips themselves. In FCE's **Edit Marker** window you have the ability to add chapter markers and compression markers. These are markers that are usually applied to sequences in the **Timeline** window. These chapter and compression markers can be exported for use with DVD creation. If you are exporting a sequence for use in iDVD or DVD Studio Pro, be sure the markers are added to the sequence timeline and not to a clip. If a clip is selected the marker will be added to the clip and will not appear on export to the DVD authoring appliction.

6.28 Edit Marker Window and Marker Display in Viewer

6.29   Audio Waveform

Using Markers

Let's return to working on our sequence. To sync up the sound in the bed with the picture of another shot, we're going to place markers on both shots. First let's put a marker in *Ceremony7*.

1. Double-click on the sound track in the **Timeline** to open it into the **Viewer**.

The first major burst of sound on the track, led by a clearly defined spike, is the sound of the drum (Figure 6.29).

2. Scrub the track until you've found the very beginning of the sound. Hit the **M** key to add a marker.

Now we want to match this frame with another shot.

3. Open *Ceremony9* in the **Viewer** and play the video from the beginning until the priest strikes the drum.

It's quite hard in the small **Viewer** screen to see precisely when that moment is, but again the audio track gives us a much better clue.

4. Click on the **Audio** tab in the **Viewer** and scrub the track until you find the drum sound. Match it with the spike on in the audio waveform.

Because the waveform gives a visual representation of the sound, it can be much easier to edit the sound in the **Audio** tab than it is by just listening to it.

5. Once you've found the sound, put a marker on the clip with the **M** key.

6. Grab the clip with the **Loudspeaker** icon, which is the **Grab Handle** at the top of the **Viewer** (Figure 6.30) and pull the clip into the **Timeline**.

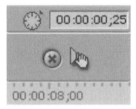

6.30 Audio Grab Handle

7. Drag the clip onto the empty track above **V1**. The audio will automatically go onto **A3/A4**. Make sure the arrow indicator is pointing downward as you drag the clip.

This will perform an overwrite edit, which is what you want to do. If you only drag the clip so that it is in the top third of a track, the arrow will be pointed to the right. This will slice everything on all unlocked tracks and push it down the timeline. This can be very useful, but in this case that would be a bad thing.

Lining Up the Clips

If you need to get a closer look to line up the clips better, remember that you can use **Option-+** to zoom in and **Option- -** to zoom out.

> ☞ *Tip*
> ___
> ***Zoom a Marquee:*** You can also use the **Zoom** tool to drag a marquee along a section of the **Timeline** (on a screen if you're in the **Viewer** or **Canvas**) to zoom into just that portion of the Timeline.

1. With **Snapping** toggled on (**N** key), slide *Ceremony9* along the **Timeline** until the markers line up as in Figure 6.31.

You'll probably find that by coincidence, the beginning of the two shots line up. If you grab the clip at the marker to drag it the markers on the two clips will actually snap to each rather than the clips snapping to edit points.

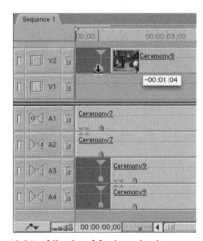

6.31 Aligning Markers in the Timeline

👍 *Tip*_____

Deleting a Marker: To delete a marker on a clip, make sure the clip is selected, and with the playhead sitting on the marker, press **Command-`**. Or you can hit the **M** key to call the dialog box and click the **Delete** button. Remember you can move to go to the next marker with **Shift-M** (or **Shift-Down** arrow) and **Option-M** (or **Shift-Up** arrow) to go to the previous marker. You can use the menus delete all the markers in a clip with **Mark>Markers>Delete All**. You can also use the keyboard shortcut **Control-`**. You can extend the duration of a marker with the keyboard shortcut **Option-`**.

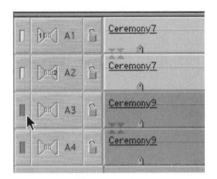

6.32 Toggling Sound Track Off

6.33 Shortcut Menu>Clip Visibility

2. Once you've got the clips lined up, play through the area. If the clips sound slightly out of sync, the drums not banging together, slide *Ceremony9* up or down the **Timeline** until the sounds match up.

3. As you line up the sounds, it may be helpful to toggle one of the sound tracks off so you can tell exactly which of the tracks you're hearing. To toggle off and on a track, click on the green button light on the left edge of the **Timeline** (Figure 6.32). The length of track will dim as you toggle the sound off.

Once you've got the first strike of the drum lined up, you'll notice that the rhythm is not very consistent and wanders fairly quickly.

👍 *Tip*_____

Invisibility: You can also switch off the visibility of an individual clip or audio track. To switch off just the audio portion, **Option**-click the audio to select it separately from the video. From the menus choose **Modify>Clip Visibility** (**Control-B**). You can also use the **Clip** shortcut menu to **Control**-click on the audio and choose **Clip Visibility** (Figure 6.33). You can also solo items. If you wish to see only one video track or hear only one audio track, you can **Option**-click it to select it and choose **Sequence>Solo Item(s)** or use the keyboard shortcut **Control-S**. This function is not available in the shortcut menus.

4. Because you probably don't want to hear both tracks of audio, toggle off the sound for *Ceremony9*. Don't delete the track for *Ceremony9*; you may still want to hear it while you're working on the scene. But once the scene has been edited, you can safely delete the audio on **A3** and **A4** from the **Timeline**.

Waveform in the Timeline

It might also be beneficial to turn on the waveform display in **Timeline** window

1. Click on the **Timeline Options** tab

2. In the **Timeline Options** window, check the box marked **Show Audio Waveform**.

Because displaying the **Audio Waveform** in the **Timeline** takes a good deal of computer processing power—prereading the audio and then displaying it—the redraw ability and video playback capabilities of the computer are markedly slowed down. So it's a good idea to toggle the waveform display on and off as needed. Fortunately there is a simple keyboard shortcut to do this, **Command-Option-W**.

5. When you do want to do that, **Option**-click on the audio for *Ceremony9* to select it separately from the video, and then simply delete it.

You can get away with two drum hits, but I would suggest cutting away from the wide shot of the priest just before the third drum strike to mask the creeping loss of synchronization.

6. Use the **Blade** tool (**B**) to cut *Ceremony9* just before the third strike of the drum. Your timeline should look something like Figure 6.34.

Second Edit

Rather than deleting the remainder of the shot, let's open the second part of *Ceremony9* in the **Viewer** from the **Timeline** and look at it. There is a zoom into the kneeling priest in white at the end of the shot. We'll use that next, but we'll cut out the zoom itself.

1. Go down to about 16;16 and mark a new In point.

2. Now pull the shot up against the first part of *Ceremony9* as in Figure 6.35.

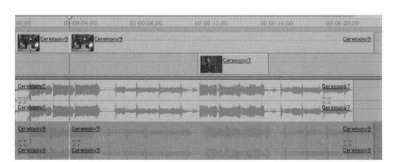

6.34 Timeline with Bladed Clip on V2

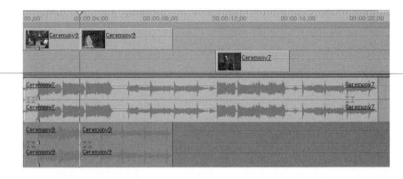

6.35 Timeline after Second Edit

3. You might want to lock **V1** together with the audio on **A1** and **A2**. Just click on the **Lock** icons at the head of the tracks.

4. After cutting the clip with the **Blade**, you could also use the **Ripple** tool to pull up the beginning of the shot in the **Timeline**, watching the two-up display until you find where you want the second shot to start.

In this case, the ripple technique will work, but in other circumstances, where you're not working at the head of a sequence, you can get in trouble because you'll be rippling the shot on **V1** as well, pulling it out of the sync with the material edited onto **V2**.

5. Play the scene a couple of times.

I think you'll see that the shot of the kneeling priest probably needs to be shortened. The nature of editing is that it creates patterns of rhythm. In this case, because of the music, the patterns are quite strong. We have also created a visual pattern. By cutting the long shot of priest before the third beat of the drum, we have determined to some extent the visual rhythm we'll follow for this short scene. If you play the sequence, you'll find a natural edit point after the call of the priest with the drum to the response of the gathered men. We need to find a shot for this.

Third Edit

At the beginning of the *Ceremony8* is the response of the acolytes, so this is what we'll use next. We want to place this shot onto **V2** cutting into the second portion of *Ceremony9*.

6.36 Track Target Buttons

1. Park the Timeline playhead at the point you'll make the edit, about 5:15 into the sequence.

2. Now target the correct tracks—**V2**, **A3**, and **A4**—with the **Target** buttons on the left edge of the tracks (Figure 6.36).

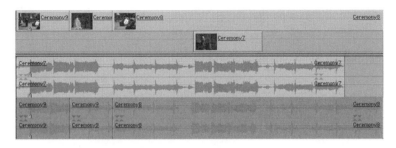

3. Open up *Ceremony8* from the **Browser** into the **Viewer**.

4. When the tracks are targeted, cut *Ceremony9* by either:

   - Pulling *Ceremony8* to **Overwrite** in the **CEO**, or
   - Pressing **F10**.

After the edit, the **Timeline** should look like Figure 6.37.

Fourth Edit

Obviously we have much more of *Ceremony8* than we need. Let's cut that down further. The logical place to make the cut is to let the shot extend until it reaches the video on **V1** or the base shot *Ceremony7* (Figure 6.38).

Fifth Edit

After the priest's call in *Ceremony7*, the acolytes make another response to end the scene.

1. Open up *Ceremony8* from the **Browser** again.

Notice that toward the end of the shot the camera pushes into a closer shot of the men in the corner. We'll use this portion of the shot next.

2. Mark an In point after the camera settles, about 9;16.

3. Drag the shot onto **V2**, butting it to the end of the shot on **V1** (Figure 6.39).

6.39 Timeline after Fifth Edit

Be careful you don't drag the shot onto **V1** or it will cut your primary audio track, unless you've locked the audio track already.

Sixth Edit

I probably wouldn't want to end the scene with this shot. I'd rather repeat the wide shot of the priest again. We'll make the cut just before the response concludes so we see the drum being struck in *Ceremony9*, the wider shot. Again the problem is syncing the drum hits, and also that the sound runs out on *Ceremony7*. To do this, we'll again set markers in the audio of the base shot *Ceremony7* and in the **Browser** clip *Ceremony9*

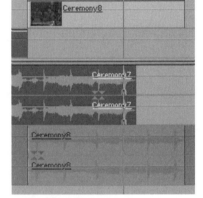

6.40 Setting Markers in the Audio Clip

> 👉 **Tip**
> **Scrubbing:** If audio scrubbing isn't be working for you, make sure that you have it switched on. It can be toggled on and off under **View>Audio Scrubbing** (**Shift-S**). It defaults to being on, and I generally leave it on all the time.

With the waveform switched on in the **Timeline** it's easy to see where the drum beats come.

1. Scrub in the **Timeline Ruler** (where the time increments are at the top of the **Timeline**) until you find the fourth drum strike exactly. This is the one we're going to match the pacing to for the drum strike on *Ceremony9*.

2. Click on the *Ceremony7* clip in the **Timeline** to select it and hit the **M** key to add a marker. Because the clip is selected the marker is added to it. If you didn't select the clip first, the marker would be added to the **Timeline** itself (Figure 6.40).

3. Open *Ceremony9* from the **Browser** and play the clip up to the first drum.

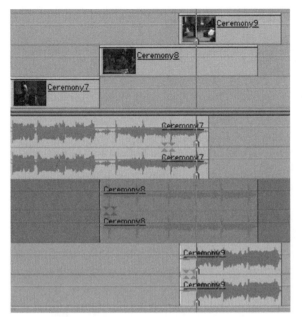

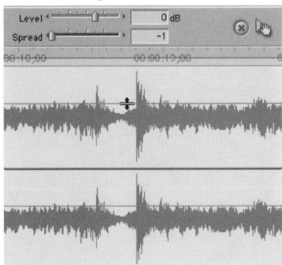

6.41 Timeline after Sixth Edit (left)

6.42 Line-Moving Cursor (below)

4. If there isn't one there already, set a marker on the first drum strike. Again, this is easiest to do in the **Audio** tab of the **Viewer**.

You don't want to cut the shot at the drum strike. You really want to cut to the shot before the strike so that you see it happen, rather than cutting on the strike, when all you would see in the shot is the hand coming away from the drum.

5. Pull *Ceremony9* from the **Viewer** into the **Timeline** and drop it onto the area above **V2** to create yet another video track, as in Figure 6.41.

6. Slide *Ceremony9* in the **Timeline** until its marker lines up on the second marker on *Ceremony7*.

This time, however, we're not going to mute the audio for *Ceremony9* as we did for the audio on **A3/A4**; we're going to mix the two tracks using the level controls.

Controlling Audio Levels

You can adjust audio levels in two primary areas:

- Viewer
- Timeline

We'll look at adjusting levels in the **Viewer** first.

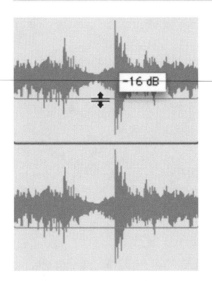

6.43 Decibel Level Change Indicators

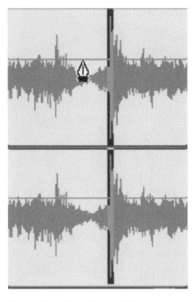

6.44 Pen Tool in the Viewer

In the Viewer

1. Open the audio of *Ceremony7* from the **Timeline** into the **Viewer** by double-clicking on the audio track.

Notice the mauve line in the center of the audio track. As you move the cursor over the line, it changes to a line-moving tool (Figure 6.42).

At the top of Figure 6.42, you'll notice the **Level** slider and its **Decibel Indicator** window. It's currently at 0, which is the level at which the audio was captured

2. With the line-moving cursor, grab the audio level line and push it up or pull it down to try it out.

This moves the level for the overall audio level of the whole clip. As you move the line up or down, both the **Level** slider and the **Decibel Indicator** window at the top move. A small window appears in the waveform as well that shows the amount in decibels (dB) that you're changing the audio level (Figure 6.43).

You often don't want to move the whole level of the audio, just a portion. To do this, you need to put keyframes on the **Audio Level** line, which allow you to bend the line, ramping the audio level value up or down.

☞ Tip

What is a Keyframe?: We'll be talking more and more about keyframes as we get further into the book. A keyframe is basically a way of defining the values for a clip at a specific moment in time, at a specific frame of video. Here we're dealing with audio levels. We're saying at this frame we want the sound to be at a particular level. By then going to a different point in the clip and altering the levels we will have created another keyframe, defining the sound level at that particular frame. The computer will figure out how quickly it needs to change the levels to get from one setting to the other. The closer together the keyframes are, the more quickly the levels will change; the farther apart they are, the more gradually the change will take place. To add a keyframe, you need to select the **Pen** from the bottom of the **Tools** or call it up with the **P** key. The cursor then changes into the **Pen** tool (Figure 6.44).

3. Click with the **Pen** on the **Level** line to add a keyframe. A little diamond-shaped mark will appear.

4. Go farther along the timeline, about a second will do, and add another keyframe with the **Pen** tool.

5. Then pull that keyframe down so that the audio fades out over time (Figure 6.45).

There are several ways to delete an audio keyframe:

- Grab it and pull it down out of the audio timeline until the cursor changes to a trash can and the keyframe snaps off the line.

- While you're using the **Pen** tool, hold down the **Option** key when you're over the keyframe. The cursor will change into the **Pen Delete** tool (Figure 6.46).

- Use the shortcut menu by clicking on the keyframe and selecting **Clear**.

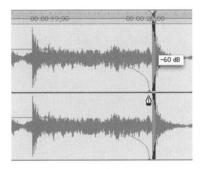

6.45 Audio Fade Out

👉 *Tip*

No Switching Necessary: If there already is a keyframe on the level line, then you don't need to switch to the **Pen** tool. The cursor will automatically change to a crosshairs as you move over the audio node. If you are working with the **Pen** tool and you want to switch to the straight-level line- moving tool, hold down the **Command** or **Shift** key.

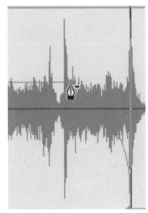

6.46 Pen Delete Tool

To delete all the keyframes in the audio, click the **Reset** button, the button with the red **X** next to the **Grab Handle** at the top of the panel.

To move a keyframe, grab it and slide it left and right along the line.

Delete any keyframes you may have added to the clip. Though the **Viewer** allows for more precision, I'll show you another way to do this, right in the **Timeline**.

In the Timeline

It's often easier to control audio levels in the **Timeline** itself. The controls work in exactly the same fashion as in the **Viewer**. The first step to take is to activate the **Clip Overlay** lines, which normally remain hidden—a good thing, so that you don't accidentally grab the **Level** line and change the setting when you're grabbing a clip.

👉 *Tip*

Fixing Soft Audio: Sometimes audio is just too low to be as forceful as you'd like, even after you crank it up with FCE's level controls. A neat little trick is to double up the audio tracks. Just put another copy of the same sound on the track below and push that audio level up as well. Double your pleasure. It's saved me more than once in a pinch.

Spread and Pan

In a stereo clip, such as we're working with here, both audio tracks appear in one panel. When there is a stereo pair of audio, there is a slider at the top of the **Viewer** that controls **Spread** and is defaulted down to −1 so that the two tracks are centered between the speakers. Spreading the audio will move the stereo sound farther and farther apart. When you work with a stereo clip, called a **stereo pair**, changing the level of one track with automatically change the level of the other track.

A stereo pair can be changed into multitrack audio from the **Modify** menu by selecting **Stereo Pair**. This will toggle the audio between being a stereo pair with both audio tracks changing level in unison and being two separate channels of audio whose levels can be controlled separately. This is important if your video was shot with distinct audio channels, for instance, a lavaliere mic on one channel and a shotgun mic on the other.

When you switch to a multitrack audio, instead of there being a single **Audio** tab in the **Viewer**, there are now two separate tabs one for each channel. In the **Timeline** you might also notice audio clips with pairs of inward-pointing triangles. The triangles indicate that the clip is a **stereo pair**. When the triangles are missing, the clip has separate audio channels. In addition to the **Level** line in the **Viewer**, there is now a **Pan** slider instead of the **Spread** slider (Figure 6.47). The **Pan** slider allows you to move the audio from one side of the stereo speakers to the other. **Pan** defaults to a value of zero, centered between the two speakers of a stereo system.

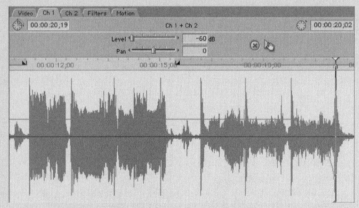

6.47 Multitrack Audio in the Viewer

Using the **Pan** line, you can shift the sound to come from either the left side or the right side. Moving the **Pan** slider to the left to −1 will move all the sound to the left speaker, and moving the **Pan** slider all the way to the right to 1 will move the sound to the right speaker. Like **Levels**, **Pan** values can be keyframed. The classic example is the racing car that approaches from the left with all sound coming from the left speaker, roars by and disappears to the right, while the sounds sweeps past to the right speaker.

To turn on the **Clip Overlays**:

- Click on the **Clip Overlays** button on the lower left corner of the **Timeline** (Figure 6.48) or
- Use the keyboard shortcut **Option-W**.

6.48 Clip Overlay Button

When the **Clip Overlays** are activated, red lines appear in the middle of the audio tracks, which are the **Level** line. Black lines appear near the tops of video clips. These are **Opacity** controls. We'll look at those in later lessons.

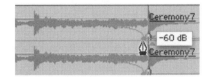

6.49 Fade Out in the Timeline

As when editing in the **Viewer**, you can shift the red **Level** line up and down. Selecting the **Pen** tool will allow you add a keyframe. By adding another keyframe farther down the line, you can pull down the level in a curve that fades the sound out (Figure 6.49).

Let's now add a crossfade to the clips in our sequence.

1. On *Ceremony7*, set the first level keyframe after the drum strike, just a little past where *Ceremony9* begins on **V3**.

2. Place the second keyframe and pull it down to do the fade out of the audio shortly before the next drum strike, the second marker we placed in *Ceremony7*.

3. Fade up the sound on *Ceremony9* as shown in Figure 6.50 so that the drum strike after the cut you hear is the sound on *Ceremony9*.

You have now created a crossfade between the tracks on **A1/A2** and **A5/A6**.

4. As a final touch you might want to **Option**-click on the edit point at the beginning of *Ceremony9* and shorten the shot a bit so that you cut to it just a moment before the drum strike. You use **Option**-click because you want to make it a split edit, leaving the sound crossfading before you cut to the picture.

6.50 Crossfading Audio Tracks

Other Audio Tools

FCE has other tools that help with editing and controlling your audio levels. It's sometimes useful to select entire tracks to adjust the audio for the whole track. You can select a single track, multiple tracks forward and backward, a single track forward and backward, or a whole track of audio and adjust their levels globally. Though we don't need these track selection tools for this exercise, I'm sure you can see how useful they could be.

6.51 Track Tool

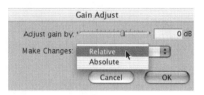

6.52 Audio Controls

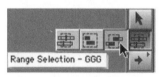

6.53 Range Selection Tool

Paste Attributes

Attributes from Ceremony7:

☑ Scale Attribute Times

Video Attributes:
- ☐ Content
- ☐ Basic Motion
- ☐ Crop
- ☐ Distort
- ☐ Opacity
- ☐ Drop Shadow
- ☐ Motion Blur
- ☐ Filters
- ☐ Speed
- ☐ Clip Settings (capture)

Audio Attributes:
- ☐ Content
- ☑ Levels
- ☑ Pan
- ☐ Filters

Cancel   OK

6.54 Pasting Audio Attributes

6.55 Shortcut Menu Audio Cross Fade

Select the items or the track with the **Track** tool (**T**) (Figure 6.51). Once you have your track or clips selected, go to **Modify>Levels** (**Command-Option-L**)

This command calls up a dialog box that allows you to adjust the audio levels of the clips (Figure 6.52). The slider or the value box will change the gain setting for all the clips selected. The **Relative** and **Absolute** popup sets how the gain is affected. **Absolute** will make the level you set affect the whole of all the clips, eliminating any fades. Using the **Relative** setting will change the value of the levels relative to each other. This global levels control not only works on audio, but also works on other levels, such as opacity. Note that you can also change the **Relative** or **Absolute** levels of a group of audio keyframes. Use the **Range Selection** tool (Figure 6.53) to select the area that includes the audio keyframes. If you then apply the **Levels** tool, it will raise or lower the relative or absolute values of the keyframes in the selected area.

You can also copy the values of an audio clip to others clips. Copy an audio clip by selecting it and pressing **Command-C**. Now select with the marquee or **Command**-click the clips you want, and then use the **Paste Attributes** function from the **Edit** menu (or press **Option-V**). Check the attributes you want to paste to the other clips' **Levels** or **Pan** values (Figure 6.54). We shall look at pasting attributes more closely in later lessons.

Though keyframing audio in either the **Viewer** or the **Timeline** gives you greater control and flexibility, FCE does also allow you the ability, as we saw in the lesson on transitions, to add audio crossfades as audio transitions. These can be added from the **Effects** menu, **Audio Transitions**. You can also call up the default audio crossfade by **Control**-clicking on the audio tracks at the edit point and selecting the default crossfade from the shortcut menu (Figure 6.55).

There are two crossfades available: **Cross Fade** (0dB) and **Cross Fade (+3dB)**. The latter is the default. The **0 Cross Fade** ramps the audio smoothly downward producing a lowering of the level halfway through the transition. This works best for crossfading different music tracks for instance. The **+3 Cross Fade** is a curved audio fade such as you get when you're keyframing in the **Viewer** or in the **Timeline**. This produces a smoother fade, without apparent level reduction halfway through the effect.

For normal speech it's probably best to keep the recording around −12dB, perhaps a little higher for louder passages, a bit lower for softer ones.

Many audio CDs are very heavily compressed, right up to the limits of digital audio. If you see your audio meters hitting the top of the scale, lighting up the two little orange boxes at the top, bring down your audio levels a few dB. You'll probably find you have to do this for most audio CD material.

Monitor not only single tracks, but also monitor and listen to your mixed track. Often a single track will not exceed peak level, but a mix of all your tracks may send your meters well into the red.

Voice Over

Final Cut Express has a feature called **Voice Over** that allows you to record audio tracks directly to your hard drive while playing back your **Timeline**. **Voice Over** is most valuable for making *scratch tracks*, test narrations used to try out pacing and content with picture. It could be used for final recording, though you'd probably want to isolate the computer and other extraneous sounds from the recording artist. Many people actually prefer to record narrations prior to beginning final editing so that the picture and sound can be controlled more tightly. Others feel that recording to the picture allows for a more spontaneous delivery

⭐ *Tip*

A key tool for working with audio in Final Cut is its audio meter (Figure 6.56). The standard audio level for digital audio is −12dB. Unlike analog audio that has quite a bit of headroom and allows you to record sound above 0dB, in digital recordings 0dB is an absolute. Sound cannot be recorded at a higher level. It simply gets clipped off. Very often on playback of very loud levels, the recording will simply seem to drop out completely and become inaudible as the levels are crushed beyond the range of digital audio's capabilities.

iMovie Sound Effects

It is possible to bring iMovie3 sound effects into Final Cut Express, like those great new Skywalker Sound Effects. The trick is to know where they are and to copy them to somewhere else. Do this very carefully.

1. **Control**-click on the iMovie3 application inside your *Applications* folder.

2. From the shortcut menu select **Show Package Contents**.

3. Go inside the *Contents* folder to the *Resources* folder and find inside that the *Sound Effects* folder.

Most of the iMovie sound effects are in there as AIFF files. Copy what you need from that folder. Do not move them. The Skywalker sounds are MP3s and should be converted to AIFF using iTunes or the Quick-Time Pro Player, if you have that.

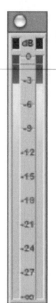

6.56 Audio Meters

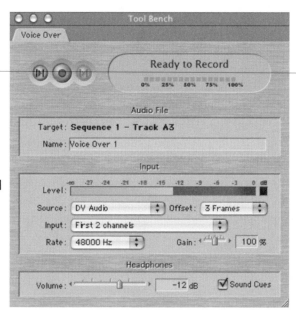

6.57 Voice Over Tool

from the narrator. However you use it, **Voice Over** is an important tool in the application.

Voice Over is found under the **File** menu. This brings up the window in Figure 6.57.

More RAM for VO: Because **Voice Over** works in RAM, storing the sound before recording it to disk, you may need to put more RAM into your computer over and above the minimum requirements asked for by FCE because the audio is buffered in RAM as it's recorded. 48kHz audio consumes 6MB per minute. So a half-hour track would take 180MB. Once they are recorded, all of these recordings are stored in your *Capture Scratch* folder with the project name.

The first steps you'll have to take are to configure your recording setup for your **Source, Input,** and **Sampling Rate.**

Source defines where the sound is coming from: the computer mic input, a USB device, a camcorder, or an installed digitizing card.

Input controls the type of signal being received, whether it's line level, balanced audio in, digital audio, or whatever your source device is capable of handling.

DV Input: If you're recording through a DV camcorder or other DV device, make sure that **Video** (at the bottom of the **View** menu) is switched to **Real Time**. If it's set to **FireWire**, the playback signal will be going out through the cable, which prevents you from recording from it. Two sets of signals going in opposite directions just won't work. If you have **FireWire** selected in the **View** menu, you'll get the error message in Figure 6.58. Also make sure your camera is in camera mode and not in VCR mode. It has to be in camera mode to get the input from the microphone.

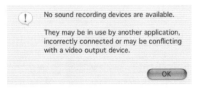

6.58 DV Device Error Message

Offset adjusts for the delay taken by the analog to digital conversion. USB devices typically take one frame. DV cameras can be three frames or more.

Let's look at some of the controls in this panel. The large red button, the middle of the three in the top portion of the window, is the **Record** button. It will also stop the recording, as will the **Escape** key. The button to its left is the **Preview/Review** button and will play the selected area of your sequence. The button to the right is the **Discard** button. Immediately after a recording or after aborting a recording, pressing the **Discard** button will bring up the warning dialog in Figure 6.59.

6.59 Discard Warning Dialog

The **Gain** slider, next to the **Input** popup, allows you to control the recording level based on the horizontal LCD display meter. This is fine for scratch tracks, but for finished work, it would probably be better to have a hardware mixer before the input for good mic level control.

The **Headphones** volume does just what it says. If there is nothing jacked into the headphone output of your computer, the sound will come out of the computer speaker itself. To avoid recording it or the **Sound Cues**, uncheck the **Sound Cues** box.

Playback Levels: Don't be fooled by FCE's vertical audio meters. These display the playback levels, and do not show the recording level.

FCE gives the recording artist elaborate **Sound Cues**, which are turned on with the little checkbox. Together with the aural sound cues in the headphones, there is visual cuing as well, which appears in the window to the right of the **Record** button. As the recording starts, a countdown begins, with cue tones as the display. It starts pale yellow (Figure 6.60) and becomes darker and more orange until when recording begins. Then the display changes to red (Figure 6.61). There is a cue tone at 15 seconds from the end of the recording as well as beeps counting down the last five seconds to the end of the recording (Figure 6.62). Recording actually begins during countdown and continues two seconds after the end of the recording during **Finishing** (Figure 6.63). Though this doesn't appear in the **Timeline** after the recording, you can simply drag out the front and end of the clip if the voice started early or overran the end.

I think the best way to work with **Voice Over** in the **Timeline** is to define an In and Out point, as in Figure 6.64. If no points are defined, recording will begin at the point at which the playhead is parked and go until the end of the sequence, or until you run out of available memory, whichever comes first. You can also simply define an In point and go from there, or define an Out and go from the playhead until the Out is reached. Because the **Timeline** doesn't scroll as the sequence plays, it might be helpful to reduce the sequence to fit the **Timeline** window. **Shift-Z** will do this with a keystroke.

Recording is always done to a targeted track that has free space. If there is no free space within the defined area of the recording, **Voice Over** will *always* create a new track. So if you record multiple takes, they will record onto the next lower track or onto a new track. The **Audio File** window (Figure 6.65) will give you the track information. If there is no free space, a new track will be created. You can name the recording in the **Audio File** window, and each take will be numbered incrementally.

After recording, the new voice over clip appears selected. You can play it back for review, but if you want to record further takes, use **Control-B** to switch off the clip audio so you don't hear it during playback of the next take.

After a discarded take, **Voice Over** will record to the previously assigned track with the previously assigned name. After a few takes, you may want to discard a previous take and reassign the targeted track so that **Voice Over** will work with the empty tracks you vacated, as shown in Figure 6.66, which shows an aborted recording on a higher track.

The next recording will take place on a new **A9** below *vo6*. Or I could simply discard *vo2*, retarget and the next recording will be on the blank **A5** again, using the recording name *vo7*. Also, you should switch off previous takes as you go so that the talent doesn't hear the previous recording in the headphones while recording.

6.60 Starting

6.61 Recording

6.62 Recording Counting Down

6.63 Finishing

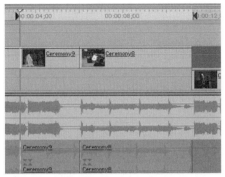

6.64 Timeline Marked for Voice Over

6.65 Audio File Window (below)

6.66 Timeline after Recording Takes

After a recording session with **Voice Over**, it would not be a bad idea to go into your hard drive and root out old tracks that aren't needed and may be filling up your drive. Those takes you recorded that you no longer want can be deleted from your sequence, but they aren't automatically deleted from your hard drive. Also remember, the recordings are only a part of your sequence and will not appear in your Browser at all, unless you put them there.

Summary

In this lesson we looked at working with sound in Final Cut. Performing split edits, overlapping sound, cutting with sound, overlapping and crossfading tracks, transitions, meters, as well as FCE's **Voice Over** tool. Sound is often overlooked, seeming insignificant or of minor importance, but it is crucial to making a sequence appear professionally edited.

In the next lesson we'll look at the many titling options available in Final Cut Express.

> **✎ Tip**
> **No Timecode in Voice Over:** There is no timecode or other identifying information other than the assigned name with any **Voice Over** recording, if you need to reconstruct your project at a later date. It may be an idea to keep this recording preserved on tape or on disk if you want to use it again.

Lesson 7

Adding Titles

Every program is enhanced with graphics, whether they are a simple opening title and closing credits or elaborate motion graphics sequences illuminating some obscure point that can best be expressed in animation. This could be simply a map with a path snaking across it or a full-scale 3D animation explaining the details of how an airplane is built. Obviously, the latter is beyond the scope of both this book and of Final Cut Express alone. But many simpler graphics can be easily created within FCE.

In this lesson, we will look at typical titling problems and how to deal with them. As always, we begin by loading the project.

Loading the Lesson

This should be familiar to you by now. Let's begin by loading the material you need onto your media drive.

1. If you don't already have it there, drag over the *Media* folder from the DVD's *FCE DVD ROM Contents* folder.

2. Also drag *Lesson 7* from inside the *Projects* folder on the DVD into your *Shared* folder or your *Documents* folder.

3. Open the *Lesson 7* folder on your hard drive. Double-click on the project file *L7* to launch the application.

4. Reconnect the media file and reassign the scratch disk if needed.

5. If you did not load Boris Calligraphy when you first installed FCE, now would be a good time to do so. Put in your install CD and run the installer. Make sure the Boris Calligraphy checkbox is marked, and press **Install**. The software will be put into your *Plugins* folder in *Library>Application Support>Final Cut Express System Support*.

Setting up the Project

Inside the project in the **Browser** you'll find some sequences, which we shall look at in the course of this lesson. One of the sequences, *Sequence 1*, is empty, ready for you to use. There is also the master clip, *Damine.mov*, and the **Clips** bin.

1. Begin by opening *Sequence 1*.

2. Drag a clip, let's say *Dance2*, from the **Clips** bin and drop it onto **Overwrite** in the **CEO** (**Canvas Edit Overlay**).

Text Generator

Now let's look at the **Titler**, which FCE calls a **Text Generator**.

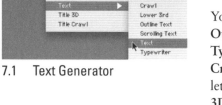

7.1   Text Generator

1. To get to it, click the small **A** in the lower right corner of the **Viewer**.

2. Go into the popup menu, drop down to **Text**, slide across, and pick **Text** again, as in Figure 7.1.

You'll notice that in addition to **Text**, there is also **Lower Third**, **Outline Text**, and the basic animations **Scrolling Text**, **Crawl**, and **Typewriter**, as well as the Boris title tools **Title 3D** and **Title Crawl**. We'll look at the Boris tools a bit later in the lesson, but let's start by looking at the way FCE's basic **Text** tool works. **Title 3D** and **Title Crawl** will not appear if Boris Calligraphy has not been loaded.

Text

This is for very basic text graphics indeed, simple on-screen words. Select **Text** from the **Generator** popup, which immediately loads a generic text generator into the **Viewer** (Figure 7.2).

Notice that this generator has:

- A default duration of 10 seconds
- A default length of two minutes

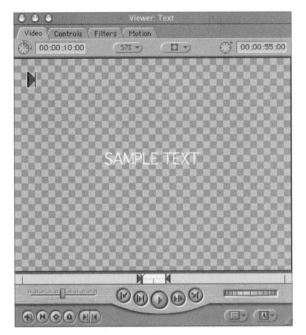

7.2   Generic Sample Text in Viewer (left)

7.3   Supered Text in the Timeline (below)

You can designate any duration for a text file up to four hours. However, once the text file has been placed in a sequence, its duration can no longer be extended beyond the designated duration. So if I accept the default length and I place the text file in a sequence, I can no longer make the duration go beyond two minutes. If you know you're going to need to make a very long text file, change the duration before you place it in the sequence. You can always make it shorter, but not longer. It's a good way to create a video bug, that little graphic that's always in the bottom right of your TV screen—or your warning that a tape is only a sample copy and not for distribution.

The first point to realize about this text generator is that at the moment it only exists in the **Viewer**. Usually the next step I take is to put it somewhere useful, either into the **Browser** or the **Timeline**. If you park the playhead anywhere over the shot that's in the **Timeline** and then drag the generic text generator from the **Viewer** to the **CEO** to **Superimpose**, the text will appear above the shot, with the same duration as the shot (Figure 7.3). Notice that the application ignores the marked Out point, but rather takes its duration from the length of the shot on **V1**.

⭐ Tip

Launching Text Generator: The default, basic text generator can be opened into the **Viewer** with the keyboard shortcut **Control-X**. It's handy if you need to create a lot of basic titles quickly.

7.4   Viewer:Text

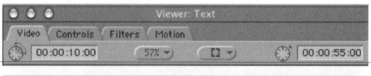

7.5   Viewer:Text from Sequence 1

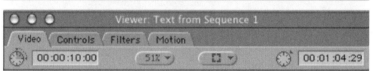

👈 Tip _____

Background: I always leave the playhead in the **Timeline** parked over the middle of the clip with the text supered on it. That way whatever I do in the **Text** controls appears a moment later supered on the clip in the **Canvas**. If you place a clip in the **Timeline** over nothing, the blackness you see in the **Canvas** behind the clip is the emptiness of space. You can make it a variety of colors, including checkerboard under the **View>Background** menu, but this is only for viewing purposes. If you want an actual color layer, use the **Generators** to make a color matte. Make it any color you want and place it on the layer below all other material.

You can also simply drag and drop the generator into the **Timeline** onto an empty track or the space above the tracks. Either way, you'll immediately see that the render line above the clip in the **Timeline** changes color. If your system has real-time capabilities, the line will be green. If not, it will be red, telling you that section of the sequence needs to be rendered.

Whether you drag the generic text generator to the **Timeline** or the **Browser**, remember that you are creating a copy of that generator. Be careful not to do anything to the generator in the **Viewer**. I've seen countless people do this. They lay the generator in the **Timeline**, work in the **Viewer**, and then wonder why the text in the sequence still says "Sample Text."

First, you should open the new generator you created in the **Timeline**. Open it by double-clicking on the **Text Generator** in the **Timeline** window. The **Viewer** screen will look exactly the same, of course, except now you'll be working on the generator in the **Timeline**, which is what you want. The label area at the top of the **Viewer** will tell you where the text came from. Figure 7.4 shows the label for text generated in the **Viewer**. Figure 7.5 shows the label for text that's been opened from a sequence.

The other telltale sign that indicates whether a title or a clip has been opened from the **Browser** (or generated in the **Viewer**) or has been opened from a sequence is in the **Scrubber Bar** at the bottom of the **Viewer**. In Figure 7.6 the clip has been opened from the **Browser**. The **Scrubber Bar** is plain. In Figure 7.7 the clip has been opened from the **Timeline**. The **Scrubber Bar** shows a double row of dots, like film sprocket holes.

Now we're ready to start making that graphic.

1. After you've opened the generator from the **Timeline** into the **Viewer**, click on the **Controls** tab at the top. You might also want to stretch down the **Viewer** to see all the controls (Figure 7.8).

7.6   Plain Scrubber Bar on Clip Opened from Browser

7.7   Dotted Scrubber Bar on Clip Opened from Timeline

These are the default settings. At the top is the text input window in which you type whatever you want to appear on the screen.

2. Click on **SAMPLE TEXT** and type in *Dance*, then do a return, and type *Title*.

3. Click out of the window, or tab to the **Size** box. The default is 36 point, which is quite small for video display.

4. Type in a size of *72* and press **Enter**, which loads the size setting.

Above the **Size** slider is the **Font** popup, in which you can pick whatever TrueType fonts you have loaded in your system. If you have fonts on your computer that are not showing up here, then they are most probably PostScript fonts. Unfortunately FCE's **Text** tool does not work with PostScript, only TrueType fonts. Boris Calligraphy—that is, Title 3D and Title Crawl—will work with both TrueType and PostScript.

An important point to note: the **Font** popup and all the settings in the text block will change all the letters for everything in the text block. You cannot control individual letters, or words, or lines of text. This applies to all of Final Cut Express's text generators except for Boris. Both Title 3D and Title Crawl have full text control, as we shall see.

The **Style** popup lets you set text styles such as bold and italic. Below **Style** is the **Alignment** popup, what's usually called **Justification**.

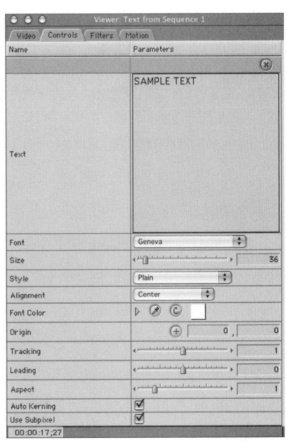

7.8   Text Control Window

Note
No Word Wrapping: FCE's titler is limited in many ways, and word wrapping is one of them. You have to put in the line breaks where appropriate, or your text is liable to run off the screen.

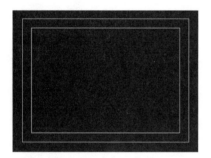

7.9   Safe Action and Safe Title Areas

7.10   View Popup

A word of caution: though the default setting is **Center**, the words in the text window are left justified. Ignore that. The popup rules; the text window just doesn't display intelligently.

The left and right alignment is not to the screen but to the **Origin** point, the way it works in Illustrator and Photoshop. So if you want left alignment on the left side of the screen, you have to move the origin point about −300 or a little less to keep it in the **Safe Title Area**, if you also set the **Alignment** to **Left**. This only applies in the **Text** tool. Other tools such as **Scrolling Text**, as we shall see, align to the screen as you might expect, with left as the left edge of the **STA**, and right as the right edge of **STA**.

Televisions have a mask on the edge that cuts off some of the displayed picture area. What you see in the **Viewer** and the **Canvas** is not what you get—far from WYSIWYG—and can vary substantially from television to television. That is why the **Canvas** and **Viewer** are thoughtfully marked with a **Safe Action Area** and a smaller area still that is defined as the **Safe Title Area**, the marked boxes seen in Figure 7.9. These are turned on with the **View** popup at the top of the **Viewer** and **Canvas** (Figure 7.10). Make sure that both **Overlay** and **Title Safe** are checked to see the **Safe Action** and **Safe Title** areas. What's within the **SAA** will appear on every television set.

Because television tubes used to be curved, and many still are, a smaller area was defined as the **Safe Title Area** in which text could appear without distortion if viewed at an angle. Titles should remain, if possible, within the **Safe Title Area**. This is not important for graphics destined only for web or computer display, but for anything that might be shown on a television within the course of its life, it would be best to maintain them.

That said, more often you're seeing titles that are well outside the **STA** and lying partially outside even the **SAA**. Also note that FCE uses an **SAA** and **STA** that are smaller than most other editing systems, which usually only reduce the area 10–20%. The *Extras* folder on your DVD contains a 720×534 format image called *SafeTitle.pct* that shows a more conventionally scribed **Safe Title** and **Safe Action Area**. It's in PICT format with an alpha channel so it will lay over video in FCE. The *Extras* folder also contains a 720×534 PICT file that has been scribed with a grid. I find this helpful to lay over an image. I use it as a guide in the **Canvas** to line up graphic and video elements in a composition. Why these images are 720×534 we'll see a little bit later in the lesson.

Font Color is self-explanatory. It includes a color picker and a color swatch as well as a disclosure triangle that twirls opens to show the **HSB** sliders and **Value** boxes.

The small icon between the **Eyedropper** and the **Color Swatch** serves no function in FCE.

The default color for the titles is white—pure, unblemished, high–luminance value white. In fact, it's whiter than white, at least as far as NTSC video goes. This white exceeds the standards set for maximum luminance in NTSC. The black that FCE generates is blacker than NTSC black. It's important that you try to keep your luminance and chrominance values within the correct range. Oversaturated colors or video levels that are too high will bloom and smear on a television set. Set the HSB value so that brightness is no more than 92%. This may look pale gray on the computer screen, but as far as NTSC video is concerned, this is white, and it will look white on a television screen.

This is often a problem with using artwork which hasn't been specifically designed for video. Interlacing, limitation in how satu-

Fonts and Size

Not all fonts are equally good for video. You can't just pick something you fancy and hope it will work for you. One of the main problems with video is its interlacing. Video is made up of thin lines of information, each line is essentially switching on and off 60 times a second. If you happen to place a thin horizontal line on your video that falls on one of those lines but not the adjacent line, that thin, horizontal line will be switching on and off at a very rapid rate, appearing to flicker. The problem with text is that a lot of fonts have thin horizontal lines called serifs, the little footer that some letters sit on (Figure 7.11).

7.11 Serif Fonts

Unless you're going to make text of a fairly large size, it's generally best to avoid serif fonts. You're better off using a sans-serif font for most video work. You should probably avoid small fonts as well. Video resolution is not very high, the print equivalent of 72dpi. You can read this book in 10 point comfortably, but a 10-point line of text on television would be an illegible smear. I generally never use font sizes below 24 and prefer to use something larger if possible.

rated a color can be and how bright it can be, the chrominance and luminance range limitations of NTSC, moire patterns, compression, all sorts of issues affect images used in video. Unless the artist makes the necessary adjustments while creating the work, it often looks unsatisfactory when incorporated into a video production.

You can set the origin with a **Crosshair** button or with x,y values. You can use the crosshairs by clicking on the button and then clicking wherever in the **Canvas** you want the center point for the origin of the text to be. The value windows are more precise, of course. The first window is the horizontal, or x value; the second window is the vertical, or y value. The default is the center of the screen. This is centered on the baseline of the first line of text, in this case somewhere right under the **n** in **Dance**.

Tracking is the spacing distance between letters. The higher the tracking value, the farther apart the letters will get. Small increases in tracking will have a large impact on letter separation. As you move tracking down below zero, the letters will scrunch together, and if you go low enough into negative values, the letters will actually flip over.

Leading (pronounced *ledding*, as in little bits of lead spacing used in hot metal typesetting) is the spacing between lines. The default is zero. A setting of –100 moves the text up so that it's all on one line like in Figure 7.12. A value of 100 moves the text down a whole line.

Aspect adjusts the vertical shape of the text. Low numbers stretch text, and higher numbers squeeze the text (Figure 7.13).

Be careful with the **Aspect** control. Very little movement from the default of 1 will cause ugly antialiasing (stair-stepped edges) to appear around the text.

Auto Kerning adjusts the letter spacing based on the letters' shape rather than absolute values (Figure 7.14). Personally I think **Auto Kerning** is too tight for most video, where any blooming will run the letters into each other, particularly serif fonts at smaller font sizes. You might want to add a little **Tracking** to the default setting to spread the letters slightly.

Note
Tracking: The Auto Kerning check-box near the bottom of the controls has to be checked on or Tracking will not function.

7.12   Leading at –100

7.13   Left: Aspect with a Value of .4 Right: Aspect with a Value of 4

7.14   Left with Auto Kerning Right without Auto Kerning

Tip

Flickering Text: Interlace flickering caused by serifs and other fine lines can be alleviated somewhat by smearing the image across the interlace lines. It is easiest to do this with text created in Photoshop, where you can simply applying a one-pixel vertical motion blur. You don't have to soften the whole image like this. If there are particular portions that appear to flicker, you can select them with a marquee or lasso, slightly feathered, and then apply the vertical motion blur to just that portion of the image.

Or in FCE you can duplicate the **Text Generator** in the sequence and stack one on top of the other. Apply a slight **Blur** or **Antialias** filter to the bottom copy. Only the slightly blurred edge that sticks out from underneath the unblurred copy will be visible, smearing the edge. You can also darken the lower copy to give the text a slightly harder edge.

Lower Thirds

A lower third is the graphic you often see near the bottom of the screen, like those identifying a speaker or location that you always see in news broadcasts. They're simple to create in Final Cut, though they are fairly limited. If you want to create something more exciting or stylish, you'll probably find it easier to do in Photoshop or in **Title 3D**, which we'll look at later on page 178. Because **Lower Third** is so limited, it's easy to use.

Click on the **Generators** button, and in the menu drop down to **Lower Third**.

Figure 7.15 shows the simple lower third Final Cut generates. It's set down in the lower left corner of the **Safe Title Area** for you.

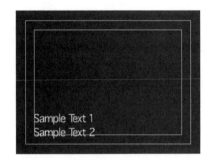

7.15 Lower Third

You can create the graphic in the **Viewer** before you move it to the **Timeline**, but remember once you've moved it to the **Timeline**, what's there is now a copy. I like to move the graphic to the **Timeline**, because once it's there, you can put the playhead over it and quickly see what you're doing in the **Canvas**. Open the **Controls** tab in the **Viewer** (Figure 7.16), and you'll see that the **Controls** are quite different for lower thirds. You have some new parameters, and you are missing a property as well. There is no **Alignment** popup.

You have two lines of text. Unlike the regular text window, each of the two text boxes here can only hold one line of text. Each text box can be set to any font, size, or color. You can make a line as long as you want—of course, if you make it too long, it will run off the screen. At the bottom of the controls, you have the ability to create a background for the text (Figure 7.17) and to adjust the opacity of the background.

Viewer: Lower 3rd from Sequence 1

Video | Controls | Filters | Motion

Name	Parameters
Text 1	Sample Text 1
Font	Geneva
Style	Plain
Size	36
Tracking	1
Font Color	
Text 2	Sample Text 2
Font	Geneva
Style	Plain
Size	36
Tracking	1
Font Color	
Background	None
Opacity	100
Color	
Auto Kerning	☑

00:00:03;11

7.16 Lower Third Controls

Font Color	None
Background	Bar
Opacity	Solid

7.17 Lower Third Backgrounds

7.18 Lower Third with Bar and Background

Bar appears as a line between the text blocks. Despite having an opacity of 100%, it will still show some of the underlying video through it. **Solid** is a block of color that appears behind the two text blocks. You can apply one or the other, but not both. You could always add another lower third beneath it, with no text, just the background, as shown in Figure 7.18.

Scrolling Text

FCE's **Scrolling Text** is called up the same way as the other text elements in the **Text Generator** menu. It looks startling at first because it opens in the **Viewer** with a blank screen, checkerboard, or black. Don't panic. Drag it to the **Timeline** or **Browser** and then double-click the new version to open it back into the **Viewer**. Go straight to the **Controls** tab (Figure 7.19), which looks pretty familiar, especially the top few items.

The control called **Spacing** is actually **Tracking**. I have no idea why it's called **Spacing** here. It does not mean vertical spacing. For that you use **Leading**. I'm not sure either why **Leading** is represented as a percentage rather than value, as in other **Generators**.

Indent only works with left- or right-justified text. With the left-justified (or aligned), the text indents about 10%, close to the safe title area. To move the text block farther to the right, use the **Indent** slider (Figure 7.20).

Gap Width lets you set the spacing between vertical columns of text. This space is often called the gutter. **Gap Width** only works with center alignment. You activate it by typing an asterisk in your text where you want the column to separate, as in "Producer*Dorothy*Cox" (Figure 7.21). You can't make your font size too large because the text will quickly run off the screen. To add a second line for each title as in Figure 7.21, you have to enter an asterisk on each line to maintain the gutter.

Fade Size is an interesting control. It allows the scroll to fade in as it comes in off the bottom of the screen and fade out as it disappears off the top (Figure 7.22).

Direction is set in a popup and can be the conventional upward movement, or it can be changed to downward.

How fast the scroll moves is determined by the length of the scroll in the sequence. The longer the scroll, the slower the movement. Unfortunately, the only way to test the speed is to render part of the scroll. You don't have to render the whole thing, just enough to show you how fast the text is moving. If it's too slow, make the scroll shorter; if it's too fast, make the scroll longer. Change the duration either by typing in a new duration in the **Viewer**, or by dragging the end of scroll in the **Timeline**.

Crawl Text

Crawl is the horizontal version of a scroll. It produces text that moves across the screen, such as the ticker seen on the bottom of all cable news channels. The controls are a little different, but they should be pretty familiar by now (Figure 7.23).

Spacing again is tracking. The **Location** slider defaults to 85, which is the bottom of the **Safe Title Area**. Reducing the number will move the crawl higher up in the screen. A value of about **20**, depending on the font and size, puts it at the top of the **Safe Title Area**.

Typewriter

Let's look at **Typewriter** next. It looks especially good if you use a typewriter monospace font such as Courier.

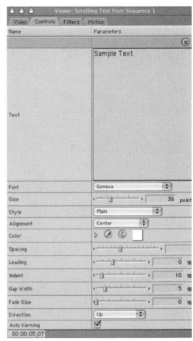

7.19 Scrolling Text Controls

7.20 Indent Set to 20%

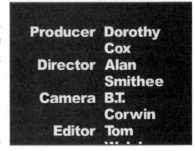

7.21 Guttered Scroll

7.22 Fading Scroll

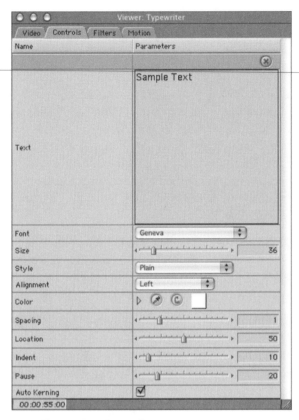

7.23 Crawl Controls

7.24 Typewriter Controls

The controls give you a small degree of flexibility (Figure 7.24).

Alignment defaults to **Left** so that the typing begins on the left edge of the **Safe Title Area** and works its way across. Be careful with the line layout, because it's easy to type right off the screen. Because the text doesn't wrap, you have to put in a return wherever you need a line break.

Location sets the vertical height of the typing. The default is 50, the center line of the screen. A setting of about 20 moves the text block to the top of the **Safe Title Area**, which is probably where you should start if you have more than a few of lines to type on.

Indent sets how far in from the edge the text is set if it is either left or right aligned.

Center alignment has an odd effect. The typing happens in the center of the screen, and the line of text spreads out from the center. It's unusual and may be worth playing with.

The default **Pause** value of 20 produces the action of a brisk typist, depending on how much text there is to type. The way it works is that the higher the **Pause** value, the longer the text is held on the screen before the end of the clip. So the three variables are:

- The length of the clip
- How long the text holds after the typing is completed (that's the **Pause** value)
- How much you have to type

If you have a lot to type, set the **Pause** value fairly low. If you set the **Pause** value very high—for instance, 100—no typing will occur; the text will just be there and spend 100% of the time paused on the screen.

Outline Text

I saved **Outline Text** for last because it's the most complex of FCE's **Text Generators**, with the greatest number of controls. Figure 7.25 shows only part of the controls. We'll examine the rest of them in a moment.

Because **Outline** is meant to be a big bold text, perhaps with video in it, the default font size is 64. It defaults to white text with a broad black outline.

In the **Outline Text** controls, **Tracking** returns instead of spacing, and **Aspect** returns as well. This is useful if you want an image to fill the letters. It lets you make the lettering taller or shorter. Again, be careful of antialiasing if you pull it around too much.

Line Width is more conventionally called *stroke*. It's the edging around the letter. You can make it disappear to nothing, or you can make quite large, up to 200 (Figure 7.26). You can, as we shall see in Lesson 10, "Adding Video" on page 268, insert video into the outline itself to make some really quite bizarre visual effects.

The **Softness** setting is for the stroke. It defaults to 5. I wouldn't put it any lower; the edges would start to look quite blocky. If you push the values up near 100 with a very large stroke, you get a kind of wispy background (Figure 7.27).

The **Text Opacity** control is self-explanatory, though I'm not quite sure why it's here. Note that this controls the opacity for all the text as well as the stroke. You cannot, unfortunately, use this tool to create an outline with a transparent interior. I'll show you

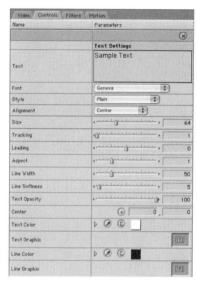

7.25 Default Outline Text Controls

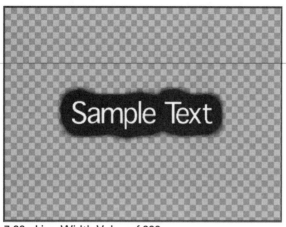

7.26 Line Width Value of 200

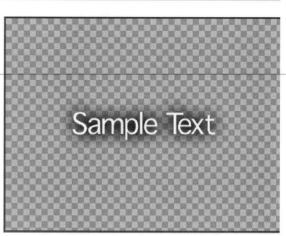

7.27 Line Width 200 and softness at 75

the way to do this using FCE's **Filters** and **Compositing** tools in Lesson 10, "Empty Outline Text" on page 272.

Center is what's called **Origin** in the standard **Text** tool, 0,0 being the middle of the screen.

Now we come to **Text Graphic** and **Line Graphic**. These allow you to insert still images into the outline using the **Well**. We saw the **Well** on page 121 in Lesson 5 on transitions, and it works the same way here: simply drag the image or clip from the **Browser** and drop it in. It would be nice if the sequence played the video inside the **Outline Text**; it doesn't, unfortunately, neither in the text nor in the **Line Width**. It only displays the In point of the video. Don't despair, though. It's possible, even simple, using FCE, to have video moving inside your text. We'll look at that also in Lesson 10 on compositing.

Let's look at the rest of **Outline Text**'s text control panel (Figure 7.28). The default is for the background to be off. You turn it on by increasing the horizontal and vertical size. The horizontal size acts in relationship to the amount of text you have—the less text, the less effect the horizontal value has; the more text, the farther the background extends (Figure 7.29).

Horizontal and **Vertical Offsets** set the screen position relative to the text, so it's not strictly an origin point. If the text is set high in the screen, so will the background. On the other hand, with the text high in the screen and the **Vertical Offset** set to negative numbers, the background will be pulled down lower in the screen (Figure 7.30).

Tip

Seeing the Border: Because Outline Text starts out as white with a black border, when you put the **Timeline** playhead over the title on V1, you probably won't see the border being black on black. The easiest way to make it visible is to change the background of the **Canvas** to checkerboard by going to View>
Background>Checkerboard 1.

7.28 Background Settings Panel

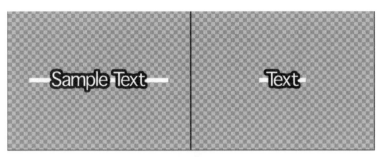

7.29 Both with Background Set
with Horizontal Size 150
Vertical Size 20

Nesting

In the project **Browser** is another sequence called *Title and Background*, which is made up of a number of FCE titling tools. The output appears in Figure 7.31, but if you open it in FCE, you'll see it in color. I'll show you how it was built up.

If you open the sequence *Title and Background*, you'll see that it is made up of two layers. On **V1** is the video clip *Dance2*, and on **V2** is a text block called *Title Composite* and another called *Title Composite Japan*. These are nests. Nesting is an important concept to understand in Final Cut. Because you can have sequences within sequences in FCE, you can also group layers together into nests to form a sequence of their own. You'll notice in the **Browser** there are sequences called *Title Composite* and *Title Composite Japan*. These are the elements that appear on **V2** in *Title and Background*. Let's build these nests together.

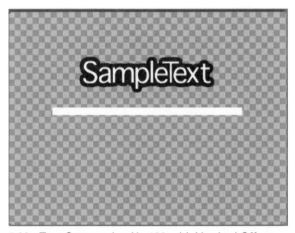

7.30 Text Centered at Y −100 with Vertical Offset
Set to −100

7.31 Title and Background

Text

1. Start by duplicating *Sequence 1* in the **Browser**. Select the sequence and use **Edit>Duplicate (Option-D)**.

2. Rename the sequence *Title Composite 2*, to distinguish it from the one that's already in the **Browser**.

3. Open the duplicate *Title Composite 2* by double-clicking on it, or simply electing it and hit **Enter** or **Return**. Delete anything that may be in the sequence.

4. In the **Viewer**, from the **Text Generator** popup select **Outline Text**.

5. Drag the **Sample Text** block onto **V2** of your sequence, leaving **V1** empty for the moment.

6. Double-click it to bring it back into the **Viewer** and go to the **Controls** tab.

7. First change the text to *DAMINE*, the name of the village where this video was shot.

8. You can, of course, use whatever text, color, or settings you want, but this is how I built this image:

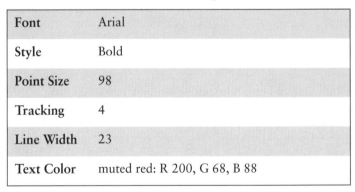

Font	Arial
Style	Bold
Point Size	98
Tracking	4
Line Width	23
Text Color	muted red: R 200, G 68, B 88

7.32 System Color Picker

9. To set the color values, I used the system color picker by clicking on the color swatch and using the RGB sliders as in Figure 7.32.

10. Because the letters looked too jammed together, I set the **Tracking** to 4.

That's it. You have the basic text block. Now let's set the background white glow.

Background

1. In the **Viewer** create a new **Outline Text** block.

2. Drag it to **V1** and open the new **Outline Text** clip from the **Timeline** back into the **Viewer**. In the **Canvas** you'll text *Sample Text* behind *Damine* as in Figure 7.33. Notice I'm using a checkerboard background.

This is going to be the background white glow.

3. In the text block, hit the spacebar 13 or 14 times; that is, type in 13 or 14 empty spaces. Use the default font size, which is fine.

We've now made a blank area of spaces for the background to work with. If we simply it empty, there would be nothing for the horizontal and vertical background controls to be applied to.

4. Scroll to the **Background** controls and set the following:

Horizontal	200
Vertical	200
Back Soft	50 (blurs the background considerably)
Opacity	100

Your **Canvas** should like something like Figure 7.34.

5. Placing the cursor on the **Filmstrip** icon at the head of **V1**, hold down the **Control** key, and from the shortcut menu, select **Add Track** (Figure 7.35).

6. Do this three times so that you have a total of three empty tracks between the two layers with the **Outline Text** blocks.

7. In the **Viewer** from the **Generators** button, select **Matte>Color**, as we did to make the color backing for the Page Peel transition in Lesson 5. Again this will fill the screen with midtone gray.

8. Drag it to **Timeline** and place it on the empty **V2** you created.

9. Double-click the **Color** in the sequence to open it back into the **Viewer**.

10. Go to the **Controls** tab and set the color to the same dark rose as the DAMINE title. Use the color picker if the title is visible in the **Canvas**. It should be if the playhead is sitting over the clips.

> ☆ **Tip** _____
> **Renaming:** It's helpful to rename the **Outline Text** before we create a new one. **Control**-click on the **Outline Text** on the top track and select **Properties** from the menu. In the **Item Properties** dialog you might want to change the name to something like **DAMINE**.

7.33 Two Outlines Texts in the Canvas

7.34 Text and Background Layers

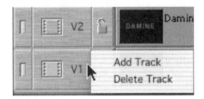

7.35 Adding Tracks

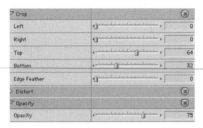

7.36 Crop and Opacity Settings in Motion Tab

11. After setting the color, go to the **Motion** tab and twirl open the **Crop** controls (Figure 7.36). I used these settings:

Top Crop	64
Bottom Crop	32
Opacity	75

We'll look at the other controls in the **Motion** tab in detail in the next lesson.

12. Open another **Color Matte**, and place it on the track above the red bar you just created.

13. Make the color of this matte green (R 20, G 96, B 19), and in the **Motion** tab set:

Top Crop	64
Bottom Crop	38

14. One more color matte to make. Generate the matte and bring it to the sequence below the top **Outline Text** block.

15. Set the same green color and these **Crop** values:

Top Crop	70
Bottom Crop	32

Your sequence should have five layers in it (Figure 7.37):

- **Outline Text** block on **V1**
- Three color mattes on the layers above
- At the top, another **Outline Text** block, the one that holds the actual text DAMINE.

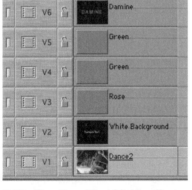

7.37 Timeline After Making Text and Matte Layers

Putting It All Together

1. Duplicate *Sequence 1*.

2. Open the duplicate and delete anything that may be in it.

3. From the **Clips** bin select the clip called *Dance2*. Use **Overwrite** in the **Canvas** or drag it directly onto V1 of the empty sequence.

4. Target **V2** and untarget the audio tracks **A1/A2**.

5. Move the playhead back to the beginning of the sequence.

6. Drag *Title Composite 2* from the **Browser** to **Overwrite** in the **Canvas** or directly onto **V2** in the **Timeline.**

Drop Shadow

You thought I forgot the drop shadow on DAMINE. Here is the beauty of nested sequences.

1. Double-click the nest. It opens as a whole separate sequence in a new tab in the **Timeline** window.

2. Double-click on the **Outline Text** block at the top to open it in the **Viewer.**

3. Go to the **Motion** tab, and check the box for **Drop Shadow.** Enter these settings:

Offset	4
Angle	135
Shadow color	Green: R 62, G 139, B 54
Softness	15
Opacity	80

The drop shadow is done. Click back on the parent sequence, *Sequence 1*. You'll see the drop shadow there as well. This change will now appear in every iteration of that sequence wherever it appears anywhere in my project.

Here's what else makes this beautiful: suppose I've built this complex text block, and I want to change the actual text, but nothing else.

1. Duplicate *Title Composite 2* in your **Browser.**

2. Change the name of the duplicate to *Title Composite Japan 2* and open it by double-clicking on it.

3. Double-click on the top outline text block to open it into the **Viewer,** and replace the word *DAMINE* with the word *JAPAN.*

Nothing else changes, just the text block and its drop shadow. Easy, isn't it?

A nested sequence is like a clip in a sequence. If you want to apply an effect to a nest or reposition the block—lower in the frame for instance—you can do this without adjusting each layer individually. We'll look at applying effects in a later lesson, as well an animating images about the screen.

Title 3D

The tools we have used so far in Final Cut Express are text tools. Boris Calligraphy, through **Title 3D** and **Title Crawl**, provides us with a titler. These really supersede the FCE text tools in many ways, giving the user great control and flexibility with text. It is a hugely feature-packed tool, an application within itself really. I'm going to show you some of its principal tools, but for a thorough look at its capabilities, there is a PDF in the *Extras* folder on the Final Cut DVD that details its operation. Just be warned that it makes much reference to animation of text, capabilities which are not available in Final Cut Express.

Boris Calligraphy really should be installed when you install FCE. Because they are built into FCE's **Generators**, they are very much an integral part of the application.

Call up Title 3D from the **Generators**. It will launch a separate titling window that is part of the Boris interface (Figure 7.38). This is the first of five tabbed windows that allow you access to Title 3D's powerful and complex tools. In fact, Title 3D has so many controls that there seem to be controls for the controls.

The first tabbed window is obviously the text window.

Unlike the FCE text box, it is truly WYSIWYG. Most importantly, each control can be applied to each letter or group of letters separately. So now, with little trouble, you can make a garish combination of colors and fonts, such as I have done in the sequence *Calligraphy.*

Before you do anything in this window, you may want to click on the second tab and change the default **No Wrap** to **Wrap** (Figure 7.39). You can leave the wrap default at 512. 512 will give you word wrapping that will fit inside a standard 720 video image's **Safe Title Area**.

The **Top-down Text** and **Right-to-left Reading** checkboxes at the bottom of the window are great if you want vertical text or if you're doing Hebrew or Arabic text.

After you've set **Word Wrapping**, go back to the text window to enter your text. The main window allows you to enter and select

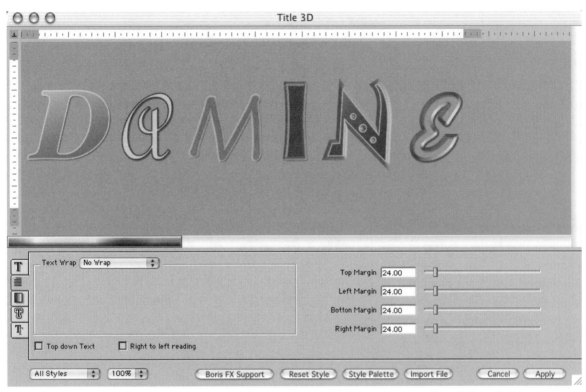

7.38 Title 3D Interface

text, which you can then adjust with the controls at the bottom part of the window.

The text window works very much like most text applications, such as Word. At the top of the **Text** window is a ruler that allows you to set tabs for precise positioning of text elements (Figure 7.40). Use the **Tab** key to navigate from one tab indent to the next. After you've set a tab, you can double-click on it to toggle from left justified, to right justified, to center justified. This tool is especially useful when making long scrolls like movie credits that often use columns and indents for different sections.

The white area seen in the ruler is the active text part of the screen, while the gray area is beyond the word wrapping.

7.39 Word Wrapping

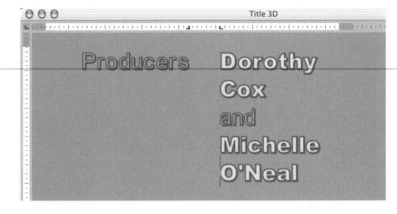

7.40 Title 3D Text Window Ruler

Let's look quickly at some of the phenomenal text control in Calligraphy. In the bottom portion of the screen, the first popup obviously sets the font. The two buttons to the right will move you up and down through your font list. Below the Font popup is a **Point Size Value** box. The two buttons to the right will incrementally raise and lower your point. To the right of the font controls are six buttons that let you set:

- Normal
- Bold
- Italic
- Underline
- Superscript
- Subscript

Below that, three **Paragraph** buttons let you set justification:

- Left
- Center
- Right

The **Tracking** slider adjusts the letter spacing globally.

Kerning adjusts the spacing between individual pairs or groups of letters without affecting the overall spacing. It allows you to control individual letter spacing. It's important for many fonts, especially when you are writing words like AVE, where you need to slide the A and V closer together than fonts normally place them.

Leading controls the line gap between all the lines in the window.

Bitmap or Vector

When you scale text created with the FCE titler, the image quickly became jagged around the edges, yet in Title 3D you can scale the text, twisting and skewing the letters, and you'll see no apparent antialiasing or stair-stepping on the edges of the letters. This is possible because Calligraphy works with vector graphics, while FCE text creates bitmapped graphics.

When a bitmapped graphic is created, the color and position of each pixel in the image is defined. If you then scale that image, you have to scale the pixels, trying to create pixels where none previously existed. When a vector graphic is created, no pixels are actually defined. Only the shape, based on lines and curves, is defined. So if you scale a vector graphic, you're simply redefining the shape; no actual pixels need be created until the image is displayed on the screen.

Figure 7.41 shows what happens when a bitmapped text file (Apple Chancery 76 point) is scaled 300% and when a vector-based text file is scaled the same amount. The scaling for the vector graphic has to be done within **Title 3D** and not using the **Scale** slider in the **Motion** tab.

7.41 Left: Bitmapped
Right: Vector

The **Style** controls (Figure 7.42) allow you to skew the text on the *x* and *y* axis. These were primarily designed to be used as animation controls, but because that capability is not available in FCE, these controls can do little more than create interesting letter patterns by tilting letters in various ways.

Style Baseline will allow you to raise and lower letters separately, while **Style Scale X** and **Style Scale Y** will let you scale individual characters on the *x* and/or *y* axis independently from each other, allowing you to create interesting and unusual letter arrangements, as in Figure 7.43.

The **All Styles** popup at the bottom lets you change to **Basic Style**. You see basic limits in the text window. It does speed up preview, which can get quite slow with long text windows.

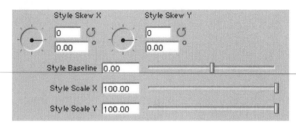

7.42   Style Controls   7.43   Skewed, Scaled and Baseline Shifted Letters

The **Percentage** popup lets you change the display size of the text window, a useful feature if you have a lot of text and want to quickly move around in it.

Boris FX Support will connect you to Boris's online web support system.

The **Reset Style** button will reset all the parameters for the words in the text window. It will not, however, reset wrapping, tabs, justification, or margins.

The **Style Palette** is a great tool (Figure 7.44). It allows you to create your own text style and to name and save it. This way you can replicate styles from file to file and even project to project simply and efficiently.

The **Import File** button allows you to bring into the **Text** window a previously created plain text file or RTF (Rich Text Format) file. All the justification and styles applied there will be honored in **Title 3D**.

Cancel and **Apply** are self-explanatory.

This is only the first couple of tabs in **Title 3D**.

The third tabbed panel, **Text Color**, lets you set the text fill and opacity (Figure 7.45). Notice the little checkbox in the upper left corner that let's you turn off the fill, so that you only have the text outline if you want. The **Text Fill** popup lets you choose to fill the text with a color or with a gradient. If you choose **Color** the **Style Color** swatch allows access to the system color picker that we saw earlier. If you choose **Gradient** you will get access to an incredibly powerful gradient editor (Figure 7.46), which allows multiple color points as well as transparency. To add color points, click below the gradient bar display.

The fourth tabbed window lets you set the width and opacity for the **Text Edge**, and not just a single edge, but up five separate

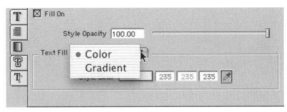

7.45   Text Color

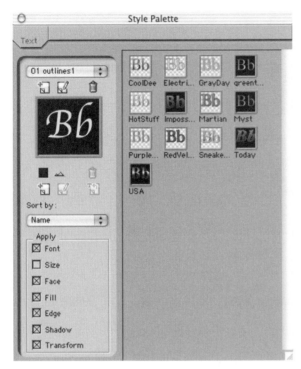

7.44   Style Palette

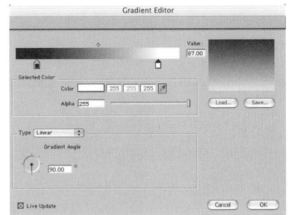

7.46   Gradient Editor

edges for each letter (Figure 7.47). Each edge can be **Plain, Bevel,** or **Glow,** and can be **Center, Inside,** or **Outside.** The slider on the right controls the softening blur for each edge. The variations possible with five edges are nearing infinite. More than anyone could need.

The fifth panel sets up to five separate **Drop Shadows.** These can be either a standard **Drop;** a **Cast** shadow, which slopes away from the text; or a **Solid** shadow with sides (Figure 7.48). **Drop** and **Cast** shadows don't have **Highlight** or **Shade** color, but they have a **Softness** control that appears when the shadow popup is changed. Each shadow also has controls for color, distance, opacity, and angle.

A major drawback of working with Boris Calligraphy is that unfortunately, while you're working in Title 3D, you cannot see the text composited on top of the image. Once you've created your text, drag it to the **Timeline** or **Superimpose** it over a clip that's already there.

7.47 Text Edge

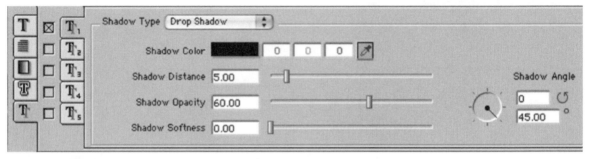

7.48 Drop Shadow

If you need to change or adjust the text, double-click the **Title 3D** file in the **Timeline** to open it into the **Viewer**. Then click on the **Control** tab to open all the controls for **Title 3D** (Figure 7.49).

To access the text window to change the letters or styles or any of the other controls, click on the **Title 3D** logo at the top of the controls panel. Again many of the features in this panel were designed primarily as animation controls which are not available in FCE.

The **Geometry** section controls the text overall, changing:

- Position
- Distance
- Scale
- Tumble
- Spin
- Rotate

While **Position** places the text in the screen, **Distance** makes the text appear nearer or farther away. The **Scale** value in this panel will allow you to get clean, large fonts. When working with **Title 3D**, scale your text here in this panel, not with **Scale** in the **Motion** tab.

Tumble, Spin, and Rotate will turn the entire text block around on the *x, y,* and *z* axes, respectively. A nice thing about Calligraphy is that if you have a real-time capable system, most of these motion settings, including drop shadow, will preview in real-time.

Pivot controls the point around which the text Tumbles, Spins, and Rotates. If the Lock to Position box is checked, the controls have no effect. With the box checked, the text will Rotate around the selected Pivot point, which can be set with numeric values or with the crosshairs button. Neither Tumble nor Spin controls function with the X/Y controls, but their movement is affected when the Z slider is activated.

Transformation affects all the letters in the text block, but it affects them individually. In Figure 7.50 the image on the left has its Geometry tumbled –45 ° and spun 50°, while the image on the right has its Transformation tumbled –45° and spun 70°. Notice that on the right each letter is moving, while on the left they are moving together.

Title Crawl

Title Crawl is accessed from the bottom of the Generators popup and shares many of the same controls as Title 3D. The text window that's evoked when Title Crawl is called up functions identically in both Calligraphy title tools. The real difference is seen in the Controls tab of the Viewer (Figure 7.51). Here there are far fewer options: no Geometry, no Transformation.

The Animation popup lets you set:

- None, the default
- Roll (Scroll)
- Crawl

Mask Start and End, Blend Start and End are the same as FCE's Fade Size tool, only with more control. Here you can fade the start and end separately as well as controlling the amount of fade, here called blend. The Reverse Direction checkbox does just that, makes a roll reverse from the default bottom-to-top direction to

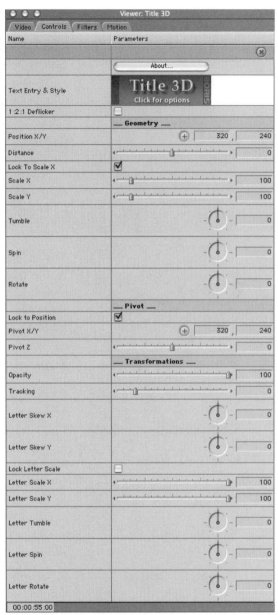

7.49 Title 3D Controls

✎ Note
Interlace Flickering: If you're doing text animation on interlaced video, check the 1:2:1 **Deflicker** box to reduce interlace flickering.

7.50 Geometry vs. Transformation

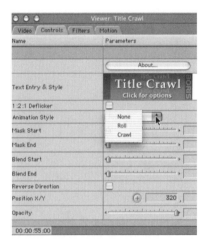

7.51 Title Crawl Controls

top-to-bottom, and reverses direction of the standard right-to-left crawl to left-to-right.

To do a **Crawl**, a horizontal stream of text across the screen, make sure **Word Wrap** is switched off.

The speed of the **Roll** or **Crawl** is determined by the amount of text in the text window and the duration of the text block in the **Timeline:** the longer the block, the slower the motion. You should be aware that though **Title 3D** is vector based, **Title Crawl** is not. It produces bit-mapped graphics.

Photoshop Titles

If the capabilities of these text and title tools aren't enough for you, there is always Photoshop or its younger brother Photoshop Elements. What great titlers these are, infinitely malleable, allowing you to create many additional graphical elements, like banners and bars and gradients. Though it could be done, it would be far more difficult to construct these items in FCE than in these great graphics applications. It seems anything you can imagine is possible with these Adobe products. I've used Photoshop often, particularly for lower thirds, and also for working with still images that need to be incorporated into a project.

What you should first know about working in PS is that you should only use RGB color space—no CMYK, no grayscale, no indexed color. They don't translate to video.

One problem with using PS is the issue of square versus non-square pixels. Because PS is a computer program, it works in square pixels exclusively, while digital video uses rectangular pixel, tall, narrow pixels that allow for greater horizontal resolution. This presents a minor problem. The important point is to understand how FCE handles still image files. It handles different types of images in different ways. Single layer files are treated one way, multilayer Photoshop files or PS files with transparency are treated another way. Single layer files are treated as graphics files and FCE understands that they're come from a square pixel world. Multilayer files are treated as sequences, and FCE would not presume to alter the dimensions of a sequence you created. It assume you did it correctly.

1. Because you're working in the DV format using rectangular pixels based on a frame resolution of 720×480 pixels, you should create your PS files at 720×534 to start with.

2. After you've made your graphic, go to **Image Size** and, making sure **Constrain Proportions** is deselected and **Bicubic** is selected, change the height of the image to 480.

This squashes the image down, distorting it, changing it to a file that FCE recognizes as using rectangular pixels.

3. Save your file.

I save out a separate PS file that has been converted to DV format and keep the original so I can correct the typos I usually make.

Figure 7.53 shows an image at 720×534. Notice that the circle in it is circular, while in Figure 7.54 the image has been squeezed down to 720×480, distorting the circle. That's fine. When it's put into a DV sequence and played back to DV the circle will become round again.

When you bring a PS file that's 720×480 into FCE, the editing software assumes it's been prepared for use in a DV sequence. When placed in a DV sequence, the image will work perfectly and be treated as a nonsquare pixel image.

There are templates for these formats as well as for the 16:9 format in the *Extras* folder of the book's DVD.

You're not always making a graphic that needs to fit in the video format. Sometimes you're making a graphic that is much larger, one you want to move around on to make it seem as if you're panning across the image or zooming in or out of the image. To do this, you need to make the image much greater than your video format, perhaps 2,000×2,000 pixels or more.

✒ Tip
Preset Sizes: If you're working with Photoshop 7, there's a feature that allows you to select preset custom sizes when you make a new file. Use the **Preset Sizes** popup and select **720x534 Std. NTSC DV/DVD** (Figure 7.52).

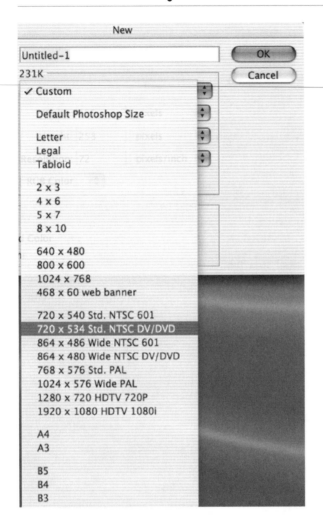

7.52   Photoshop Preset Popup (Left)

7.53   Circle in a 720x534 Image

7.54   Circle Squeezed into a 720x480 Image

Widescreen

If you're working in widescreen format, shooting and editing using the 16:9 anamorphic aspect ratio, making graphics requires different pixel sizes. The Photoshop file should be created at 960x534 for DV.

If you are working with a Photoshop layer image, you still should squeeze the image down to nonsquare pixels before you bring it into FCE. To do this, rather than using pixel values, use percentages and reduce the height of the image to 90% or, if you want to be anally precise about it, 89.886%. Again, you should not resize these images if they are single layer images without Photoshop transparency. FCE understands these are square pixel images brought into the DV world and will handle them appropriately. If they are PS layered files with transparency, FCE treats these as separate sequences and does not adjust for square pixels. The rules of the road are probably unnecessarily complex, but the bottom line is if it's a single-layer file, let FCE do the resizing; if it's a PS file, squeeze it before you import it.

➤ *Tip*

Bringing in the Layers: If you do bring your PS sequence into Final
Cut as layers, and you decide you'd rather work with it as a single-layer
file, use this easy trick: Open the PS sequence, select all the layers,
and go to the **Modify>Make Freeze Frame (Shift-N)**. That will make a
still image of all the layers. You can then drag that still into the
Browser, rename it, move it wherever you want, and use it again and
again. What's nice about this technique is that it preserves the transparency of the Photoshop file; all the layers will be merged, but the
transparency will remain intact. If you want to preserve the layers as
individual images, just select all the layers in the PS sequence and drag
them to the **Browser**. They will appear as individual images with their
PS layer names as in Figure 7.55. All the colored layers have been
pulled out of the sequence *Multilayer.psd*.

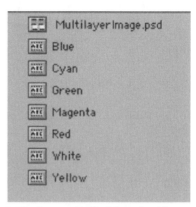

7.55 Layers Pulled from Inside
Multilayer Photoshop File

When you import an oversized Photoshop file and place it inside a
sequence, FCE will immediately scale the image. If the still is
smaller than the image resolution—say, a 500×200 image in a
720×480 DV sequence—the application will simply place it in the
center of the screen with blackness around it. If the image is, for
instance, 400 pixels wide but 800 pixels tall, FCE will scale it
down to fit inside the window, as in Figure 7.56. If you do want
to use the image at its full size, so that you can move across it, for
instance, the first step you'll have to do is to return it to its full
size.

1. Select the image in the **Timeline** and press the **Enter** or **Return**
    key. Or **Option**-double-click on it to open it into the **Viewer**.

2. Click on the **Motion** tab in the **Viewer**.

3. Set the **Scale** value back to 100.

Resolution

For people who come from a print background, the important
point to note is that video doesn't have a changeable resolution.
It's not like print where you can jam more and more pixels into
an inch of space and make your print cleaner, clearer, and crisper.
Pixels in video occupy a fixed space and have a fixed size, the
equivalent of 72dpi in the print world, which happens to be the
Macintosh screen resolution. Dots per inch are a printing con-
cern. Forget about resolution. Think in terms of size: the more

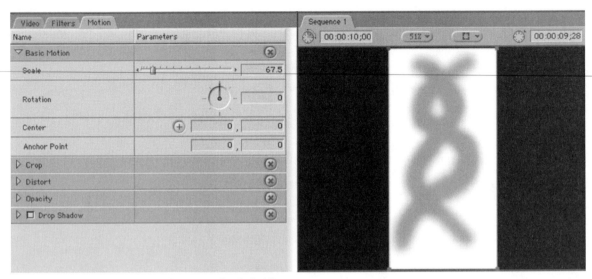

7.56 Large Image in Canvas Showing Scale in Viewer

pixels, the bigger the picture. Do not think that you can make an image 720×480 at a high resolution like 300dpi or 600dpi and be able to move it around in FCE. Certainly you'll be able to scale it up, but it will look soft, and if you scale it far enough—to 300%, for instance—the image will start to show pixelization. FCE is good at hiding the defects by blurring and softening, but the results are not really as good as they should be. FCE is a video application and only deals with pixel numbers, not with dpi.

Scanners, on the other hand, are designed for the print world where dpi is an issue. Because scanners generate lots and lots of pixels, this is very handy for the person working in video. This means that you can scan an image at, let's say, 300 or 600dpi, even a quite small image, and your scanner will produce thousands and thousands of pixels, which will translate into video as a very large image. You now have an image that's very much larger than your video format of 720×480 pixels. If your scanner can generate an image that's 2,880 pixels across, it's making an image four times greater than your DV video frame. You can now move that very large image around on the screen, and make it seem as if a camera is panning across the image. Or you can scale back the image, and it will look as if the camera is zooming back from a point in the image. Or reverse the process and make it look as if the camera is zooming into the image. We'll look at these in Lesson 8, "Animation Effects" on page 208.

Pulling Photoshop Effects

One problem many users encounter with Photoshop images is with effects applied in PS, such as drop shadows to text layers or any of the hundreds of image effects the application can do. None of the effects seem to appear when the file is imported into FCE. In fact, if you have an adjustment layer applied in the file, you will get an **Out of Memory** error message if you try to import the Photoshop document. The problem is the effects are not applied to the image, but remain with PS so they can be changed at any time without having to recreate the layer. It's like nondestructive editing in Final Cut. There is a way around this, however. Just merge the layer with the effect into an empty PS layer. Make a new blank layer beneath each layer you want to rasterize, then from the **Wing** menu of **Layers** palette choose **Merge Down** (Figure 7.57). This fixes the effect with the image onto the empty layer. Of course, now the layer effects are no longer editable.

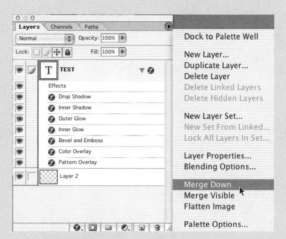

7.57   Merge Down

Another method, if you only have a few layers that you don't mind merging together, is to use **Merge Visible**. Create a blank layer at the bottom of the layer stack and then use **Command-Option-Shift-E**. Unlike the normal **Merge Visible** from the Photoshop Layer menu, this keyboard command will not collapse the layers into a single layer but will copy the content of all the visible layers and merge them into the single blank layer. With this method you still have the editable layers in the PS document. If you switch off the visibility for the upper layers in PS, when the file is imported into, the merge layer will be visible, and the other layers will be present as well, only with their track visibility switched off as they were in Photoshop.

This is something you should do at the very end: merge the layers as needed, and squish the file to its DV format, while still keeping an original PS file copy in its original format with the original images, text layers, and effects, separated and still editable.

Working with a single-layer file within FCE has one advantage: it's simpler. One of the issues that arise with PS sequences in Final Cut is the problem of doing transitions between them (see "Transitions between Sequences" on page 192).

Transitions with Still Images: If you want to put together a group of still images with transitions between them, you can simplify the process in a couple of ways. When you import the files, make sure you leave enough room in your **Still/Freeze Duration** preference to accommodate the transitions. Sequentially number the stills you want to import and place them into a separate folder on your hard drive. Next import all your stills as a single folder using **Import>Folder** so that they come in as a bin. Then drag the bin from the **Browser** straight to the **Canvas Edit Overlay** and drop on **Overwrite** (or **Insert**) with **Transition**. All the stills will miraculously dump out of the bin and appear in the **Timeline** with a Cross Dissolve between them. The technique works beautifully with flattened PS files or other image formats such as PICT files.

Fading

Very often you'll want to fade in the graphic and fade it out again. Take another look at the sequence called *Title and Background*.

1. Click on the **Clip Overlay** button (**Option-W**), the button in the far lower left corner on the **Timeline** window.

The files now have lines in them near the top. This is the opacity value of the clips. With the lines all the way to the top, their values are 100%. You'll notice that the line ramps down at the beginning and end of each of the graphics clips in the lesson sequence. This will fade in and fade out the **Opacity** from 0 to a 100 and back again. This works exactly like the control we used for audio levels.

2. Grab the level line and pull it down. The overall level will change.

Transitions between Sequences

Because FCE allows you to place sequences within sequences, such as these nested Photoshop or graphics sequences we've been working with here, it sometimes becomes necessary to create transitions between them. This presents some problems. FCE treats each sequence as a complete piece of media. So as we've seen, if you have used the media to its limits, you can't create a transition.

Though each layer in a PS sequence can be any length you want, when the PS sequence is laid into another sequence, the final sequence assumes that the limit of the media is the limit of the nested sequence. It will not go burrowing into the nest to extend the media for each layer to make room for the transition.

So if you want to create a transition between sequences, you have to ripple the outgoing sequence and the incoming sequence to allow room for the transition.

3. Use the **Pen** tool (**P**) to make opacity keyframes on the level line and to pull down the opacity as needed.

Also, the global **Levels** tool, **Sequence>Levels** (**Command-Option-L**), will also affect the levels of multiple video or title clips. We saw this feature in Lesson 6, "Controlling Audio Levels" on page 147. Unlike audio keyframes, though, you can also smooth the opacity keyframes to ease into the fade by **Control**-clicking on the keyframe. In the sequence *Title and Background*, the first clip has had the fade smoothed, while the second has not.

> **Tip**
>
> **Fading Graphics:** Another way I like to do a fade in or a fade out from a graphic is to lay a **Cross Dissolve** just before the edit point. If you place it too close to the edit, it will drop in as a one-frame dissolve, but if you place it slightly away from the edit, it will drop in as dissolve to the edit point, as in Figure 7.58. This only works if there aren't two graphics inline with each other, butted up one to the other.

7.58 Cross Dissolve to Fade Out Graphic

Summary

In this lesson we've gone through FCE's title tools, Boris Calligraphy, and the task of bringing Photoshop title files into Final Cut. But that isn't all there is to titling. There are still some issues with graphics images in Final Cut, particularly images in motion, that we'll look at in the next lesson on creating animation in FCE.

Lesson 8

Animating Images

Final Cut Express has considerable capabilities for animating images. It allows you to enhance your productions and create exciting, interesting and artistic scenes. In this lesson we will concentrate on FCE's motion capabilities.

Loading the Lesson

One more time, begin by loading the material you need onto your media drive.

1. If you don't already have it there, drag the *Media* folder from the DVD to your media hard drive.

2. For this lesson you might also want to drag the folder *Animation Media* on to your media drive.

3. Also bring the folder *Lesson 8* from inside the *Projects* folder into the *Shared* folder of your system drive or your *Documents* folder.

4. Eject the DVD and open the *Lesson 8* folder on your hard drive.

5. For this lesson you need to have Boris Calligraphy loaded on your computer. If you haven't already done so, install it from your FCE CD.

6. When you have all the software installed on your computer, double-click your copy of the project file, *L8,* to launch the application.

7. Reconnect the media, and reassign the scratch disk if needed. The item *BB.mov* is the movie that was in the *Animation Media* folder.

Motion Window

Let's first take a look at how to create motion in Final Cut.

1. Open *Sequence 1,* which is, of course, empty.

2. We're only going to deal with video tracks for much of this lesson, so the first step we'll take is to untarget the two audio tracks **A1** and **A2.** Just click on the little yellow target channels at the head of each track.

3. Next drag a clip—let's say *Archers1*—from the **Clips** bin and drop it onto **Overwrite** or **Insert** in the **Canvas Edit Overlay** (**CEO**).

Because the audio tracks were untargeted, only the video portion of the clip will appear in the **Timeline.**

4. Use the **View** popup menu at the top of the **Canvas** to select **Image+Wireframe** (Figure 8.1).

8.1   Canvas Popup Menu

Select the clip in the **Timeline,** and the image in the **Canvas** will appear with a wireframe indicator. The large cross through it defines the corners and boundaries (Figure 8.2).

5. Double-click on the clip in the **Timeline** to open it in the **Viewer,** and then click on the **Motion** tab at the top to open it (Figure 8.3).

Here are the motion elements that can be keyframed. Most of them, with the exception of **Opacity, Drop Shadow,** and **Motion Blur,** can be keyframed in the **Canvas.** We saw how to keyframe **Opacity** at the end of the last lesson. Once you start twirling open the little triangles, which the FCE manual calls *disclosure triangles,* you might need to stretch down the window.

8.2   Image+Wireframe Clip in Canvas

Once a keyframe has been set for a parameter, if you move to another point on the timeline and change the parameter values, a new keyframe will be set. The speed of the change is determined by the time between the keyframes: the farther apart in time the keyframes, the slower the motion.

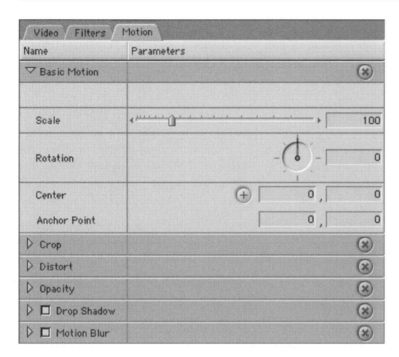

8.3   Motion Control Window

Notice that each of the control panels—**Basic Motion, Crop, Distort, Opacity, Drop Shadow,** and **Motion Blur**—has a button with a red X on it. This allows you to reset the values for that parameter.

Keyframing

The basic concept of keyframing is that you mark the properties for a clip at a particular frame. You mark it by setting a *keyframe*. If you go further forward or backward in time by moving the playhead, and change the parameter values for the clip another keyframe will automatically be set. The application calculates how fast it has to change the values to go from one state to the other. If the keyframes are far apart in time, the change will be gradual. If the keyframes are closer together the change will be more rapid.

It's easy to set a keyframe in FCE. With the clip selected in the **Timeline**, click the **Keyframe** button (the little diamond at the bottom right of the **Canvas**), or press the keyboard shortcut **Control-K** (Figure 8.4).

8.4   Keyframe Button

8.5 Filters and Motion Bar Button

8.6 Image Scaling Distorted

🐾 Note _____
Viewer Keyframe Button: The **Viewer Keyframe** button that is in the mirror position to the **Keyframe** button in the **Canvas** does not work for some reason.

This sets an initial keyframe for those properties in the **Motion** tab that are keyframable. It will not set keyframes for **Opacity** nor for **Drop Shadow**. When a keyframe is set the wireframe for the clip turns green in the **Canvas**. The wireframe will also display a number which indicates the track number of the track the clip is on.

To delete a keyframe that you've set, **Control**-click on the image in the **Canvas** and select **Delete point** from the shortcut menu (Figure 8.5).

Let's look at the parameters in the **Motion** tab that can be keyframed and what you can do with them.

Scale

The first keyframable property in the **Motion** window is **Scale**, a simple slider and value box that lets you set a size. Because FCE deals exclusively in bitmapped images, stills, video, and text files made up of pixels, it's generally not a good idea to scale upwards, not much above 110% to 120%.

👍 Tip _____
Controlling Sliders: Because there is so little travel in the slider's useful range, I usually use it while holding down the **Command** key, which gives smaller increments of movement. The **Command** key works like this in many drag movements in FCE, such as dragging clips to lengthen and shorten them in the **Timeline**. If you hold down the **Shift** key, you'll get increments up to two decimal places.

While the sliders and value boxes in the **Motion** tab give you precise control, the easiest way to scale or control the other motion parameters is in the **Canvas**. With the **Canvas** set to **Image+Wireframe**, grab one of the corners and drag. The image will, by default, scale proportionately. If you want the image to be distorted, hold down the **Shift** key while you drag (Figure 8.6).

If you hold down the **Command** key while you drag an image's corner to scale it, you add the **Rotation** tool so you can scale and rotate at the same time.

Rotation

Rotation is controlled with the clock dial or with values.

There is a limit on how far you can take rotation, no more than 24 rotations seems possible. To get there, you can either:

- Keep dialing in more and more turns of the screw or
- Type in a value

Each notch of the "hour" hand is one revolution. It would be nice if separate value boxes for revolutions and degrees had been included. At the moment, you either have to:

- Twist the dial around and around lots of times or
- Calculate, such as 22 revolutions times 360° equals 7,920°

By the way, 24 revolutions are 8,640°.

Like **Scale**, **Rotation** can be created in the **Canvas**. As you move the cursor near one of the edges of the image, it changes into a rotation tool (Figure 8.7). You can now grab the image and swing it around the anchor point, which we'll see in a minute. For the moment, rotation is happening around the middle of the image. It's a little easier to rotate the image if you grab nearer the corner, but don't get too close or you'll grab the **Scale** point.

Center is position: where the image is on the screen. FCE counts the default center position, 0,0, and counts outwards from there, minus *x* to the left, plus *x* to the right, minus *y* upwards, plus *y* downwards. The crosshairs allow you to position an image with a click in the **Canvas**.

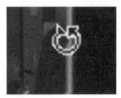

8.7   Rotation Tool

⭐ *Tip*

Rotation Tip: Holding down the **Shift** key will constrain the dial to 45° increments, while holding down the **Command** key will give you a little finer control over the movement of the dial.

Straight Motion

Let's set up a simple motion for a clip. You should have the clip *Archers1* at the beginning of an empty sequence.

1. If you have done any movement to the clip, reset the parameters by clicking on the red **X** buttons in the **Motion** tab.

2. Make sure the **Canvas** is in **Image+Wireframe** and that the playhead is back at the start of the sequence.

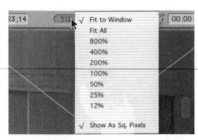

8.8 Zoom Popup

8.9 Moving Image Off the Screen

We're now going to move the clip off the screen.

3. If you need to position an image outside of the **Canvas**, first reduce the size of the display in the **Canvas** with the **Zoom** popup (Figure 8.8) to say something like 25%. You might want to stretch out the **Canvas** a little. This will show you the grayboard around the image.

4. Grab the image and move it off the screen (Figure 8.9).
    Or use the **Center** crosshairs to click on a point out in the grayboard.

5. Once the clip is positioned off the screen, use **Control-K** to set a keyframe or click the **Keyframe** button in the bottom right of the **Canvas**.

6. Go forward five seconds in time. To move the playhead exactly, make sure the clip in the **Timeline** is deselected (**Command-D**) and type **+5.** and **Enter.** You'll see the playhead in the **Timeline** move. You can also hold down the **Shift** key and tap on the **Right** arrow key five times to move forward five seconds.

7. Drag the clip across the screen to the other side, creating a line with a string of dots on it.

You have now created a straight linear motion of the image across the screen (Figure 8.10). Notice that while at the first keyframe the wireframe was green, at the second keyframe only the dot in the center of the wireframe is green. This is because only the **Center** position value has changed.

Tip

Navigation Tips

Tip 1: In the **Canvas**, the center point turns green when the playhead is on the keyframe. It's only visible when the clip is selected. When the clip isn't selected, there is no indicator.

Tip 2: If you are moving a clip or multiple clips off the screen, it's handy to use **Fit All** from the **Zoom** popup. This will adjust the **Canvas** to include all the clips off the screen.

Tip 3: The spacing of the little dots along the motion path indicates the speed of the motion. If the dots are bunched together, the motion is slow, whereas if they're more separated from each other, the motion is fast.

Curved Motion

There are two ways to create a curved path:

- Pull out the path from the linear motion.
- Create a curved path by using Bezier handles.

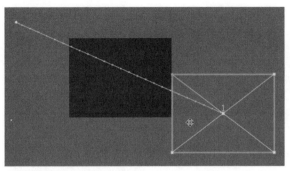

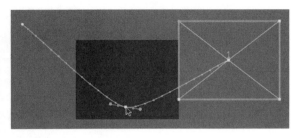

8.10 Linear Motion Path

8.11 Curved Motion Path

In the first method, when you place the cursor on the line, it changes from the regular **Selection** tool into the **Pen** tool. You can then drag out the line so that it's a curve (Figure 8.11). This creates a new keyframe.

Notice also the two bars sticking out from the dot on the curve. The bars have two handles each, represented by little dots, one slightly darker than the other. These bars are the Bezier handles.

The second method doesn't create an intermediate keyframe. There are normally no handles to adjust the arc on either the start point or the end point of the motion. You can quickly add these by **Control**-clicking on the point and selecting **Ease In/Ease Out** from the shortcut menu (Figure 8.12).

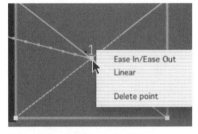

8.12 Ease In/Ease Out Menu

When you select **Ease In/Ease Out,** the handles appear. These can be used to pull the line into an arc (Figure 8.13). Unfortunately, the handles are quite small, and minor adjustments can have a major impact on the motion path. The outer handles allow you to adjust the arc of the curve. Each side of arc can be adjusted separately to make complex movements.

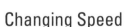 **Tip** _____

Zoom: To zoom into a portion of the **Canvas**, select the **Zoom** tool, **Z**, and lasso a rectangular area (like drawing a marquee) around a section of the screen. **Zoom** will fill the **Canvas** with that section. **Option-Zoom** will take you back out.

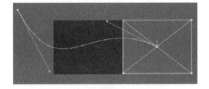

8.13 Curved Motion with Bezier Handles

Changing Speed

Normally objects don't arrive at speed instantly, nor do they stop instantly. So if your image is starting or stopping on the screen, you probably want it to accelerate or decelerate, rather than jerk-

8.14 Shortcut Menu Options

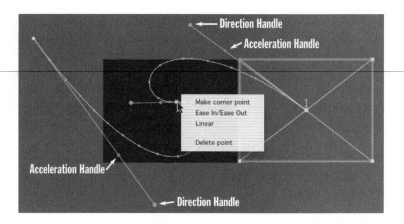

ing into motion. In graphics animation this is called *easing*: you ease into a motion and you ease out of a motion. This is what the darker set of handles, the **Acceleration Handles**, do. They control the speed at which the image moves through the keyframe, the rate of deceleration as it approaches the keyframe, and then acceleration as it leaves the keyframe. If you want the motion to smoothly pass through the point without changing speed, make sure those handles are not moved, or **Control**-click on the keyframe and choose **Linear** (Figure 8.14). If you pull the handles apart, the motion will be faster. If you push the handles inward toward the keyframe point, the motion will slow down. The image will decelerate as it comes to the keyframe, and then accelerate away. I have created a simple motion path that shows this.

1. Open *Curved Path Sequence*.
2. Render out the motion path.

You'll clearly see the deceleration and acceleration as the image passes through the intermediate keyframe. Notice that the image moves much quicker in the first part of the movement and then slower in the second portion. This happens because the first portion of the movement is shorter both in time and distance.

✎ Tip
Adjusting Bezier Handles: If you want to make the curves or the motion even more complex, you can adjust each end of the Bezier handles independently. If you hold down the **Command** key and grab a handle, it will move separately from the other (Figure 8.15).

8.15 Separate Bezier Control Handles

One great feature of FCE is the ability to move the entire motion path you've created. You can move the whole path as a single entity to whatever position on the screen you want. This can be very useful, if, for instance, you've made a horizontal movement—say, left to right across the screen—that slides a clip through the upper portion of the screen. Later you decide it would be better for it to slide across the lower portion of the screen. Rather than resetting all the motion path keyframes, simply move the entire path. To do this, make sure the **Canvas** is in **Image+Wireframe** mode. Hold down **Command-Shift,** and when the cursor is over the clip, it will change to the **Hand** tool (Figure 8.16). Grab the clip and move it. The whole motion path will move as a single group.

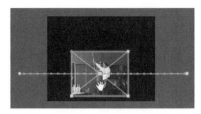

8.16   Hand Tool to Move a Motion Path

Anchor Point

The anchor point is the pivot point around which the image swings. It's also the point around which scaling takes place. For some reason that escapes me, **Anchor Point,** unlike **Center,** does not have crosshairs for positioning it. Fortunately there is a way to move it in the **Canvas** (Figure 8.17).

1.   Select the **Distort** tool (keyboard **D** for distort) and grab the center point of the clip. Drag it to where you want to position the anchor point. The point you're moving with this tool is actually the anchor point.

We'll look at the **Distort** tool on page 205.

2.   Apply a rotation to the image.

Notice that it doesn't swing around the center of the image but around this new point. If you pull it out to the upper right corner, that's where the image will pivot. Take a look at *Anchor Point Sequence.* Two images swing through the frame with opposing anchor points.

Notice also that on the second clip I have animated the center as well as repositioning the anchor point. It moves slightly differently, more tumbling than simply rotating. Be careful with animating multiple parameters: once the anchor point's been moved, it can lead to unexpected results.

8.17   Anchor Point Moved with Distort Tool

> ☞ *Tip*
>
> ***Anchor Point Keyframe:*** If the clip is deselected, the anchor point keyframe is not indicated in the **Canvas.** If the clip is selected, however, the track number will turn green to show that the playhead is over an Anchor Point keyframe.

8.18   Crop Controls

▽ Crop		⊗
Left		0
Right		0
Top		0
Bottom		0
Edge Feather		0

★**Tip**
Crop Line: If the clip is selected in the timeline, when the playhead reaches a Crop keyframe, the crop line shows as blue. If the clip is not selected, no indicator appears in the Canvas.

Other Motion Controls

Crop

Crop allows you to cut the image from the sides. This can be done with the controls hidden under the twirly triangle (Figure 8.18).

If you have specific values, or if you want to reduce the image by precise amounts—such as equally from all sides—then this is place to do it. To crop in the **Canvas**, you'll need to use the **Crop** tool as we did in the last lesson. The **Crop** tool is in the tools and can be called up with the letter **C**, just as in Photoshop (Figure 8.19). Like the other motion controls in the **Canvas**, it will only work while you're in **Image+Wireframe**.

The **Crop** tool in Final Cut doesn't work very much like Photo-Shop's. You can't simply drag a marquee across the image to define the section you want to keep.

1.   Select the image, and with the **Crop** tool grab one edge of the image.

As the tool gets near the edge, it changes into the **Crop** icon, indicating the cursor is acting in **Crop** mode.

2.Grab the edge and pull in the image to crop (Figure 8.20). Or you can grab the corner and pull in two sides at once.

Notice at the bottom of the **Crop** control panel the slider for **Edge Feather**. This softens the edges of the image and can be very attractive, particularly when there are multiple images on the screen (Figure 8.21).

8.19   Crop Tool

8.20 Cropping the Image in the Canvas

8.21 Two Clips in Canvas Cropped and Feathered to 80

Distort

This tool allows you to squeeze or expand the image, either maintaining its shape or pulling it apart. Be careful, though. Remember these are pixels you're dealing with, and making pixels bigger will make them blocky and ugly. What's remarkable is how much you can distort the image and still get away with it. As with other tools there are two or more places to do everything. We already saw one way to distort the image by grabbing a corner with the **Selection** tool and dragging the image around while holding down the **Shift** key. This distort alters the aspect ratio of the image but maintains its rectangular shape. This can also be done with the slider at the bottom of the **Distort** control panel (Figure 8.22).

Moving the **Aspect Ratio** slider to the left, into negative numbers, will squeeze the image vertically so it mashes down into a narrow slit. Pulling the slider to the right into large positive numbers will squeeze it horizontally, so that it's a tall, thin image. The slider ranges from –1,000 to 1,000. The image can't be squeezed until it's gone, but it does come close.

You could dial in values into the corner point boxes, which will move the corner points to any position you want, but the easiest way to use **Distort** is with the **Distort** tool, which is underneath **Crop** in the tools. Select it or call it up with the **D** key.

> **☞ Tip**
> **On the Fly:** If you're working with the **Distort** tool and want to change the overall scale of the image, release the mouse and hold down the **Option** key. When you grab the image and pull, it will scale proportionately.

▽ Distort			⊗
Upper Left		–360 ,	–240
Upper Right		360 ,	–240
Lower Right		360 ,	240
Lower Left		–360 ,	240
Aspect Ratio	◄———▯———►		0

8.22 Distort Control Panel

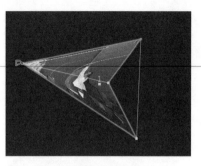

8.23 Distorted Image in the Canvas

The **Distort** tool lets you grab a corner in the **Canvas** and pull it around and really mess the image up (Figure 8.23).

☞ *Tip*

Proportional Distortion: If you use the **Distort** tool and grab one corner while holding down the **Shift** key, you will distort the image proportionately. Dragging the upper left corner in, for instance, will make the upper right corner move inward the same amount. It's a easy way to create perspective. It's also an easy way to bend the image inside out so half of it is flipped over on itself.

Anything becomes possible with these kinds of tools. Now that images are digital, they can be twisted and distorted, shaped and sized, and blended any way you can imagine. I hope you see the potential for creating almost any transition you can imagine.

I've made a simple one using **Distort**, **Scale**, and **Center** animation. Look at *Transition Sequence*. That's only the beginning. A few pulls on **Distort** tool, a little scaling, and the image shoots off. If you apply motion or any other effects to a clip, the whole clip has to be rendered out, even if for the greater part of its duration, all the values remain at default.

The simplest way to get around this problem is to cut the clip—**Control-V** or **Blade**—and separate the normal section from the twisted section. You can see what I did in *Transition Sequence*. Just be careful you don't move elements around so that the two parts get dislocated from each other.

There are still a few more elements to look at in the **Motion** panel. **Opacity** is next.

Opacity

This effect is pretty obvious. The transparency of the image decreases from a 100% opaque to zero opacity. It's a useful way to do simple fades, as we saw in the **Timeline** with titles in the previous lesson on page 360. Whatever is adjusted in the **Timeline** with the **Pen** tool will also appear reproduced here. Using the **Pen** tool, you can fade video in and out the same way you can audio.

Drop Shadow

Drop Shadow is really helpful in giving a multilayered image a three dimensional appearance. It gives titles and moving images some depth and separation (Figure 8.24). FCE's **Drop Shadow** is pretty basic, but it works fine. The control panel has all the expected features of **Offset, Angle** of offset, shadow **Color, Softness,** and **Opacity** (Figure 8.25). Note that **Drop Shadow** has to be activated with the little checkbox in the upper left corner of the control panel.

What might seem puzzling about the **Offset** slider is that it goes into to negative numbers. Just ignore those and use **Angle** to set the direction of the shadow.

The **Angle** control lets you change the direction in which the shadow drops onto the underlying layers.

Softness lets you control the amount of blurring on the edges of the shadow. Though the slider goes up to 100, I'm quite disappointed in how little effect it has. Shadow softness in FCE really reaches no more than about 10% into the shadow area, so you're forced to rely on **Opacity** to soften the shadow area, which is not the same look. It lacks the subtlety of other compositing applications.

The default drop shadow settings work well for stills and other large images, but not so well for text. If you're using this drop shadow with the basic text tool, you should bring down the offset value and push up the opacity value. For thin objects like text, the first is too high and the second too low.

Motion Blur

Motion Blur is also activated with a checkbox in the upper left of its control panel. Figure 8.26 shows FCE's **Motion Blur** at a setting of 1,000 with four samples and with 32 samples. This was

8.24 Drop Shadows against White Matte

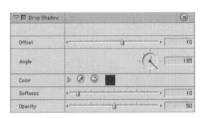

8.25 Drop Shadow Control

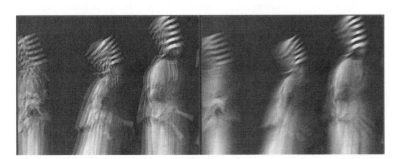

8.26 Motion Blur Set to 1,000 with Four Samples on the Left and 32 Samples on the Right

created by applying **Motion Blur** to a fast, horizontally moving clip. It gives the clip the appearance of great speed because of the added blur. Sampling goes down to 1, which produces no **Motion Blur** at all. The stepping that occurs in the lower sampling rates is ugly and best avoided. The low sample settings can be used, though, to produce interesting effects in images that contain fast moving objects. You will see a ghosting effect as the object moves through the screen.

Use **Motion Blur** if you're trying to make it look as though your animations are moving very quickly, but be warned that **Motion Blur** adds considerable time to all renders. It's a very long and slow calculation for each frame. If you are going to apply it, always add it last, just before you're finally going to render out your sequence.

Animation Effects

Pan and Scan

Pan and scan, or the Ken Burns effect, are slang terms for doing motion on large-size images such as stills. I have set up a sequence that illustrates some of the problems. If you open *Pan Sequence*, you'll see that it contains four copies of a still image. It's a PICT file called *Pict*, but it could as easily be a Photoshop file, Targa file, or TIFF. I try to work with PICT files for single-layer images because they're simpler to deal with in FCE. *Pict* is a very large image, much larger than our **Canvas**. It's 1,494×1,098.

In an earlier lesson, I said you should forget about image resolution as far as video is concerned and think only in numbers of pixels. In the print world for which scanners are designed, resolution is critically important. If you're scanning images such as this one to use in FCE, you can scan it at a high resolution, like 300 or 600dpi. Ideally you'd want to calculate the area you're going to zoom into based on an image that's a multiple of 720 pixels across at 72dpi. Often it's simpler just to scan more than you need, and adjust it in Photoshop, or even leave it to Final Cut. By scanning at high resolutions, the scanner will make lots of pixels. FCE will translate this into a very large image, not a small image at high resolution like a print system would do.

In *Pan Sequence*, I've panned and scanned *Pict* four times. Look at them one at a time. On real-time systems, these movements will not need rendering to playback on the computer screen.

> ✦ *Tip*
> _____
> **Moving Between Keyframes:**
>
> Because keyframes aren't visible in the application, it's sometimes difficult to find them. In addition to keyframes being sticky if you have **Snapping** turned on, you can also use keyboard shortcuts to move between them. **Shift-K** will take you to the next keyframe, and **Option-K** will take you to the previous keyframe.

1. In the first, the image starts out center in the screen and zooms into a point in the upper right corner of the image.

A couple of problems are apparent:

- The image jerks into motion; acceleration is not smooth.
- The zoom-in seems to get slower and slower as it progresses.

This latter is a difficult problem and pretty much impossible to deal with when using the **Motion** controls in FCE. It is totally unnatural and the bane of trying to create motion that looks like a camera moving over an image and zooming as it goes.

2. To try to solve the jerking problem, I applied **Ease In/Ease Out** to the keyframes in the second copy of *Pict*.

This obviously isn't going to work. The smoothing rate of scale and the **Ease In/Ease Out** rate of center point animation are different so that the image shoots off the **Canvas** and slowly comes back into frame.

3. The third version of *Pict* compromises by limiting how far into the corner the keyframes allow the motion to go. By leaving room for easing to overrun and swing back, the move is more acceptable. At least it doesn't shoot off the **Canvas**.

Scaling takes place around the anchor point, so if you scale to zoom and pan off to one corner at the same time, the image is moving farther and farther away from the point on which the scale is changing. To try and get around this problem and the problem of the mismatched animations, a third animation is added, the **Anchor Point**, which is not normally animated. Using the **Distort** tool I dragged out the **Anchor Point** so that rather than moving farther and farther off the screen as the image moved, it remained centered in the screen. This produces a different result, not great, but acceptable, still sometimes subject to overshoot, especially on very large images.

The bottom line is you have three basic choices:

- Live with the jerky motion and lack of acceleration and deceleration.
- Apply easing to the center keyframes and leave room for the overshoot on the zoom in.
- Or animate the anchor point as well to try and compensate for the overshoot.

Which one you use probably depends on the situation. Sometimes one might work better rather than another.

Animating Text Files

The problems of pan and scale apply equally to animating text files, such as titles created in FCE. As with graphics files, you don't want to scale images up because the text becomes pixelated (Figure 8.27).

So use a larger size and scale down, you say. That works up to a point. But what if the point size is larger than the screen and you scale down? Figure 8.28 shows what happens.

8.27 Text at 48 Scaled to 300

The text is cut off. So how do you solve this? There is unfortunately no good way to do this within the toolset FCE provides. You can't animate the text so that it's larger than the screen and scales down. The only way to do this is to generate a large text image in Photoshop or Photoshop Elements or some other imaging application and bring that into FCE and animate the scale there.

8.28 Text at 200 Scaled to 70

Split Screen

This is a common request for all sorts of purposes, for showing parallel action such as two sides of a phone conversation or to show a wide shot and a closeup in the same screen. It's easy to do if the video was actually shot for a split screen. For a phone conversation, for instance, it should be shot so that one person in the phone conversation is on the left side of the frame and the other person on the right side of the screen.

Take a look at *Split Screen Sequence* in your **Browser**. Don't bother rendering it out; they're just still frames. In the first clip, Rich was shot on the left of the screen and Anita on the right. I had to crop the picture of Anita from one side, and because neither image left enough space for the other person, I had to move Rich farther to the left and Anita farther to the right.

Some people like to add a bar that separates the two images as in Figure 8.29. That's easy to do. Use the **Generators** to create a color matte and place it on the top track, like in *Split Screen Sequence*. Crop the matte left and right so that only a narrow stripe is visible over the join of the two frames

Picture in Picture

By now you've probably figured out how to make a PIP, a Picture-in-Picture. You just scale the image down to the desired size and position it wherever you want on the screen.

8.29   Split Screen with Bar

One note of caution about PIPs: many video formats, such as DV, leave a few lines of black on the edges of the frame, as we saw when doing transitions. This is actually the rough edge of the CCD, where the pixels end. It's normally hidden in the overscan area of your television set and never seen. However, as soon as you start scaling down images and moving them about the screen, the black line becomes apparent. The easiest way to do this is to take the **Crop** tool and just slightly crop the image before you do your PIP so as not to get the black lines, which give the video an amateur look. You might also want to add a border to the PIP to set it off, but that's for Lesson 11 when we look at "Video Filters" on page 496.

A nice touch to add to PIPs is to give them a drop shadow from the **Motion** tab. This will help to separate it from the underlying image and give a screen a sense of three dimensionality.

Brady Bunch Open

This is one of the classic opens on American television. It's relatively easy to reproduce in Final Cut Express using the techniques we've learned here.

In the **Browser** is a clip called *BB.mov*. Play through it. This is the sequence we're going to build. It's based on the timing of the original show open. If you know the Brady Bunch song, sing along. In building this sequence, we'll use still images rather than movie clips to conserve storage space.

1.   Open the *Brady Bunch Sequence*.
2.   You'll probably have to render it out to play it at real speed, but it shouldn't take very long. Or use **Option-P** to play through the sequence as quickly as your computer can.

We're going to replicate this sequence. Look through it closely to get an idea of where we're going.

3. In your **Browser** is a sequence called *Brady Bunch Work Sequence*. This sequence has markers set in where events will occur.

4. To begin you might want to lay *BB.mov* on **V1** in your **Timeline** and lock the track. That way, it can act as a guide.

Sliding White Bar

The first step we have to take is to create the white bar that slides across the screen. Easy enough.

1. Make a color matte. In **Controls**, change the color from the default gray to full white.

2. This bar moves across the screen very quickly. So set the duration to about two seconds. You'll need even less than that, but if you make it too short it may be difficult to work with in the **Timeline**.

3. Crop the top and bottom with the **Crop** tool in the **Canvas**. In the **Crop** controls, the **Top** value is 48.75 and the **Bottom** value is 47.92, creating a narrow bar. You could bring it into the **Timeline** first and then bring it back to the **Viewer** to crop it, but we know we're going to create a thin white line, so we may as well do it before loading it into your work sequence.

4. Drag the bar into the blank space above **V2**, creating a new **V3**, leaving a video track free below it.

I'm assuming that you've placed *BB.mov* on **V1** as a guide and have locked that track.

5. Slide the bar off the screen to the left so that you start in black. Its coordinates should be *x* –720, *y* 0.

6. Keyframe the white bar with the **Keyframe** button at the bottom of the **Canvas**

7. Move the playhead to about 22 frames into the sequence.

8. Using *BB.mov* as a guide, slide the bar across the screen to its end position, which is when about half the bar is off the screen on the right side. Hold down the **Shift** key as you slide it to constrain the movement to horizontal. Its **Center** coordinates should now be *x* 360, *y* 0.

9. Use the **Pen** tool on the **Opacity** overlay in the **Timeline** to fade out the white bar over three or four frames.

10. When you're done with the **Pen** tool, return to the **Selector** (**A** for arrow).

Remember that although keyframes are invisible in the **Timeline,** if **Snapping** is turned on as you drag the playhead through the sequence, it will snap to keyframes inside the clips.

Fixing the Headshot

1. Open the bin in your **Browser** called **Graphics**.

It's probably best to just leave it open. In the **Graphics** bin are the headshots of this sequence and the image for the pan and scan sequence we dealt with earlier. These are mostly PICT files and a few titles made with **Title 3D**. We'll get to those later on page 219.

2. Drag *HeadshotPink.pct* to **V2** to the point where the bar stops and begins fading out (Figure 8.30).

8.30 Headshot and White Bar

Obviously at this point the headshot will fill the frame with the white bar over it. What we have to do is scale down and reposition the headshot.

3. Grab one corner of the headshot in **Canvas** and pull it in.

4. Grab the image and slide it to the right so it's positioned under the bar (Figure 8.31). I scaled it down to 52.3% and positioned it to *x* 166, *y* 0.

Next we have to crop the image.

5. Select the **Crop** tool from the tools (keyboard shortcut C for crop). With the **Crop** tool, pull in the left and right edges a little bit.

6. Then crop the top and bottom until the headshot is a narrow slit hidden underneath the bar. Or hold down the **Command** key as you drag with the **Crop** tool to proportionately crop the image from both top and bottom. The settings used in the sequence are:

8.31 Scaled and Positioned Headshot

Left	6.38
Right	11.28
Top	50
Bottom	50

7. Select the clip and set a keyframe in the **Canvas**.

8. Go forward about 14 frames in the timeline. With the **Canvas** active, type *+14* and press **Enter**.

Be careful you don't do this in the **Timeline**, because if you don't drop any selected clips, you'll actually move them 14 frames in the **Timeline** rather than moving the playhead 14 frames.

9. Pull open the top and bottom crop lines to the full height of the image or in the **Motion** tab set the **Top** and **Bottom** crop values to 0.

You've made the first part of the animation: the bar slides across the screen, stops, and fades out, and the headshot wipes open to reveal the picture. Don't worry about the lengths of the clips yet. We'll fix that later.

Middle Headshots

Now we're ready to bring in the next set of headshots.

1. Go down to Marker 1 in the timeline.

Shift-M takes you to the next marker; **Option-M** takes you to the previous marker. Three headshots appear on the left.

2. From the **Graphics** bin, drag in the image *HeadshotGreen.pct* and place it on **V3**, the track above the pink headshot.

3. Again, first we have to scale and position it so that it's in the lower left corner of the screen. The settings I used are:

Scale	29.59
Center	x –231, y 147
Crop Right	3.85

4. Then we need to fade in the image in the **Timeline** with the **Pen** tool (**P**).

This again is a fairly quick fade in, about 14 frames.

5. Select the clip in the **Timeline**.

6. Now **Option-Shift**-drag from **V3** to **V4** to make a copy of the clip on the track above.

7. Repeat to place a third copy on **V5**.

At this stage, all three copies of *HeadshotGreen.pct* are on top of each other.

8. Select the clip on **V4** and in the **Canvas** drag it upward, holding down the **Shift** key to constrain direction, and position the image about the center line of the screen.

9. Repeat for the clip on **V5**, dragging it up vertically to the top third of the screen. I used these **Center** position settings for the three layers:

V5	$x -231, y -148$
V4	$x-231, y -1$
V3	$x -231, y\ 147$

At Marker 2, where the fade-ups on the green headshots end, the screen should look like Figure 8.32.

Extending

So far so good. Next you should extend the image files in the timeline all the way down to Marker 3. You could drag them out to Marker 3 with the **Selector** tool (**A**), or you could do an **Extend** edit.

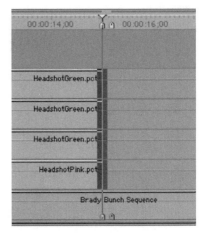

8.32 Four Headshots on Screen, Marker 2

1. **Command**-click on the edit points at the end of each clip in the **Timeline**.

2. Once all the edits are selected, move the playhead to Marker 3.

3. Press **E** to do an **Extend Edit**.

Voilà. All the clips will be extended to Marker 3, as shown in Figure 8.33.

At Marker 3, all four shots end, and we cut to black, but not for long. Next we have to bring in a new white bar from the right side.

4. Copy the white line from the beginning and paste it at the next marker on V3.

The line will appear with all its motion and opacity just like the first time you made it. The only problem is that it's moving in the wrong direction.

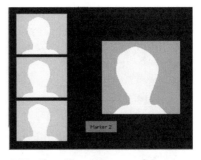

8.33 Timeline at Marker 3

5. Open the copied clip at Marker 4 into the **Viewer**.

6. Holding down the **Shift** key, slide the clip in the **Canvas**, which should still be in **Image+Wireframe** mode, across the screen to the other side.

This is the bar's new start position at *x* 720, *y* 0.

7. Go to the point where the fade-out begins, which should also be the bar's second **Center** keyframe. Scrub in **Timeline** until the playhead snaps to it.

8. Slide the bar to the left to its end position, mirrored from the first time you did it. The **Center** position should be *x* –360, *y* 0.

9. Select the clip *HeadshotPink.pct* that's on **V2** and copy it.

10. From the **Graphics** bin, drag *HeadshotBlue.pct* onto **V2** in the **Timeline**, placing it at the point where the bar begins its fade-out.

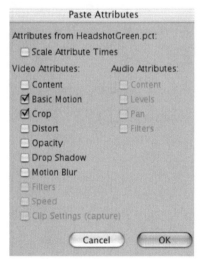

8.34 **Paste Attributes**

11. With *HeadshotBlue.pct* selected in the **Timeline**, go to the **Edit** menu and choose **Paste Attributes** (**Option-V**). This brings up the dialog box in Figure 8.34.

12. Select **Basic Motion** and **Crop** from the dialog box. Because we've lengthened *HeadshotPink.pct*, make sure that the checkbox at the top of the window for **Scale Attribute Times** is deselected. The default is for the box to be checked.

This duplicates the position and animation of the earlier shot. This ability to copy the attributes of a clip and to paste these attributes to one or more clips, pasting the copied clips motion settings as well as its filter and audio settings as desired, is a very powerful tool in Final Cut Express.

Now all we have to do is reposition the clip to the left side of the screen.

13. Holding down the **Shift** key, slide the image in the **Canvas** to the left so that it's underneath the white bar.

Adding More Headshots

1. Jump down to Marker 5 and bring in the clip *HeadshotRed.pct* from the **Graphics** bin and place it on **V3**.

2. Copy the green headshot that's earlier on **V3**.

3. Select the new red headshot and again use **Paste Attributes** (**Option-V**).

4. Apply **Basic Motion**, **Crop**, and **Opacity**. Again with **Scale Attribute Times** deselected.

Now reposition its center so that it's on the opposite side of the screen.

5. Again, **Option-Shift**-drag the copies of the clip from **V3** to **V4** and **V5**.

6. Holding down the **Shift** key to constrain movement, reposition the clips so that they appear one above the other on the right side of the screen. The **Center** values I used for these three shots are:

V5	x 215, y −148
V4	x 215, y −1
V3	x 215, y 147

7. Again, extend the green headshots and the blue headshot all the way down to Marker 7.

Again the screen cuts to black.

New Headshots

1. Go down to Marker 8 and bring in the clip called *Head-PinkSmall.pct* and place it on **V2**.

2. The image is the right size for the start of this section, but it's in the wrong place.

3. In the **Canvas**, drag it straight up to the top of the frame so that the top edge of the image is at the top edge of the screen. My setting for the **Center** was *y* −129.

4. Go to Marker 9 and set a keyframe.

It's often easier to work backwards in animation, to start with the end position on the screen and then animate the wipe on.

5. Now go back to Marker 8 and with the **Crop** tool (**C**), grab the bottom crop line and pull it upward off the screen.

This is why it's easier to make the end position first, because the two crop lines are now right next to each other, and they're much harder to separate. That's your start keyframe position. It will give you a quick wipe on of the picture.

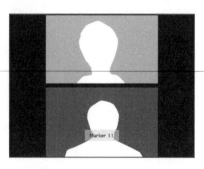

8.35 Two Headshots on Screen, Marker 11

Marker 10 is where the next image comes in.

1. Place *HeadBlueSmall.pct* on **V3**.

2. Reposition to the bottom center of the screen. My **Center** value was *y* 125.

3. Go to Marker 11 to set a keyframe.

4. Go back to Marker 10, and this time take the top crop line and drag it down to hide the image.

At Marker 11 both pictures should now be on the screen as shown in Figure 8.35. We're ready now to bring in the rest of the headshots.

Final Headshots

At Marker 12 we'll first have to place a keyframe on both the pink and blue head shots. Both images need to scale down slightly and have the left and right sides cropped so the images fit into their final position.

1. With the playhead at Marker 12, select both headshots and click on the **Keyframe** button in the **Canvas** to set a keyframe for the two headshots.

2. Change the scale of the **Timeline** window so that you can see most of the **Timeline**.

3. Position the playhead at Marker 13 to place the next head-shots. **Shift**-select the three green headshots from near the beginning of the sequence and copy them.

4. Target **V4** and paste the clips into the **Timeline**.

The three duplicate green headshots should be on **V4**, **V5**, and **V6**, leaving **V2** and **V3** for the pink and blue headshots. Next do the same for the red headshots in the timeline.

5. Select the red headshots, and copy them.

6. **Control**-click in the head of the **Timeline** above **V6**, and from the shortcut menu, choose **Add Track**.

7. Target **V7** and paste the clips into the **Timeline**.

Between Marker 12 and Marker 14 where the green and red headshots reach full opacity, the pink and blue headshots scale, crop, and slightly reposition to their final locations.

For the pink headshot, my values at Marker 14 are:

Scale	58.08
Center	*x* 1, *y* –148
Crop Left	2.83
Crop Right	5.23
Crop Top	4.29

For the blue headshot, my values at Marker 14 are:

Scale	66.5
Center	*x* 0, *y* 139
Crop Left	8.23
Crop Right	11.22

When you've positioned the clips about the screen, you should end up with the **Canvas** looking like Figure 8.36.

One more step needs to be taken before we put in the titles: extend the headshots down to the end of the sequence.

1. Move the playhead all the way down to Marker 24.

2. Then **Command**-click on the edits at the ends of all the headshots: pink, blue, the three greens, and the three reds.

3. Now do an **Extend Edit** to stretch them out to the playhead.

8.36 Eight Headshots on Screen, Marker 14

Titles

We're finished with almost all the headshots. Next we have to get the titles on the screen. I've prebuilt them for you using **Title 3D**. They are made with the *Textile* font, which the closest in the basic Apple font collection to the original title style.

1. Lay the first title, *Main Title* in the **Graphics** bin, at Marker 15 on the topmost track, **V10**.

You'll see that it's at its full size. In fact, there is a small scaling of the title in the open.

2. Go to Marker 16 and set a keyframe. This will be the end point of the main title animation.

3. Next go back to Marker 15 and set the **Scale** value in the **Motion** tab of the **Viewer** back down to 47.83.

4. Next go down to Marker 17 and with the **Razor Blade (B)**, ~~cut the title and throw away the rest of it.~~

At Marker 18, the next title, *Starring Title*, appears.

5. Drop *Starring Title* onto the same track as the main title.

6. Cut this title off at Marker 19.

7. At Marker 20 introduce *Mom Title*. Because it overlaps with the final headshot we're going to bring in, it needs to be placed on a higher track, **V11**.

8. At Marker 21 set an **Opacity** keyframe with the **Pen** tool for *Mom Title*. *The frame before* Marker 22 set the **Opacity** down to zero. This will fade it out quickly.

9. **Razor Blade** *Mom Title* at Marker 22.

Final Polishing

We're on the home straight, just a few more steps to take. At Marker 21, while *Mom Title* is fading out, one more headshot is fading in.

1. Drag one more copy of the green headshot into the center of the screen. Place it on **V10** underneath **Mom Title**.

2. The final green headshot needs to be positioned, scaled, and cropped top and bottom to fit the center square in the screen. The values I used are:

Scale	33
Center	$x -5, y\, 0$
Crop Left	1.6
Crop Top	5.12
Crop Bottom	6.11

3. Set an **Opacity** keyframe for the green headshot at Marker 21 and set the value to zero. Ramp up the **Opacity** to 100 at Marker 22.

At Marker 22 the last title, *Alice Title*, just cuts in. Place it on **V11**.

4. Cut off both *Alice Title* and the center headshot at Marker 24.

Fade to Black

The last step we want to do is to fade to black. We could keyframe and ramp down the opacity on each of 10 layers now on the screen, but there's an easier way.

1. Make a short slug and place it on the topmost video track at Marker 23.

2. Set its **Opacity** down to zero.

3. At Marker 24 use the **Pen** tool bring its opacity up to 100% so that black fills the screen.

Congratulations. You've made the Brady Bunch open. The original open was made with a good deal more precision than I invested in it, but if you want, you can precisely align and shape the images using exact values in the **Motion** tab.

Summary

In this lesson we've looked at Final Cut's animation capabilities. These are tools you can use to composite images one on top of another, using FCE's multilayer capabilities. We'll look at more compositing techniques in a later lesson, but first let's see how to use Final Cut's filters.

Lesson 9

Adding Special Effects Filters

In this lesson we're going to look at and work with Final Cut's filters to create some special effects. FCE offers a great variety of excellent effects. Unlike transitions that go between clips, filters are applied to single clips, or parts of clips. In addition to the filters included with the application, other programmers are creating effects using Final Cut's scripting software FXBuilder, such as the collection of filters written by Christoph Vonrhein. In the *Extras* folder of the DVD is a folder for *CHV-FCE Plugins*, which includes demo versions of the *3D Cube* generator, the *Storm Front* transition, and *Binoculars* filter. There is also a free *Silk and Fog* filter. There are also the filters created by Joe Maller, who wrote the free filter, *Color Glow*, that Apple gives away when you register your copy of Final Cut Express. A demo version of his filters is also available in the *Extras* folder. They will all work within FCE, except for TimeBender, which is dependent on the ability to keyframe the effect. Finally there are the demo filters from Klaus Eiperle's *CGM DVE's Vol.2+* with FCE support. Check out the HTML files and the demo movies that explain them. Klaus wrote the FXScript DVE's that are part of FCE.

For this lesson, though, we'll confine ourselves to the FCE built-in effects package, including the **FXScript DVE's**. If you have not already done so, you should install the new **FXScript DVE's** that

223

came with FCE. Just run the installer and check the box for **FXScript DVE's from CGM.**

To add new filters to FCE they need to be placed in the *Plugins* folder while the application is closed. Drag the plugins into *Library>Application Support>Final Cut Express Support>Plugins.*

★ *Tip*
Navigating Video Filters: To quickly get to any filter in the *Video Filters* sequence, **Control**-click in the **Timeline Ruler** of the **Timeline**, and from the shortcut menu select any one of the markers by name. Above each marker is the name of the filter that was applied to the shot.

Loading the Lesson

One more time, let's begin by loading the material you need onto your media drive.

1. If you don't already have it there, drag over the *Media* folder from the DVD.

2. Also drag onto your system drive the folder *Lesson 9*.

3. Eject the DVD, open the *Lesson 9* folder on your hard drive, and double-click the project file, *L9*, to launch the application.

Inside your project copy, you'll find the usual suspects in the **Browser, Clips** bin, *Damine.mov,* and other files. One of the sequences is called *Effects Builder.* This demonstrates some of the filters we'll see in this lesson. As we go through the lesson, I'll show you how the effects in this sequence was made. There is also a sequence called *Video Filters.* In it each filter has been applied with its default settings to a two-second portion of *Dance2.* For quite a few filters, such as the color correction filters, the default settings do nothing, but having them laid out like this lets you easily look at any filter and twiddle its knobs to see what it does.

You may have thought there were a lot of transitions. There are even more filters—103 of them, in fact—some of which aren't very useful, but there still quite a few that allow you to do amazing things with video. Because there is so much redundancy in the filters, different filters that do basically the same things, as well as filters that don't function well in FCE, I'll only go through some of the important ones.

Applying a Filter

It couldn't be simpler to apply an effect in Final Cut Express.

1. Select the clip in the **Timeline** or in the **Browser** and from the menu bar select **Effects>Video Filters.**

2. Pick a submenu and pick an effect.

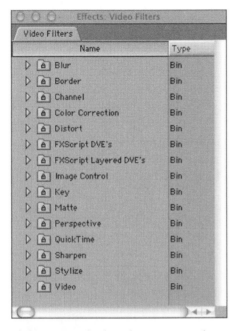

9.1   Video Effects Bin

9.2   Selected Effect in Filters Panel

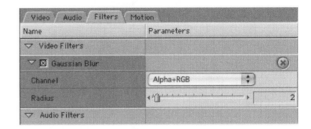

If they're applied in the **Browser**, then every time that clip is used, the filter will go with it. If the effect is applied in the **Timeline**, it's only applied to that one copy of the clip. It is immediately applied with its default settings to the clip. If you prefer, you can drag the effect from the **Video Filter** bin inside the **Effects** panel of the **Browser** (Figure 9.1).

It's just as easy to remove an effect. Simply open the clip into the **Viewer**, go to the **Filters** tab, select the effect by clicking on its name, and press the **Delete** key (Figure 9.2).

Any number of filters can be added to a clip. The order in which the filters are applied can be important. The filter order can be changed simply by dragging the filters up and down to new positions in the order. Filters can also be turned on and off with a little checkbox. This allows you to leave a filter in place, yet toggle its effect on and off to see what it's doing to the picture.

Filters can also be copied and pasted. If you select a clip that has a filter applied, you can copy the clip and use **Paste Attributes** (**Option-V**) to paste that filter or filters and their settings to any number of other clips simultaneously (Figure 9.3). You can also select a clip or a number of clips in the **Timeline**, and from the **Edit** menu choose **Remove Attributes** (keyboard shortcut: **Command-Option-V**). Make sure the **Filters** box is checked in the

Paste Attributes

Attributes from Dance2:
- ☑ Scale Attribute Times

Video Attributes:
- ☐ Content
- ☐ Basic Motion
- ☐ Crop
- ☐ Distort
- ☐ Opacity
- ☐ Drop Shadow
- ☐ Motion Blur
- ☑ Filters
- ☐ Speed
- ☐ Clip Settings (capture)

Audio Attributes:
- ☐ Content
- ☐ Levels
- ☐ Pan
- ☐ Filters

[Cancel]   [OK]

9.3   Paste Filter Attributes

Remove Attributes dialog box, and the filter or multiple filters will all be removed.

Filter values cannot be keyframed so that they can be altered over time, but you can often split a clip, apply different filter values to the two parts, and connect them with a long cross dissolve. This gives the appearance of the filter values changing over time. Look at the set of clips at Marker 1 in the sequence *Effects Builder*. The middle portion of the clip *Dance2* has the effect applied to it. By slowly cross dissolving to itself, the illusion is created that the image becomes more blurred and then less blurred.

✍ *Tip*

Selective Filtering: You can actually add a filter to only a section of the length of a clip, which can be useful if you want to ramp up an effect, while most of the length of the shot remains unchanged. To avoid having to render out the entire shot, you can apply the filter by select a section of the clip you want to effect with the **Range Selection** tool (GGG). To make the selection, stroke along the clip, the group of clips, or sections of the **Timeline** where you want to apply the filter. Choose the filter from the **Effects** menu, and you'll immediately see that only that portion of the **Timeline** picked with **Range Selection** will change the render color to red.

Let's begin by opening the empty *Sequence 1* and dragging one of the clips from the **Clips** bin into it. We'll start with *Dance3*. We'll apply some filters to this clip to see how they work.

Favorites

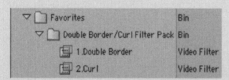

9.4   Filter Pack in Favorites Bin

Favorites are a great way to save effects, because you can not only save them as their default settings, but you can also save them as an effects pack, a number of effects that work together to produce a result. It's simple to do. Apply the effects and adjust them as you as you want them, and then with the **Filters** tab of the **Viewer** open, drag them to the **Favorites** bin, where you can rename them anything you want (Figure 9.4) Notice that I created a bin within the **Favorites** bin, in which I numbered and named the filters. By numbering them I created a stack order for the way should be applied.

The **Favorites** bin sounds great, but it has a serious downside, which is that **Favorites** are part of the application's preferences. So if you have to trash your prefs file, your favorites are gone with it. See "Favorites" on page 226 for one good solution to this problem.

Some Useful Filters

Gaussian Blur

Gaussian (pronounced *gousian*), named after the 19th century German mathematician, Karl Friedrich Gauss, produces a smooth blurring of the image. This blur does more, though, than softening the picture. It allows you to blur channels separately through a popup (Figure 9.5).

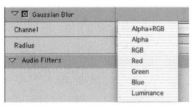

9.5 Gaussian Blur Controls

Selecting different channels can produce some interesting and unusual effects. Try applying the filter. Bring *Dance3* into *Sequence 1*. With the clip selected, choose **Gaussian Blur** from the **Effects>Video Filters>Blur** menu. If you want to blur a couple of channels, just apply the effect twice.

The order in which the effects are applied always makes a difference. Don't assume that because you apply **Luminance Gaussian** and **Blue Gaussian** you get the same effect by applying them the other way around. FCE processes the filters from the top down as they're stacked in the **Filters** tab. If you blur **Luminance** first, the color values smear, and you'll get less impact than if you blur the color value first.

The clip at Marker 2 in the *Effects Builder* sequence shows **Gaussian Blur** applied twice, first with the **Blue** channel blurred, and then with the **Luminance** blurred. A word of caution: be careful with blurring the **Luminance** value of an image. It can produce nasty blotchiness.

Bevel Border

Bevel Border is a nice touch to Picture-in-Picture effects (PIPs) and can be used to mask those nasty black edges we talked about in the previous lesson.

Bevel creates a nice edge for scaled images (Figure 9.6).

The color picker is called **Light Color**, like the color of a gel a lighting director might put over a light that's falling across the beveled edges. You can, of course, also set the angle the light is falling from.

9.6 Bevel Border with a Width of 15

Channel Arithmetic

The **Channel** filters allow you an amazing degree of control of color and compositing. We'll look more closely at compositing in the next lesson on page 251, but here the channel effects allow you to combine clips and apply color effects to them combined with compositing modes.

Arithmetic is a basic **Channel** effect. It composites a color to any one of the color channels **R**, **G**, or **B**, or all three combined, using one of the compositing modes on a popup (Figure 9.7).

FCE calls them **Operators**, but they are really compositing modes. We'll look at compositing modes in the next chapter. In the *Arithmetic* sequence in your **Browser**, I have laid out a short clip of *Dance3* 12 times. Each clip has a different **Operator** mode applied to its RGB value using the default color, gray. Look through these to get a basic idea of how the **Operators** work. Most of the **Operators** such as **Add**, **Subtract**, **Darken**, and **Lighten** are commonly known, but there are a couple of unusual **Operators**, **Ceiling** and **Floor**, that produce interesting results.

9.7 Arithmetic Channels Popup

Channel Offset

Channel Offset is a cool filter, though you can easily take it to great extremes where strange effects will happen, especially if you use the **Repeat Edges** popup. The clip at Marker 3 in the *Effects Builder* sequence shows you **Channel Offset** as applied in Figure 9.8.

Compound Arithmetic

Compound Arithmetic is based on an image placed in the **Well** (Figure 9.9). Without an image there, the **Operator** popup produces little effect. It does not change by compositing with the

9.8 Channel Offset Three Times with Channel with Large Offset and Repeat

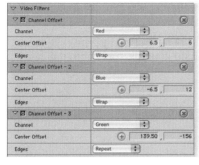

layer below, simply with itself. If an image is in the **Well**, the **Operator** will apply to the image. Try it with text such as that on the clip at Marker 4 in the *Effects Builder* sequence.

Color Correction

Good exposure and color begins in the shooting. It's actually easier and always better to do it right to start rather than trying to fix it in post. That means lighting the scene well, correctly exposing it, setting your white balance correctly, and not leaving the camera's auto exposure and white balance to guess. If you're producing work for output on a television set, it is essential that you view your color correction work on a properly set-up production monitor, not the computer monitor. The color and luminance values on television sets are very different from computer monitors. Do not trust the computer screen to display the colors and luminance values the way they will appear on TV. Watch your video monitor while you work, or at least a TV set. Don't try to rely on your computer monitor.

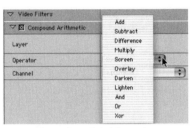

9.9   Compound Arithmetic Controls

The color correction tools are professional strength tools, so use them carefully. **Broadcast Safe** is the perfect tool to use if you suspect your video is too bright for television. Just drop it on a clip, and you'll immediately see if it reduces the video level. It will have no effect if the image does not need correction.

Broadcast Safe isn't just a magic bullet; you do have quite a bit of control on the filter to set it to whatever parameters you want (Figure 9.10). The default is be **Conservative**. The values controlled by the sliders are based on luminance value standards called IRE. A value of 100 is considered peak white, while 0 is pure black. In practice, most cameras, especially consumer camcorders and prosumer equipment, shoot at levels much higher than 100, up to 120 and beyond, what's called superwhite. Television are designed to accept a video signal with peak white at 100, though they too have a good deal of tolerance, and most newer TV sets can readily accept values around 110 and 120IRE.

Notice that as the default you limit both the luminance values and the chrominance values. If you want to keep the luminance in an acceptable range but do something outrageous with the color, you have to make sure **Custom—Use Controls Below** is selected from the popup. Then uncheck the **Saturation Limiting** checkbox and go to town.

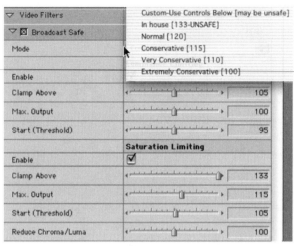

9.10 Broadcast Safe Controls

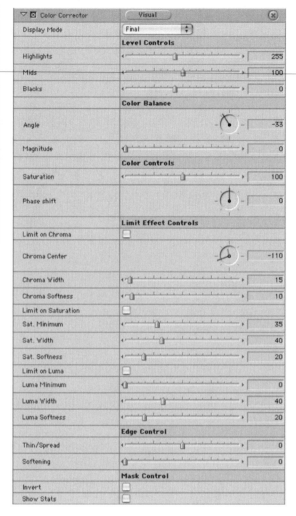

9.11 Top of the Viewer Window with Color Corrector (above)

9.12 Color Corrector Filter Controls (right)

Color Corrector

Unlike most filters, **Color Corrector,** as well as the **Chroma Keyer** in the **Key** submenu, has two panels in the **Viewer** (Figure 9.11). One marked **Filter** has sliders and numerical controls to adjust the values (Figure 9.12), and a useful button at the top that lets you switch to the **Visual** display. The second panel with the name of the filter has the visual interface that you are most likely to use (Figure 9.13).

Some important functions are on the **Filter** panel only. One is the little button with the red **X** to reset the entire filter. The other items are the whole group of controls for **Limit Effect Control, Edge Control,** and **Mask Control.**

Let's take a look at the visual controls for **Color Corrector.** At the top is a grouping of useful buttons (Figure 9.14). The **Numeric** button takes you to the **Filter** panel. There is also the little checkbox that allows you to toggle the filter on and off. The **Eye** icon simply tells you that you're in the **Visual** panel, if you didn't realize that already. Below the little timeline are the basic timeline controls and timecode reference.

There is the **Grab Handle,** which lets you pull the effect onto a clip, similar to the **Grab Handle** in the audio panel. On either side of the **Grab Handle** are some very useful buttons. The first to the right, with the number **1** on it, allows you to copy your **Color Corrector** settings to the next clip in the **Timeline.**

The second button to the right, marked with the number **2,** can be even more useful. This copies the settings not to the next clip in the **Timeline,** but to the second clip down the **Timeline.** For instance, if you have a two-camera set-up for a wedding or a theatrical performance that basically switches back and forth between the two cameras and you want to color balance one camera to the other, you need to color correct every other shot in the **Timeline.** Clicking the **2** button will copy the settings to the next shot for that camera. You can quickly copy the settings to every other shot in the **Timeline.**

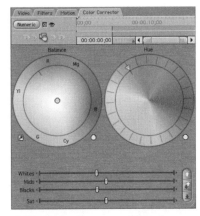

9.13 Color Corrector Visual
       Display

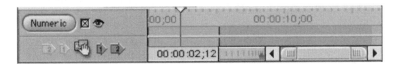

9.14 Top of the Color Corrector
       Visual Panel

The two buttons marked with a **1** and **2** to the left of the **Grab Handle** act similarly. They let you copy the **Color Corrector** settings to the clip you're working on from either the shot before, the **1** button, or from the shot before last in the **Timeline,** the **2** button.

Let's take a look at the central control panel in **Color Corrector,** which has two color wheels, four sliders, and a few buttons.

✦*Tip*

Limiting Color Effect: Without having the visual interface for the **Limit Effect Controls** and the other functions, they very difficult to use, though with some care you can effectively limit color control to only particular portions of the image. Take a look at the two stills at beginning of the sequence called *Color*. The color effect is changing the color of the woman's jacket. I did this by turning on the **Limit Effect Controls** and isolating the color of the jacket. I could do that by turning down the color saturation to zero and then turning the **Chroma Center** dial until I found the color that was being desaturated. Then by increasing the color width, I was isolating just that area of color. Turning the **Phase Shift** in the upper portion of the controls changed the jacket color from its original lime green to a more conservative tan. Notice that there are two clips stacked in the *Color* sequence. That's because I used the **Crop** tool to limit the area that I had to color select. A garbage matte would be the more natural solution, but it's broken when **Limit Effect Controls** is switched on.

The left wheel controls the color balance of the image, while the right changes the hue, just like the hue knob on a television set. Below are four self-explanatory sliders. The first controls the white levels; the second, the midtones; and the third, the black level. The fourth slider adjusts the **Saturation** or amount of chroma in the image. The three buttons stacked together on the right are auto setting buttons. These are the best place to start with any image. From the top the buttons are **Auto White, Auto Contrast,** and **Auto Black**.

In the *Color* sequence take a look at the pair of images at Marker 2. The first is probably a bit darker than it should be. The image right after it has the **Color Corrector** filter applied.

To use the filter you should begin by clicking the **Auto Contrast** button, the middle of the three-button stack. Do not click on it repeatedly. You'll just keep shifting the contrast. Just click once. Next set the **Auto Black** and then the **Auto White**. Again, just one click for each button. Always adjust the luminance, whites, mids, and blacks before you start adjusting the colors. I usually start with the mids. A little adjustment there will spread the contrast levels nicely and brighten the image without increasing the overall level. Remember, as with almost all FCE sliders, if you hold down the **Command** key, you'll "gear down" the drag, giving you finer control.

The image at Marker 3 in *Color* has been overexposed. With it is an attempt at fixing the problem. As you can see, you'll usually get a better result fixing an image that's been underexposed than one that's overexposed and washed out.

Color Corrector obviously is for color as well as luminance and contrast. At Marker 4 in *Color* is another still image. Something's certainly gone wrong here. It looks like the white balance hasn't been set correctly. CC is the easiest tool to fix this. To correct it, start with the **Auto Contrast** button, and then set your luminance levels to what looks correct to you. It's not going to take much work. The exposure is correct; just the color is wrong.

What we're going to do is pick white in the picture and use that to set the correct color balance. There are a couple of tricks to this.

1. First, take the **Saturation** slider and crank it way to the right, terribly oversaturating the image.

What this does is to emphasize any color cast in the image, making it easier to pick out what's wrong. The second trick is to find the right bit of white. The temptation is to use something that's very bright, but the problem is that what's very bright often is quite washed out and has almost no color information in it. Look for something that's white but not at full luminance or something that's neutral gray. Here's how you do it with **Color Corrector**.

2. Just to the bottom left of the **Balance** wheel is a tiny **Eyedropper**. Use this to pick something in the scene that should be white or gray. In this image there isn't really anything that's very oversaturated, so I'd pick something off the white roof of the van.

This will immediately pull the color back toward a truer representation of the image. You'll also notice that the button in the center of the **Balance** wheel has shifted toward the red direction. When I pulled the white, it gave the image a slightly more magenta tinge than I would have liked. Again, this was apparent because the **Saturation** was turned up. You'll want to fine tune the color more toward the yellow-red direction of the **Balance** wheel.

3. Before you do that, slide the **Saturation** slider back down to normal, and you'll see the image is close to looking correct.

4. Finally, push the **Balance** button in the center of the **Balance** wheel a little farther to yellow-red.

There's a little gotcha here. All the color wheels are geared down by default. So you have to move the button a lot to get any effect. In the color wheels, like **Balance**, you use the **Command** key to gear up. This is the only place in FCE that this occurs.

The little white buttons to the lower right of the **Balance** wheel and the **Hue** wheel are reset buttons.

FXScript DVE's

Four-Point Garbage Matte

A garbage matte allows you to roughly cut out a section of the image by selected points on the screen that define the four corners of the picture. There is another FCE **Four-point Garbage Matte** as well, but this one has superior capabilities. FCE also has an **Eight-point Garbage Matte**, which we'll look at shortly.

Tip

Color Balance: If you want to color balance two cameras or two shots that have a slightly different color cast, open one shot into the **Viewer** and go its **Visual** control panel. Now select the shot you want to match it to and open it into a new **Viewer** (**Shift-Enter**). You can now use the **White Balance Eyedropper** to pick white out of the second shot in the new **Viewer**. You're now balancing the white of one shot to the white of the other. It's a good first step in color matching.

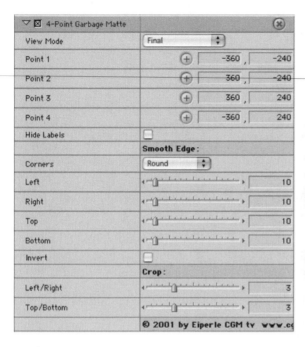

▽ ☒ 4-Point Garbage Matte		⊗
View Mode	Final	
Point 1	⊕ −360 ,	−240
Point 2	⊕ 360 ,	−240
Point 3	⊕ 360 ,	240
Point 4	⊕ −360 ,	240
Hide Labels	☐	
	Smooth Edge :	
Corners	Round	
Left	◄–◻– – – – – – – ►	10
Right	◄–◻– – – – – – – ►	10
Top	◄–◻– – – – – – – ►	10
Bottom	◄–◻– – – – – – – ►	10
Invert	☐	
	Crop:	
Left/Right	◄ – – – ◻ – – – – ►	3
Top/Bottom	◄ – – – ◻ – – – – ►	3
© 2001 by Eiperle CGM tv www.c		

9.15 FXScript DVE's 4-point Garbage Matte Controls (left)

9.16 4-Point Garbage Matte used for a Diagonal (below)

Matte Preview: If you want to see how the image will look while you're trying to garbage matte it, click one of the points' crosshairs in the **Filter** panel and then mouse down in the **Canvas**, which will update as soon as it can. If you hold the mouse down and drag the point around the screen, the image will be pulled around on the screen as quickly as your computer can manage it. The faster your computer, the sooner this will happen.

The controls in **4-point Garbage Matte** allow you to set four points on the image, beginning with Point 1 in the upper left corner, Point 2 in the upper right, Point 3 in the lower right, and finally Point 4 in the lower left (Figure 9.15).

To make a diagonal, for instance, you could simply move Point 3 over to where Point 4 is, cutting the screen from the upper right to lower left, as in Figure 9.16. You can soften the edges of the garbage matte with the **Smooth Edge** controls.

Using the **FXScript DVE's 4-point Garbage Matte** you can also create split screens with a soft edge down the middle, which you cannot do using just the **Crop** tool. Set the points as in Figure 9.17: Point 2 near the top middle of the **Canvas**, and Point 3 near the bottom middle of the **Canvas**. I extended the points out into the grayboard so as not to show the underlying image around the edges.

I've laid out the two shots at Marker 5 in the *Effects Builder* sequence so that you can see the settings and way the effect is constructed.

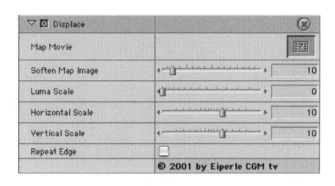

9.17   Soft Edge Split Screen using FXScript DVE's 4-point Garbage Matte

9.18   FXScript DVE's Displace Controls

Displace

Displacement or bumpmapping filters are common tools in compositing and special effects. All of these effects are most useful for creating motion in images, and are often used to create movement on background layers for motion graphics.

FXScript DVE's Displace filter brings a unique capability to FCE. This is the only place where clips can interact with each other based on a moving image placed in a well (Figure 9.18). This is unique to this filter. By putting a clip in the **Map Movie** well, the movement of the luminance value will displace the image that the filter is applied to. Take a look at Marker 6 in the *Effects Builder* sequence. *Dance3* is being displaced by the movement in the clip *Temple2*.

Luma Scale will increase or decrease the contrast range of the clip in the **Map Movie** well.

Horizontal Scale and **Vertical Scale** control how much the image is displaced by the **Map Movie**, which doesn't have to be a movie, of course. You can also put a still image in **Map Movie**.

Replicate

Replicate is cool filter (Figure 9.19). The default output produces only four images on the screen, but if you push the sliders, you can get 16 horizontal and 16 vertical. That's 256 very small images on the screen. It's a nice effect when it steps back 2, 4, 8, 16.

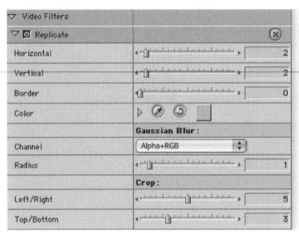

9.19 Replicate Controls and Default Output

Look at the strings of clips in *Effects Builder* at Marker 7. This was made up by blading a couple of clips and changing the replicate values up and then back down again. Be warned this is a fairly slow render on older machines.

There is also a FCE version of **Replicate**, but this one has the additional feature of being able to add borders to the images with a slider.

Desaturate and Sepia

Desaturate

This is the quickest, easiest way to remove color. The default **Amount** of 100 is a fully desaturated image, pure black and white. I find it makes a somewhat flat-looking black and white. **Desaturate** does not only *de*saturate, it will also *over*saturate. **Desaturate** can go into negative values, which overchromas the image. It won't take much of a push into the negative numbers to get excessively colorful, especially if the scene already has a lot of color, particularly reds. To do anything other than desaturate quickly, you should really use FCE's Color Correction filters.

Sepia

9.20 Sepia Controls

The default setting generates a rich brown color, without being too orange (Figure 9.20). Bringing down the **Amount** slider to around 60, blending in the underlying color, makes an interesting look.

Though the filter is called **Sepia**, the color picker allows you to tint the image any color you'd like. **Sepia** also has a **Highlight** slider, which increases the brightness in the highlight areas, punching them through the tint color. Pulling the **Highlight** slider into negative numbers will deepen the shadow areas.

Sepia should really only be used for a fast-and-easy tint of the image. For finer and more subtle control, the **Color Corrector** would be better.

Keying

Keying is used to selectively cut out areas of the image. The most efficient way to do this is chromakeying, the technique of removing one specific color from an image. It's how weather reporters stand in front of weather maps. The two commonly used colors are blue and green. Because of the way the DV format works, it's easier to chromakey green with DV than blue. On the other hand, if your subject has to wear green for St. Patrick's Day, you'll have to use blue.

The key to keying is to shoot it well. Poorly shot material just will not key properly. For chromakeying, the background blue or green screen must be evenly lit and correctly exposed so that the color is as pure as possible. Video, of course, and DV even more so, have many limitations of color depth and saturation that make good keying difficult.

FCE has tools to do chromakeying, the best of which I think is the **Chroma Keyer.**

In your copy of the *L9* project is a bin called **Keying**, which holds the elements we'll work with in this part of the lesson. Open the *Keying* sequence. This has a couple of still images to work with. On **V1** in the sequence is a still of the Stanford University clarion tower called *Background.pct*, while on **V2** is the image to chromakey called *Blue.pct*. We're going to work with a quite difficult blue screen image.

Chroma Keyer

If the material is properly shot and lit, there is really no trick to chromakeying in FCE. I would ignore the **Blue and Green Screen** and **Color Key** filters and just work with the **Chroma Keyer.** Let's

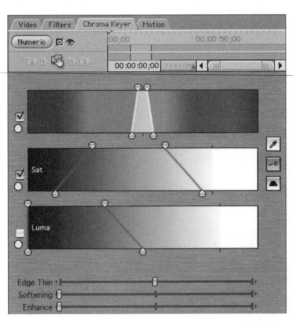

9.21 Chroma Keyer Controls (left)

9.22 Chroma Keyer Buttons (right)

9.23 Matte Display (below)

start by examining some of the controls in this perhaps daunting-looking filter.

1. Begin by applying **Chroma Keyer** to *Blue.pct* on **V2**.

2. Open the **Chroma Keyer** panel into the **Viewer** (Figure 9.21).

The controls show a **Color Range** slider at the top, the rainbow-colored bar. Below that is the **Sat** (saturation) control and **Luma** (luminance) control. Each has a round radio button that allows you to reset the parameter and a square checkbox that lets you toggle the parameter on and off. Each of the controls has handles that can be adjusted. Pulling the buttons on the top of the sliders will increase or decrease the range of the effect, while pulling on the buttons at the bottom of the slider will control the tolerance, how widely the control will be applied to adjacent colors or saturation or luminance values.

> **✎ Note**
> **Important:** The Key icon toggle does not function when the **Canvas** is in **Image+Wireframe** mode.

On the right are three important buttons (Figure 9.22). At the top is the critical **Eyedropper**. Below that, in the middle, is a three-way toggle switch with a **Key** icon. Its default position is colored gray, which shows the final output of the image. Click it and it will change to white, which will show you a black-and-white representation of what you're keying. Click it again and the button goes blue, which shows you the original source material. The bottom button with the **Keystone** icon will invert the key, which can be useful in some instances.

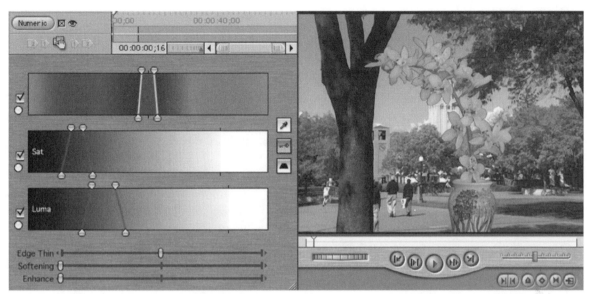

9.24 Nearly Keyed Blue Screen

3. Click on the **Eyedropper**, click in the blue screen behind the flowers in the **Canvas**, and you're practically done.

Almost instantly the bulk of the blue has disappeared.

4. Check the matte by clicking on the **Matte/Key** icon. You'll see most of the background has been keyed out, as you can see in Figure 9.23. This is a grayscale representation of transparency. What is white is opaque in the *Blue.pct* clip, and what is black is transparent.

5. Widen the **Color Range** slightly with the button pulls at the top and broaden the **Luma** controls a bit, and you'll have a pretty good key (Figure 9.24).

If you look closely, though, you'll see a rather unnatural color fringe around the edges of the flower. This is fairly easy to get rid of.

6. Push up the **Edge Thin** control a bit.

7. At the very end of the **Softening** control is a tiny little triangle. Give it a few clicks. This will move **Softening** incrementally.

8. Try adding a little **Enhance**, but not too much, or the edges will start to turn yellow.

⚑ Tip

Color Selection: If you hold down the **Shift** key you can click on multiple points and the **Chroma Keyer** controls will extend the range of values, color, saturation, or luminance as needed. Also, if you hold down the **Shift** key and drag a line through the area you want to sample, the tool will use the range of values along the line to set up the controls.

9.25 Spill Suppressor Control   9.26 Matte Choker

Spill Suppressor-Blue and Spill Suppressor-Green

The **Spill Suppressors** are used if there a blue or green cast on the edges of the image (Figure 9.25). This often happens when you get reflected light for the blue screen wall falling on the edges of a curved object, like a person's shoulders. The **Spill Suppressor** takes the blue in the image and replaces it with black, like a shadow area. This is fine on the object you want to leave, but if the background color has not been keyed out sufficiently, it can leave a dark edging on the screen.

Lower the **Suppressor** slider substantially. Usually only a small amount will be sufficient to do the work.

Matte Choker

Adding another tool in the mix here may be helpful. The **Matte Choker** is useful here, but it isn't in the **Key** package, but in the **Matte** package, which we'll see in a moment. The **Matte Choker** is mostly commonly used as a keying tool, however, and adding it to the key will improve the image.

The controls are basically the same as the **Edge Thin** and **Softening** controls in the **Chroma Keyer** (Figure 9.26), but adding a second line of choking to the key's edges will make it easier to get a tight, sharp line between the edges and the background. If you find your keying is cutting too much into the image, the **Matte Choker** can also be applied again, and by pushing the slider down into negative numbers, to bring back some of the cut-off image.

Mattes

Note

Labels: These are only visible when the **Canvas** or **Viewer** is not in Image+Wireframe mode. When you're in **Image+Wireframe**, labels are automatically hidden.

Eight-Point Garbage Matte

This filter works similarly to **FXScript DVE's 4-Point Garbage Matte** except that it allows you to crudely draw shapes on the screen with up to eight separate points. Look at the controls in Figure 9.27.

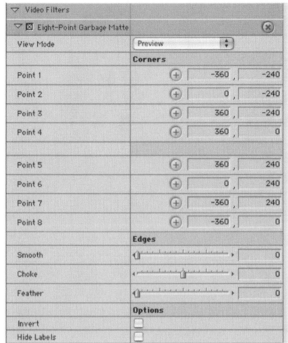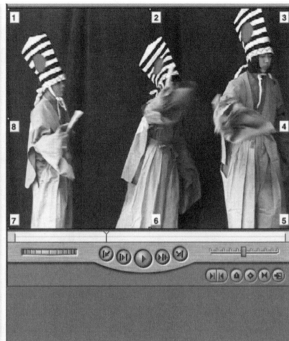

9.27 Eight-Point Garbage Matte Controls and Canvas Display

As you can see from the controls, there are eight points which can be placed anywhere on the screen using the **Crosshairs** button. Click in the crosshairs for **Point 1** and click in the **Canvas**. The point will be placed there. It's as simple and as difficult as that.

Basically the points go around the screen starting in the upper left corner. It's best to try to keep the points in those relative positions. Because lines connect the points to each other—**1** to **2** to **3** to **4** and so on—it's important to avoid having the lines cross each other. Bizarre shapes can be created with your image if the lines cross.

The three **View Modes** can be selected from a popup at the top of the controller.

- **Final** is the output as seen on the screen along with the underlying layers, but without any point markers. The **Hide Labels** checkbox has no effect.

- **Preview** is the same as **Final,** only with the points indicated and with the point numbers. The number display can be toggled with the checkbox.

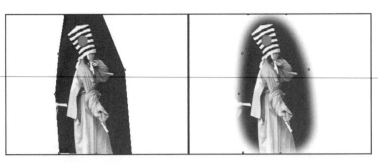

9.28 Matte without Smooth, and
with Smooth and Feather at 20

- **Wireframe** shows you the matte outline but only on the layer on which you're working, without cutting away the rest of the image to reveal the underlying layer.

Below the points are some important tools. The first is **Smooth**. This rounds out the corners in your matte. You can combine it with **Feather** to create soft-edged mattes with interesting organic shapes (Figure 9.28).

Without **Smooth** applied, **Choke** is a subtle adjustment of the matte shape. Moving **Choke** into negative numbers will slightly reduce the matte, while pushing the value up will increase the size of the matte. The more smoothing that's applied, the more powerful **Choke** becomes. With maximum smoothness, **Choke** can double the size of the matte. If pushed down to –100, it will make the matte disappear.

Finally, an important but often overlooked checkbox is **Invert**. This feature allows you to create a matte around an object that you want to remove, and then rather than keeping the area you defined, by checking the **Invert** box, you'll cut it out.

Extract

Extract is a real beauty of a filter. It's a little unpredictable to work with, but with luck it will create interesting combinations of matte shapes, especially when used with a garbage matte to define a core area (Figure 9.29).

Extract gives you deceptively simple controls with a three-up display in the **Canvas**:

- **Source**
- **Matte**
- **Final**

The bottom right corner is empty. A popup lets you select if you want the extraction applied to RGB or to the alpha channel of the

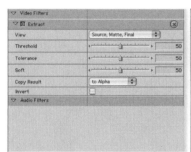

9.29 Extract Controls and Three-Up Display

image. Applying it to RGB will make a high-contrast black-and-white image. By adjusting **Threshold, Tolerance,** and **Softness,** you can vary the image substantially.

It gets really interesting when you apply it to the alpha channel instead of the RGB value. Then you cut through to an underlying layer with a great amount of control. It's useful for pulling an alpha channel from an image that doesn't have one.

Look at the TIFF file in the **Browser** called *TIFF.tif.* Apply the **Extract** filter to it with **Copy Result to Alpha Channel,** and you'll see that with hardly a tweak of the sliders, the white will disappear from around the word.

👉 *Tip*

NightScope: If you apply **Color Corrector** to a clip, taking down the black level a bit, then use the **Extract** filter, followed by **Color Corrector** again with a green tint and the white level brought down considerably, as well as the mids choked down, you can create quite a credible NightScope look for your image. Look at the clip at Marker 8 in *Effects Builder.* It needs a little fiddling, depending on the image, but it's fun, especially if you can add a little blurred glow to it with a composite mode, which we'll talk about on page 264 in Lesson 10.

Mask Shape

Mask Shape is a useful filter that lets you easily control the shape the image. The controls allow basic shapes (Figure 9.30) and have **Horizontal** and **Vertical** sliders that let you adjust the default shapes. I'll show you a practical application.

An interesting use for **Mask Shape** is to create borders using color mattes. It's simple to do. Look at the clip stack at Marker 9 in *Effects Builder.* On **V1** is the dance clip with **Mask Shape>Round Rectangle** applied. On **V2** is a color matte in pale yellow. The color also has **Round Rectangle** applied to it twice. The first time it's applied inverted. This leaves the matte with the picture showing through and fills the rest of the screen with the color. Apply-

9.31 Widescreen Controls

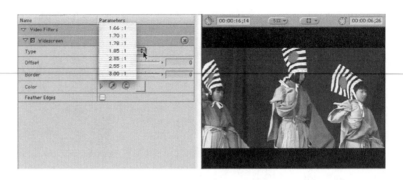

ing the shape again, only slightly larger and not inverted, will cut the color outside in the **Round Rectangle**. I also used **Mask Feather** to soften the aliasing a little.

Widescreen

This filter lets you to take a standard 4:3 video and crop it to one of seven standard cinema shapes (Figure 9.31).

This is a crop, not an overlay, so the area outside the image is empty. If you want to place a color there, you should put a color matte underneath it.

The **Offset** slider allows you to move the image up and down without altering the position. Negative numbers drag the image downward; positive numbers move the image upward, opposite of the way the *y* axis functions in the **Text** tool, for instance.

Making a Sequence Widescreen

If you want to make a whole sequence **Widescreen**—which is probably the point, rather than applying it to individual clips—nest the whole sequence, and apply the filter to the nest.

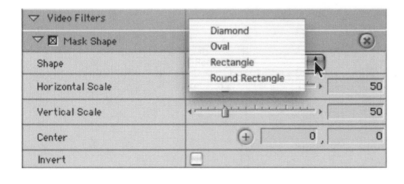

9.30 Mask Shape Controls

1. Make a new sequence, naming it something useful like *Final Widescreen*.

2. Drag your edited sequence into the new open **Timeline** window. This is now a nested sequence, with the edited sequence nested inside the new sequence.

3. Select the nested sequence in the **Timeline** and apply the **Widescreen** filter.

4. To access the settings for the filter, simply select the nest in the **Timeline** and hit the **Enter** key to open it into the **Viewer**. You can now go to the **Filters** tab to change the settings.

If you need to use **Offset,** you may not want to do it here because it will offset all the clips in the nest. Better would be to open the nest, use the **Motion** tab of any shots you want to offset, and move them up or down in the frame as necessary.

There are other ways to create the widescreen effect. You can use **FXScript DVE's 4-Point Garbage Matte.** Simply create the shape you want for the masked area, and then use the **Invert** button.

Or for a simple widescreen without the border, you could also use the **Crop** tool. This has the advantage that it renders much more quickly than other methods, as well as having real-time preview on your computer screen.

Or you could make a mask in Photoshop, a black area at top and bottom with transparency in the middle. Personally I like this way best, particularly for projects like commercials, because it lets me create interesting effects with the mask edges, graphic elements that overlap the widescreen line, different color masks, text, logos, etc.

Perspective

Basic 3D

Basic it is, but it does the job and can be used effectively for customized effects and transitions from tumbles to spins to bow ties. The controls for *x,y,z* axes are self-explanatory (Figure 9.32).

Notice the **Center** and **Scale** controls. Set these functions here and not in the **Motion** window. If you scale or reposition in **Motion,** the 3D will be cut off by the bounding box on the right, as in Figure 9.33.

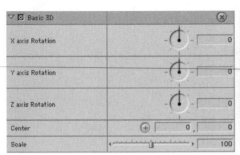

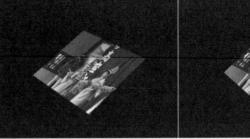

9.32 3D Controls

9.33 3D Scaled in Motion Tab and Scaled in 3D Controls

★ **Tip**
_____
Constraining Dials: Holding down the **Shift** key will constrain the dials to 45° increments.

Star Wars Scroll

Let's do something useful with this. Let's create the classic *Star Wars* scrolling title, the one where the scroll seems to disappear toward the horizon. It's tricky, but it can be done.

I started by creating a 720×2,000-pixel Photoshop file. I didn't care at all about the contents of the two layers, I just wanted to be able to import the file as a sequence. This would allow me to create a very tall sequence within FCE. In fact, inside FCE, if you look at the file called *Scroll.psd,* you see that I've switched off both of the PSD file layers to make them invisible. I could have deleted them if I wanted to. The text block called *Scrolling Text,* was made with the FCE's **Title Crawl** tool using roll animation. I placed *Scroll.psd* inside a sequence called *Star Wars Scroll.* By nesting *Scroll.psd* inside another sequence, the image can be tilted without being cut off by the bounding box.

If you open *Star Wars Scroll* and **Option**-double-click the nested sequence *Scroll.psd* inside it, you'll open it in the **Viewer.** If you look at the **Filters** tab you'll see I set the **Basic 3D** filter to *x* –74, which tilts the image backwards away from us. Because of the tilt, the text does not now appear immediately. In fact I lopped off a second and a bit from the beginning of the nested sequence so that it would start scrolling close to the beginning of the sequence.

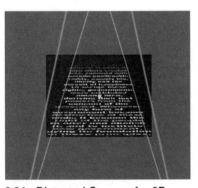

9.34 Distorted Corners for 3D Perspective

In addition to using **Basic 3D,** I also used the **Distort** tool to emphasize the keystoning of the perspective even further, as you can see in Figure 9.34.

I also added **FXScript DVE's 4-Point Garbage Matte.** This cuts off the top of the screen. I smoothed the top edge, which allows the *Scroll.psd* to fade out and disappear as it nears the top.

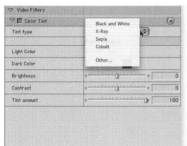

9.35 Color Tint Controls with
      X-ray Image

Be warned: all of this is going to be a pretty slow render even on a
fast computer.

Bow Tie

A bow tie is broadcasting term for two images that on the screen
at the same time, often tilted toward each other to create the illusion of perspective. Take a look at the stack at Marker 10 in
Effects Builder. That's a bow tie, most commonly used in two-
ways (interviews from a remote site). Both clips are tilted backwards on the y axis, one 45° and the other −45°. The center
points are shifted to move the images left and right, and both are
scaled down to 60 to fit the screen. You can add all sorts of
graphical embellishments like borders and bars and logos across
the bottom and top if you wish.

QuickTime Color Tint

Color Tint has one feature that is difficult to duplicate with any
other tools. It allows you to create an X-ray negative effect
(Figure 9.35). It also has a subtle sepia tint, much less garish and
orange than FCE's **Sepia.**

Color Tint also has **Other,** a wonderful tool. It allows you to set
extremely different colors for light and dark. You can have a
warm light color and a cold dark, a very nice duotone effect.

The **Brightness** and **Contrast** controls really help with the duotone, letting you put in rich color while keeping the luminance
from looking too washed out. Take a look at Marker 11 in
Effects Builder. It shows you the type of duotone effect **Color
Tint** can create.

Video De-interlace

This has got to be the most-used filter in FCE, if for no other reason than that it's used to remove video interlacing when making still images. If you don't remove the interlacing on an image with movement, you get a still that looks like Figure 9.36.

If you place that image back into a video stream, it will flicker horribly as the interlacing switches on and off. The way around the problem is to apply the **De-interlace** filter before you export the frame. In that case, the frame will look like Figure 9.37. This frame will now play back smoothly when edited into video.

The **De-interlace** filter has only a single control, a popup that lets you select a field. Choose whichever looks better.

Including in **De-interlace** is the **Flicker** functions. **Flicker** is used to overcome that horrible shimmering effect you get when there are thin, horizontal lines across the screen, such as serifs in text, thin lines of newsprint on the screen, stripes in a shirt, Venetian blinds in the distance, and a host of other possible causes. These are all caused by interlace flicker, and **Flicker**, which probably should be called **De-Flicker**, helps to remove it. It's particular useful for minimizing flickering that can occur during scrolling titles as serifed fonts run up the screen.

The other important use for the **De-interlace** filter is to help make video look more like film. The high temporal resolution of NTSC video, giving 60 discrete fields every second, is one of the reasons that makes video look like video, while film, which has a lower frame rate and no interlacing, produces a more blurred motion, a

9.36 Interlaced Still Frame

9.37 De-interlaced Still Frame

softer look which we associate with film. Removing interlacing is the first step toward trying to recreate that ever-popular film look.

Film Look

This recipe was created by Hiroshi Kumatani, who shared it with fellow Final Cut users on the 2-pop forums, http://www.2-pop.com.

1. Lay two copies of a clip, one on top of the other.

2. Apply **De-interlace** to both clips, with upper dominance on the top clip and the lower dominance on the bottom.

3. Reduce **Opacity** on the upper clip by 50%.

You can also composite a little noise on the clip, but we'll look at that in Lesson 10 in "Noise Exercise" on page 257.

Summary

This is just the tip of the iceberg of the some of the filters in FCE. I urge you to look through them and use the *Video Filters* sequence to explore its capabilities. By now you should have a fairly good idea of what you can do with this application and should be well on your way to creating exciting, interesting, and original video productions.

We need to explore one more aspect of FCE before we're ready to put our creations out on tape, the web, or some other delivery format, and that is compositing, the topic of our next lesson.

Lesson 10

Compositing

Compositing is the ability to combine multiple layers of video on a single screen and have them interact with each other. This capability really adds great depth to FCE. Until now we have been looking primarily at horizontal editing. In compositing we're dealing more with vertical editing, building stacks of layers. Compositing allows you to create a montage of images and graphics that can explain some esoteric point or enhance a mundane portion of a production. This kind of work has become the staple of wedding video production, for instance. Good compositing work can raise the perceived quality of a production. Compositing is used for a great deal of video production work on television—commercials, of course—but also on news programs and for interstitials, the short video that appears between sections of a program. Be warned, though, that compositing and graphics animation is not quick and easy to do. Most compositing is animated, and animation requires patience, skill, and hard work.

Loading the Lesson

Let's load the material you need onto your media drive.

1. If you don't already have it, drag over the *Media* folder from the DVD. Also drag the folder *Lesson10* onto your drive and put it in your *Shared* folder or your *Documents* folder.

2. Eject the DVD, open the *Lesson10* on your hard drive, and launch the project *L10*.

3. Reconnect the media.

Inside your copy of the project *L10,* you'll find the **Clips** bin, *Damine.mov,* and a number of sequences.

As in the previous lesson, a couple of sequences contain examples of effects used in the lesson. They're called *Composite Stacks* and *Composite Modes.* Before we get into compositing, we should take a quick look at the **Generators**, because these provide us some useful compositing tools.

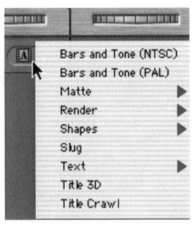

10.1 Generators

Generators

We used the **Generator** popup to create text files, but let's take a moment to have a look at what else is under that little **A** (Figure 10.1). There's **Bars and Tone, Matte,** which we've worked with already, **Render, Shapes,** and **Slug.** We're going to look at a few of the **Generators.**

Render

The **Render** generators are a great tool and a hidden secret inside FCE's **Generators.** They allow you to create compositing tools that will alter the shapes and textures of video and graphics images. Be aware that the blackness you see in **Render** items and in the **Shapes** is not the emptiness you normally see in the **Viewer** or **Canvas** around text or animated images. What you see in the gradients and shapes is actual opaque black without any transparency, such as in the **Highlight** in Figure 10.2.

Custom Gradient

Custom Gradient lets you create gradient ramps or radials, either from the default black and white or from two colors (Figure 10.3).

As with titles, you can create one in the **Viewer** and pull it into the **Timeline,** double-click on it, and use the controls in the **Viewer** while seeing your work updated in the **Canvas.**

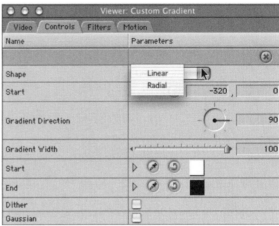

10.2 Default Highlight

10.3 Custom Gradient Controls

The default is a white-to-black gradient. The crosshairs let you pick where the white point or start color begins, and **Gradient Direction** obviously controls the angle at which the gradient proceeds, the default being pure white on the left and going to pure black on the right. In a **Radial Gradient** only the crosshairs have effect; there is no direction, of course. Generally you should leave **Dither** off. However, when a gradient shows *banding*—when what should have been a smooth transition from one color to another instead appears as sections of color with a clear edge where one color changes to another—then **Dither** should be turned on. **Dither** will add some noise to the image to break up the banding, which is usually due to the way codecs compress the video. They often are not able to make the fine distinctions in color and tone needed to produce smooth gradients. **Gaussian** makes the gradient tighter looking and seems to have less of a ramp.

Creating gradients allows you to make wonderful, complex layered images using traveling mattes, as we shall see on page 260. By animating the motion of the gradients, you can make opacity vary and change over time, revealing and fading out layered images and graphics.

Highlight

The **Highlight** render is great for generating quick highlights that race across images or text (Figure 10.4).

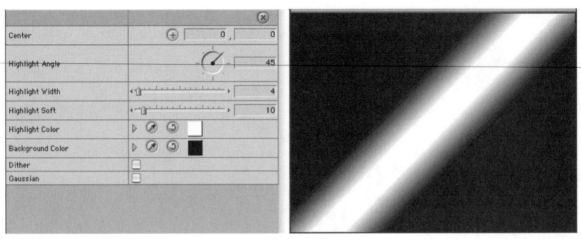

10.4 Highlight and Its Controls

The default sets the highlight to 90. I usually use it at 45 and with a much narrower highlight width than the default 10. When you combine it with a compositing mode, it produces effects that give a quick sparkle to your images.

Noise

Using composite modes, this render generator can be used to create film grain–type noise that blends with your video (Figure 10.5). It's perhaps a bit too "noisy" for most film grain, but it helps to enhance the illusion. Small quantities of **Noise** can also be used to break up banding, similar to the effect of **Dither** in the **Custom Gradient**.

Noise defaults to black and white, but the checkbox at the bottom of the controls can set color noise as well. You can also randomize it, which you probably want. Otherwise the noise looks stuck on top of the image.

Compositing Modes

One of the best ways to combine render elements with images is to use compositing modes. If you're familiar with Photoshop, you probably already know that a compositing mode is a way that the values of one image can be combined with the values of another image. Final Cut has 13 compositing modes, including two traveling mattes, which we'll look at on page 260. For the moment, we'll deal only with the first 11:

• **Normal,** the way clips usually appear

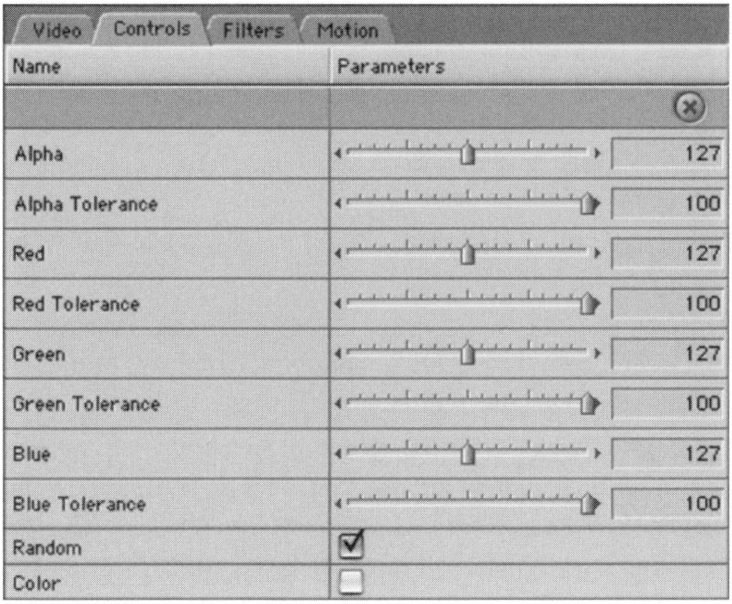

Video	Controls	Filters	Motion
Name	Parameters		

Name	Parameters
	⊗
Alpha	127
Alpha Tolerance	100
Red	127
Red Tolerance	100
Green	127
Green Tolerance	100
Blue	127
Blue Tolerance	100
Random	☑
Color	☐

10.5 Noise Controls

- Add
- Subtract
- Difference
- Multiply
- Screen
- Overlay
- Hard Light
- Soft Light
- Darken
- Lighten
- Travel Matte—Alpha
- Travel Matte—Luma

Compositing Exercise

1. Open up the sequence *Composite Modes*.

This sequence contains 11 iterations of two clips, one on top of the other. Each clip on **V2** is composited onto the clip on **V1** using a different compositing mode. A marker on the first frame of each section identifies the compositing mode applied to the clip stack. I put it on the first frame only so it doesn't obscure the image.

No two compositing modes are the same, though the differences are subtle. Some will make the output darker; some will make it lighter, but all in a slightly different manner. It's a wonderful tool for controlling image quality.

The two last **Composite Modes, Travel Matte—Alpha** and **Travel Matte—Luma,** have special uses that we'll look at shortly.

2. To change the compositing mode of a clip, select the clip on **V2** and from the **Modify** menu choose **Composite Mode.**

3. Choose a type (Figure 10.6).

You can also select the clip in the **Timeline** and with the **Control** key bring up the shortcut menu and select **Composite Mode** (Figure 10.7).

One very useful composite mode is **Screen,** which will remove black from an image. It screens out portions of the image based on luminance values. Pure black will be transparent, pure white fully opaque. Any other shade will be partially transparent. This is great for creating semitransparent shapes that move around the screen, very useful for making animated backgrounds.

Instant Sex

Let's look at some of what you can do with **Composite Modes.**

1. Begin by opening the blank *Sequence 1* and bringing in a clip from the **Clips** bin. Let's use *Ceremony8* because it has some nice highlight areas that will show off the effect.

2. Lay another copy of the same clip on **V2,** making identical copies on **V1** and **V2.**

You can also use **Option-Shift**-drag the clip from **V1** to the space above to make a copy of the clip and create **V2.**

3. To the top layer, apply a generous amount of **Gaussian Blur** of about 30. The image looks very out of focus now.

4. Turn down the **Opacity** of the clip on **V2** to something like 40%.

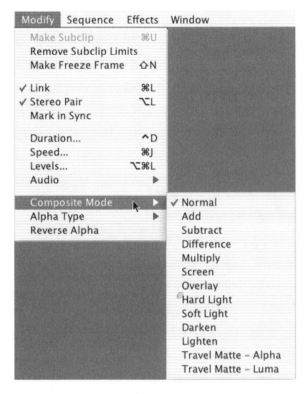

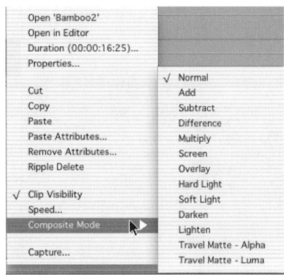

10.6 Modify>Composite Mode Menu (left)

10.7 Clip Shortcut Menu>Composite Mode (below)

5. Go to **Composite Mode** and change the clip's setting to **Add.** I prefer **Add,** but try some of the others, such as **Screen.**

6. Try adjusting the **Blur** amount and the **Opacity** levels to different settings.

This is the great After Effects artist Trish Meyer's recipe for Instant Sex. Though it was created for After Effects, it adapts readily to Final Cut. The soft, blooming highlights make a wonderful dreamy, romantic effect.

Noise Exercise

Next let's bring up the noise. We can use **Noise** to add a film-grain effect.

1. Go to the **Generators** popup, and from **Render** select **Noise.**

2. Drag it onto **V3,** above the Instant Sex stack, or target **V2** and use **Superimpose** to bring it into the **Timeline.**

3. Change the noise layer's compositing mode to **Screen.**

Note

NTSC Warning: If you are going to output to NTSC analog to be seen on a television set, be careful in using **Compositing Modes,** particularly **Add.** It will brighten the image, often beyond the luminance and chrominance values allowable for broadcast transmission. If the image is too bright or overchromaed, especially in red, it may bloom objectionably and smear easily when analog copies are made, particularly VHS copies.

4. Remember, the piece in the **Timeline** is a copy of the one you created in the **Viewer**, so double-click it to bring it back into the **Viewer**.

5. Go to the **Controls** tab to make sure the **Random** box is checked and the **Color** box unchecked.

In **Color** mode, **Noise** is too strong and generates too many sparkling bits to be useful for our purposes.

Toning It Down

10.8 Snowy Noise

At this stage the **Canvas** should look like a very snowy television picture (Figure 10.8). Now we need to reduce the effect of the **Noise**.

1. First, set the **Alpha** level all the way to zero and pull down the **Alpha Tolerance** to something around 10 or 20, depending on how much graininess you want to introduce.

2. Try also using the **Soft Light** composite mode, but with **Alpha** turned up to around 120.

Text

Let's not stop there. On top of your video, which should still have strong, glowing highlight areas, as well as a sprinkling of grain, let's add a text element.

1. Use the standard **Text** tool or **Title 3D** to create the word *JAPAN* in any font you like, fairly large size and a nice, bright color.

I used *Textile* because it's in the Apple basic font set. I used a size of 153 in bright red, **R 200, G 18, B 18**. Create whatever text block you like, using any available font.

2. Place your text block on **V4**. I also used **Image+Wireframe** to move it lower in the frame.

3. **Option-Shift**-drag the *Text* clip to the space above to create a copy on **V5**.

Your stack should look like Figure 10.9.

4. In the controls for the text file on **V5**, change the color to bright yellow.

5. Next, apply a **Gaussian Blur** filter to the text, maybe something in the 20 range.

6. Change the composite mode to **Add** so that it combines with the layers beneath.

The layer blurred out and composited will make it look like a glow over the image (Figure 10.10). But you may not want that top glow layer on the image all the time.

7. Ramp up the **Opacity** quickly over a few frames.

8. Hold **Opacity** for four or five frames.

9. Quickly ramp it down again, so it's just a quick flash of yellow glow.

Look at the sequence *Composite Stacks*. I've build the five-layer stack with the quick animation at the beginning of the sequence at Marker 1. For some reason the render output will show a much more pronounced effect than the wispy glow you see in the **Canvas** before rendering.

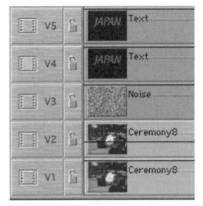

10.9 Two Video Layers, Noise Layer, and Two Text Layers

Drop Shadow Exercise

Another variation is to use a composite mode to create a different kind of drop shadow, using this type of glow layer technique only behind the text rather than on top of it (Figure 10.11). Rather than using yellow in the glow layer, simply keep the same color as the text layer.

1. Start with two copies of the text stacked on top of each other.

This time, rather than working with the upper text layer, work on the lower text layer.

2. Scale the lower text layer up in the **Motions** tab of **Viewer** to about 110%.

3. Add a little **Gaussian Blur** next, something around 10.

4. At this point the color will be too rich, so change the composite mode to **Multiply** or **Darken**.

The drop shadow glow layer stack is built in the *Composite Stacks* sequence at Marker 2.

10.10 Composited Layers and Effects

10.11 Drop Shadow Glow Layer Behind

Travel Mattes

Technically these are compositing modes as well, though they function in a special way. The two **Travel Mattes** are **Luminance** and **Alpha**. In a travel matte the layer to which it's applied will take its shape from either the **Luminance** value or the **Alpha** (the transparency) value of the layer directly beneath it. Because it tracks the layer, any animation or change in the layer below will be reflected in the tracking layer. This makes **Travel Matte** an extraordinarily powerful tool.

Area Highlight

You can use a **Travel Matte** to highlight an area of the screen. Start by creating a sandwich of three layers.

1. On **V1** place the image to be highlighted. I used *Dance 3*.
2. Drag the same image and drop it into the gray area above **V2** to create a new track, **V3**. It's important that the two clips on **V1** and **V3** are lined up exactly.
3. In between, on **V2**, place an **Oval** shape.
4. To the clip on **V3**, apply **Composite Mode> Travel Matte— Luma**.

At the moment you're not going to see anything happen because the two layers are identical, whatever is removed from the clip on **V3** will be visible in the clip on **V1**.

5. To the clip on **V1**, apply **Brightness and Contrast (Bezier)** from the **Image Control** submenu **Video Filters**. Adjust the **Brightness** value down to about –60.

The **Oval** should now be clearly visible in the center of the screen.

6. Open the **Oval** controls and set the **Aspect** down to about 0.6 and the **Size** to 35%, which will make a tall narrow oval.
7. In the **Motion** tab for the **Oval** shape, move the *x* point so that it's off toward the left, around –140, and the *y* value to 50.

You will now have a highlight area of normal exposure spotlighting the photographer, while the rest of the image is darker and obscured. (Figure 10.12).

10.12 Highlight Area Using Oval Shape

Highlight Matte

Next we're going to create a **Highlight Matte**. Let's set up a simple animation. We'll use the two layers of *Ceremony8* that we used earlier. You can copy them out of *Composite Stack* and then fine tune them in your own sequence.

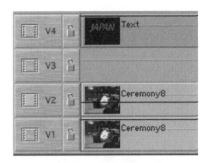

10.13 Video Tracks in Timeline

1. Use only the first five seconds of the clips for these layers that are just background to the title. The layer on **V1** is normal; the layer on **V2** as before with **Composite Mode Add**, **Gaussian Blur** about 30, and **Opacity** about 40.

2. Next add two tracks of video to your sequence above **V2**.

3. Create your text block using a large font with a bright red as we did earlier. Make it the same five-second **Duration** as the other clips.

4. Instead of placing it on **V3,** place it on **V4** as in Figure 10.13.

It's difficult to see in the grayscale figure, but I've targeted **V2**, because I'm going to superimpose the next element into the empty track above it.

5. Select **Highlight** from the **Render Generator** popup and superimpose it on **V3** between the text and the background, which will disappear, of course.

Let's work on the highlight.

6. Double-click the highlight to bring it into the **Viewer**. Go its **Controls** tab and move the **Highlight Angle** around to 35°.

7. Set the **Width** and **Softness** to about 20 and 10, respectively.

8. Leave off **Dither** and **Gaussian**; the latter only tightens the sharpness of the fall off.

Your **Canvas** should look something like Figure 10.14.

10.14 Highlight Under Text

Animating the Highlight

The next step will be to animate the **Highlight**.

1. Put the playhead at the start of the clip.

2. In the **Motion** controls tab of the **Highlight**, set the **Center** *x* axis to –640, which should take it off screen left, at least away from the text file on **V4**.

3. Make sure the **Highlight** clip is selected in the **Timeline** and create a keyframe with the **Canvas Keyframe** button.

10.15 Highlight Text with Drop Shadow

4. Move to the end of the clip (**Shift-O**). Now set the **Center** *x* point to 680.

Over the five seconds of the clip, the **Highlight** bar will sweep slowly across the screen. Of course, we still don't see the background layer.

5. Next set the **Composite Mode** of the text file on **V4** to **Travel Matte—Luma**.

If you're at the start or end of the clip, everything except the background will suddenly disappear. As you scrub through the sequence, you'll see the text will softly wipe onto the screen and then wipe off again as the **Highlight** layer slides underneath it. The text file's transparency is being directly controlled by the luminance value of the layer beneath it. The matte layer, the **Highlight** in this case, is itself invisible.

6. Try applying a drop shadow to the text layer in its **Motion** tab. It should look Figure 10.15.

Notice that the drop shadow wipes on and off with the text file. The stack at Marker 3 in *Composite Stacks* uses a **Drop Shadow Offset** of 3, with **Softness** at 50 and **Opacity** at 80.

Glints

We've seen how we can put a glow on an image and how to use a traveling matte to highlight an image. Next we're going to do something a little more complex, creating a traveling highlight, but one that only goes along the edges of a piece of text, a highlight that glints the edges.

1. We'll begin again with our two base layers, two copies of *Ceremony8*, stacked as before with the top layer blurred, the **Opacity** turned down and composited with **Add** mode.

2. Next we add the text to **V3**.

I made it a little bigger this time, font size 180, nice and fat, right to the edges of the **Safe Title Area** and beyond. Next we'll create a moving highlight area.

3. Use FCE's **Custom Gradient** from the **Generators** popup, **Render>Custom Gradient**.

4. Set the **Duration** for the **Custom Gradient** to five seconds because that's how long the animation will be, and drag the **Custom Gradient** into the **Timeline** onto **V4**.

5. Open the **Custom Gradient** from the Timeline and the **Control** tab of the **Viewer**; change the **Shape** popup to **Radial**.

6. Set the **Gradient Width** to 35.

7. Make sure both **Dithering** and **Gaussian** are not checked.

Animating the Radial

We want the glint to run along the top edge of the letters, so we'll position the radial gradient higher in the frame.

1. First let's move the start position of the **Radial** Gradient to *x,y* of 0,–100 in the **Controls** tab as in Figure 10.16.

To animate the gradient, we want it to move from left to right across the screen and then back again, staying at the its current height. At the start you want the gradient off one side of the screen.

10.16 Radial Gradient in the Viewer

2. Make sure you're at the beginning of the clip. In the **Motion** tab set the **Center** *x* point to –450, leaving *y* at 0, and keyframe it.

3. Deselect it and type *+215* to go forward 2:15 (two and one-half seconds), about halfway through the clip.

4. Set the **Center** *x* point way over on the opposite side of the screen, about 500.

5. At the end of the five-second clip, set the *x* value back to its start position of –450.

Over the five seconds of the clip, the radial gradient will sweep across the text and then back again. So far so good.

6. If you scrub the timeline, or play through with **Option-P**, you should see the gradient swing from left to right and back again.

We now have to get rid of the black and just leave the gradient across the text. We could do this by changing the composite mode of the gradient layer to **Screen**. This gets rid of the black and is useful when you want to use these kind of gradient elements on a picture.

Here, though, the gradient appears not only on the text, but on the background image as well. In this case, we want to confine the gradient to affect only the text portion of the image, so we'll leave the radial gradient layer at normal, not composited.

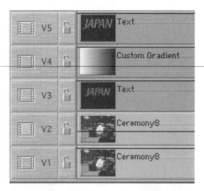

10.17 Five Layer Video Layers in Sequence

10.18 Text with Glow Composite

10.19 Glint on Text

7. To make the glow appear only on the text, start by copying the text layer on **V3** and placing the copy on **V5**, on top of the gradient.

Your stack should look like Figure 10.17.

8. Open the top text layer into the **Viewer** and use the controls to change its **Color** to white, pale yellow, or whatever glow color you want to use.

This layer will be the glow on top of the text, the radial gradient will be the matte it follows.

9. To the top text layer, apply **Composite Mode>Travel Matte—Luma**.

Immediately the gradient will disappear and the glow will be composited on top of the bottom text layer (Figure 10.18).

Polishing the Glow

That's a nice effect. You could be happy with it and stop there, with the glowing layer animated across the screen with the **Custom Gradient** layer.

What we really want, though, is for the glow not to race across the whole text, but to run just along the top edge of the text. It's not hard to do. We just need to add a few more layers.

1. **Option-Shift**-drag two more copies of the text layer on **V3** up to the top of the stack onto **V6** and **V7**.

These will, of course, completely hide the glow, so what we want to do is create a mask that will hide most of the text except for the very edges.

2. Open up the controls for the topmost layer and set its **Center** point slightly to one side, away from the side the glow starts from.

3. Also set it slightly lower on the screen if the glow is traveling above the text or slightly higher if the glow is traveling below the text.

I added 4,4 to the text layer's *x,y* values. This will make the text look slightly fatter than it really is, so what we want to do is make a matte that cuts off the bits of text that protrude beyond the correct shape of the text. That's what the layer beneath is for.

4. To the top layer, apply **Composite Mode>Travel Matte—Alpha**.

The **Travel Matte** layer disappears, and you're left with just a glint that travels along the edges of the text (Figure 10.19).

One More Touch

At the moment, the glint brushes across the upper left edge of the letters as it moves back and forth across the screen. If you want to be really crafty and add a little something special, you can shift the glint side as it swings back and forth.

1. For the first pass of the **Radial** Gradient, leave the settings as they are.

2. When the glint reaches the far right side of the screen at 2:15, set a keyframe on the uppermost offset text layer on **V7**.

3. For the next frame, while the **Radial** Gradient is still off to the right, change that offset text layer's **Center** x values to –4, leaving the y value as it is.

Now when the glint passes back from right to left, the glint will be on the upper right edge of the letters.

The glint stack is at Marker 4 in *Composite Stacks*.

Video in Text

I hope you're getting the hang of this by now and are beginning to understand the huge range of capabilities that these tools make possible. Next let's try an even more complex animation with traveling mattes, the ever-popular video-inside-text effect, the kind of technique that might look familiar from the open of another old television program.

To look at what we're going to do, open the *Composite Stacks* sequence and go to Marker 5. If you click on the clip on **V2** called *Damine Nest* and hit **Command-R**, you will render out the section of sequence defined by the length of the clip. That's what we're going to build.

If you want to make really enormous letters that fill right to the top and bottom edge of the screen, you will have to create this in Photoshop or Photoshop Elements. As we saw earlier, we can use Photoshop to create oversized sequences that we can work within in FCE. This would become a stage sequence. The stage sequence is an intermediary sequence, usually larger than your final output, that lets you work with a very large text file without cutting it off. The problem usually is that the word will extend beyond the edge of frame, so you need to make an image that is as tall as your final is, but a lot wider. For this project, for instance, we'll use a sequence that's 1,220×480, 500 pixels wider than the normal frame, but the same height.

Start out by creating the multilayer text file in Photoshop or use the one called *Stage.psd*. You may want to duplicate before you start working with it.

Making Text

We need to start with really big blocks of text.

1. In Photoshop I started with a 1,220×534 pixel image at 72dpi.

2. I created the text with the **Text** tool using the word *DAMINE*, the name of the mountain village in Japan where the clips were shot.

3. Pick a chunky, broad font type. Don't use a thin, wimpy, serif font. I used Arial Black, but you can use whatever you have at hand.

4. Make the type size large, something in the 270 range.

We're going to not only move images in the text, but we're going to move a different image in each letter of the text.

5. You can make this easier by kerning the text a little. I opened up the space between the *D* and the *A*.Don't worry about the text going outside the **Safe Title Area**. As long as it stays within the confines of the screen, it will be okay.

6. Because text starts in the center of the screen, a large text block like this will stretch right off the top of the image, so set the text low in the frame, fairly close to the bottom edge.

7. To make the letters taller, I used Photoshop's **Transform** function. Dragging out the top of the letters until they were as close to the top of the image as from the bottom (Figure 10.20).

8. Finally, I squeezed the image down to 1,220×480 and imported the Photoshop file into FCE with a duration of five seconds.

10.20 Large Title Block in Photoshop

If you don't have Photoshop or Photoshop Elements available, use a duplicate of *Stage.psd*.

Separating Letters

The text file will be the matte for the video that's inside it. Because we want different video in each letter we need to separate the word into its individual letters. We also don't need the background layer, which is only there to create the multilayer image.

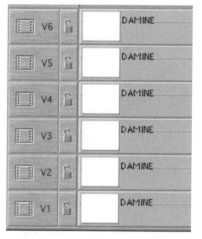

1. Begin by deleting the black background and dragging the text block onto the bottom layer.

2. **Option-Shift**-drag the text layer from **V1** onto the layers above again and again, until you have a stack six text layers tall, or one for each letter (Figure 10.21).

Next we want to create a layer for each letter.

After you've created the layer stack, then you need to crop each letter so that only it is visible.

3. If the **Canvas** is not already in **Image+Wireframe** mode, switch to it now.

10.21 Six Layer Stack of Text Blocks

4. Select the text on **V1** and use **Control-S** to solo it, so that none of the other layers are visible.

5. Use the **Crop** tool to pull in the right side of the text layer that's in your sequence. **Crop** it between the *D* and the *A* until only the *D* is visible (Figure 10.22).

6. Select the text layer on **V2** and solo it with **Control-S** to make only that layer visible.

The number in center of the **Canvas** will tell you which layer is selected.

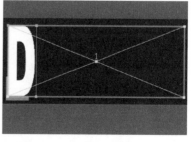

10.22 Cropped Text Layer

7. With the **Crop** tool, move the right crop line from the right until you are between the *A* and the *M*.

8. Move the left crop line so that it's between the *D* and the *A*.

9. Select the text on **V3** and repeat, moving the right crop line to the right until all of the *M* is visible.

10. Then move its left crop line so that it's between the second and third letters, *A* and *M*.

11. Repeat for the other four layers until each layer has one letter visible on it.

Adding Video

We're ready now to put in some video. We'll work only with video here.

1. Target **V1**, untarget any audio tracks, and make sure the playhead is at the beginning of the stage sequence.

2. Find a clip in the **Browser** you want to place above the text on **V1**.

I used *Bamboo1* starting at 4;00. I chose that point in the shot because there was some movement in the frame.

3. Drag the clip to the **Canvas** to **Superimpose**, slotting the clip into a new **V2** between the *D* on **V1** and the *A* now on **V3**.

4. Roughly position the clip in the **Canvas** so that it's sitting on the left side of the frame over the letter *D*.

The next step will be to apply a **Composite Mode**.

5. With the clip on **V2** selected, use the **Control** key to see the shortcut menu, and choose **Composite Mode>Travel Matte—Alpha**.

10.23 Distorted Image Composited over Text

Actually, with white text we could use an alpha matte or a luma matte, and the result would be the same. Remember, the image doesn't have to be the whole size of the frame or positioned in the center of the frame. It can be placed anywhere at any size, so long as it covers the letter.

6. Grab a corner of the image and resize it. Hold the **Shift** key and distort image shape, if you want. (Figure 10.23).

Next we need to add some more video to the other layers.

7. Target **V3** and find a clip in the **Browser** to superimpose over it.

I used *Ceremony7* from right at the beginning of the subclip.

8. **Superimpose** it onto **V4** and change its **Composite Mode** to **Travel Matte—Alpha**.

9. Scale the image in the **Canvas** and position it so that it covers the letter *A*.

The next clip will take its matte from the clip now on **V5** and fill the letter *M*. I used the beginning of *Temple2*.

10. Find a clip to use and **Superimpose** it above **V5**.

11. Set the composite mode to **Travel Matte—Alpha**.

12. Scale and position in the **Canvas**.

I used the beginning of *Dance3* to super above **V7**.

13. Repeat the process to create a new **V8**, above the letter *I*.

14. I used *Food3* above **V9**.

15. Repeat the process to create a new **V10** to be matted by the letter *N* on **V9**.

I used *Ceremony1* to super above **V11**.

16. Repeat the process for **V12**, making a new top video layer taking its **Travel Matte—Alpha** from the letter *E* on **V11**.

Your 12 layers in the sequence should now be made up of six layers of text interspersed with six layers of video scaled and positioned to fit the text layer below it (Figure 10.24).

Nesting

So far we've created the text in a stage sequence with very large letters, and we've placed moving pictures inside each letter. Next we need to animate the whole composite over another image so that the stage sequence itself moves across another image. The stage sequence we created is a nest of material. The one I've created, called *Damine Nest,* is in your **Browser**.

1. Open a copy of *Sequence 1* and lay a clip of video in it.

I used the first five seconds of *Village1*.

2. Next place your stage sequence on **V2** above the video on V1.

Sequence 1 is, of course 720×480, so when you place the much larger stage sequence in it, the stage sequence, *Damine Nest,* will shrink down to fit into the **Canvas**.

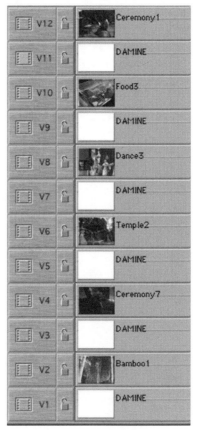

10.24 Twelve Layer Stack

10.25 Damine Nest Composited on Video

3. **Option**-double-click the nest on **V2**, which will open it into the **Viewer**.

4. Go to the **Motion** tab and reset the **Basic Motion** with the red **X** button. This will extend the layer beyond the sides of the **Canvas** as in Figure 10.25.

Next we'll want to animate the text so that the whole nest slides across the screen from right to left.

1. In the **Motion** tab, set a **Center** *x* value at the start of the clip to 968, which will push the nest off the right side of the screen.

2. At the end of the clip, set a **Center** position of *x* −978, which will move the nest off the left side of the screen.

Over the course of the five seconds the text will travel from right to left on top of *Village1*. I have build the animation at Marker 5 in *Composite Stacks*.

Variation with Fades

At Marker 6 in *Composite Stacks* is a variation in which each letter fades in one after the other.

1. Place the background layer *Village1* on **V1** in a new sequence, and your stage sequence on top of it on **V2**.

For this animation we're going to need the text sequence with the word to fit into the **Canvas**. Rather than rebuild all the text files, with all the all the layers and all the cropping, we'll simply rescale the stage sequence so that it fits into the 720×480 sequence.

2. Use the **Zoom** popup at the top of the **Canvas** and set it to **Fit All**, which should show you the full width of the stage sequence, as on the left of Figure 10.26.

3. Grab a corner of the image and pull in to reduce the scale-as on the right of Figure 10.26.

4. Double-click the nested sequence on **V2** to open it up with all its 12 layers.

10.26 Resizing the Image

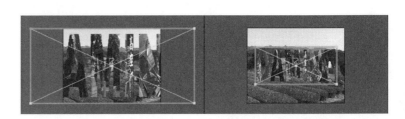

5. Select the video clip on **V2**. With the **Clip Overlay** button turned on, take up the **Pen** tool.

6. With the **Pen** tool set an **Opacity** keyframe on the clip and drag it down to zero.

7. Move the **Playhead** forward half a second, 15 frames, and ramp the **Opacity** up to 100.

8. Now go to on the video clip on **V4**. You're half a second into the clip. Set an **Opacity** keyframe with a value of zero here.

9. Go forward to the one-second mark. Change the **Opacity** to the clip in **V4** to 100.

10. Bring the **Opacity** on the video clip on **V6** down to zero-with the **Pen**.

11. Bring the **Opacity** up to 100 15 frames later.

12. Do the same for the clips on **V8**, **V10**, and **V12**, bringing up the **Opacity** for each 15 frames after the one before.

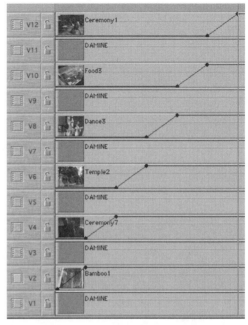

Each letter will now fade onto the screen one after the other, in half second intervals. One last touch will polish it. Your stack in the sequence should look like Figure 10.27.

10.27 Twelve Layer Stack with Opacity Keyframes

Drop Shadow Finale

1. Go back to your final sequence, the one with the rescaled stage sequence and *Village1*.

2. **Option**-double-click on the nested sequence on **V2** to open it in the **Viewer**.

3. In the **Motion** tab, set a **Drop Shadow**.

Now as each letter fades on, its drop shadow will fade on with it. This is easier than doing it for each letter in the nested sequence. The finished sequence is at Marker 6 in *Composite Stacks*.

Outline Text

Let's look at a technique for getting video inside outlined text. It's simple to do once you understand the principles behind compositing modes and travel mattes.

1. Start off by creating the outline text from the **Generator** popup.

2. In the **Controls** tab, type *DAMINE* in the **Text** box. Leave the default black-and-white colors.

3. Again use Arial Black or some other fat font, and set the size up to about 120.

4. Change the **Aspect** to 0.4. This will make the text much taller so that you'll see more of the image through it.

5. In **Controls** give the word a large amount of **Line Width** and some **Line Softness**.

I used a **Line Width** of 180 and a **Line Softness** of 50.

6. Lay this outline text in *Sequence 1* on **V2**.

7. Put a video clip as a background layer on **V1**.

I used *Village1* again.

8. Before we go further, **Option-Shift**-drag the outline text from **V2** to **V3** to copy the text.

9. You can now open up the outline text layer on **V2** and make the **Line Color** anything you want. I went for a bright yellow.

10. Put a video clip that you want to appear inside the outline text on **V4**, above the two layers of outline text.

I went for *Bamboo2* this time.

11. The final touch is to apply a **Compositing Mode>Travel Matte—Luma** to the video clip on **V4**.

Because a travel matte will always hide the matte layer, the outline text on **V3**, which provides the matte information for the video clip on **V4**, disappears, leaving you to see the outline color on the layer below. The Canvas should look something Figure 10.28. The stack is at Marker 7 in *Composite Stacks*.

10.28 Video in Outline Text

Empty Outline Text

Remember in "Outline Text" on page 171 in Lesson 7 I said I'd show you how to make outline text that was only an outline and empty where the letters are? You probably can guess how to do this already using **Composite Modes**. The stack of clips that show this technique is in *Composite Stacks* at Marker 8.

To make this effect, we'll start as we did before, by making outline text in black and white.

1. Select **Outline Text** from the **Generator** popup.

2. In the **Controls** tab, again type *DAMINE* in the **Text** box.

3. Again use Arial Black at 120 with the **Aspect** set to 0.4.

4. In **Controls** again make **Line Width** 180, **Line Softness** 50.

5. Lay this outline text in a new sequence on **V2**.

6. Put a video clip as a background layer on **V1**.

I used *Village1* again.

7. Again **Option-Shift**-drag the outline text from **V2** to **V3** to copy the text.

We haven't finished working with outline text on **V2**. To that text block on **V2**, we add a filter from the **Effects** menu.

8. Select **Video Filters>Channel>Invert**. Leave it at its default **Amount** of 100 and the **Channel** at RGB.

This inverts the color of the outline text on **V2**; what was black becomes white, and what was white becomes black.

9. Now open the copy on **V3** into the **Viewer**.

10. In the **Controls** tab, leave all the settings untouched, except the **Line Color**. Make that whatever you like.

I chose a bright yellow. Next we want to apply a composite mode to this layer.

11. Use **Composite Mode>Travel Matte —Luma**. Your composite should look like Figure 10.29. The stack is at Marker 8.

10.29 Empty Outline Text Over Video

Grunge Edges

Next we'll do something different. We're going to grunge up the edges of a clip.

1. Start out in Photoshop, making a new image that FCE will resize for digital video. Start at 720×534. If you don't have Photoshop or Elements, the file I made up is in your **Browser**. It's called *Grunge.psd*.

2. Make the new image completely black.

3. Take the **Rectangular Marquee** tool and draw a rectangle that's about 50 pixels in from the edges of your image.

10.30 Grunge.psd

4. Next fill the selection with white.

5. Now have some fun. Drop the selection and grunge up the edges of the white box. Start with PS's **Smudge** tool (**R**), with which you can pull the white into the black and black into white. Or you can use one of the PS filters from the **Distort** group, maybe **Ripple** or **Ocean Ripple** set to a small size, but a high magnitude. Or combinations of various tools.

I like to smudge up the edges a bit first and then apply the filter so it doesn't come out too repetitive. Do it by mostly pulling the black into the white because the filter will expand the schmutzing effect. Avoid doing an effect that goes beyond the edges of the frame. It will look cut off when you composite it with the video. You should end up with something that looks like the *Grunge.psd* image in your **Browser** (Figure 10.30).

6. Import your PS file into Final Cut.

7. In a new sequence place your PS file on **V1** and place a video clip on top of it on **V2**.

8. Apply **Composite Mode>Travel Matte—Luma** to the clip on **V2**.

In the **Browser** is a sequence called *Grunge Sequence* that contains *Ceremony2* on **V2** and the Photoshop file *Grunge.psd* on **V1**. To the video clip I applied **Composite Mode>Travel Matte—Luma**.

10.31 Scaled and Rotated Grunge-Edged Clip

Look at Marker 9 in *Composite Stacks*. Here I've laid a gray color matte on **V1**, while on **V2** I placed the nested sequence *Grunge Sequence*. With the **Canvas** in **Image+Wireframe** mode, I scaled and rotated the nested sequence in the **Canvas** (Figure 10.31). As you can see, you can work up millions of variations on the basic idea.

Bug

A bug is an insect, a mistake in software coding, and it's also that little icon usually in the lower left corner of your television telling you what station you're watching. There are lots of different ways to make bugs, but I'll show you one using Photoshop and compositing modes. In your **Browser** is a PS file called *Logo.psd*. Double-click it, and it will open as a sequence with two layers. The bottom layer, which has the visibility switched off, has the bug already made up with the Photoshop effect. The top layer that is visible in the **Canvas** doesn't have the effect applied, and that's the one we're going to work on. If you want to just work with the bottom layer that's made up for you already, you can skip the first section of this tutorial.

1. Make sure in your **Preferences** that your **External Editor** for still images is set to **Photoshop**.

2. **Control**-click on the visible layer in the *Logo.psd* sequence, and from the shortcut menu choose **Open in Editor.**

3. Once Photoshop has launched, select *Layer 2,* and from the little **F** in the bottom left of the *Layers* palette, add a **Layer Style,** choosing **Drop Shadow** (Figure 10.32).

4. Change the **Drop Shadow Angle** to 145 and the **Distance** to 15. Leave the other controls the same (Figure 10.33).

5. Check the **Inner Shadow** check box to add the shadow. Set the **Distance** to 5, and the **Choke** and **Size** to 10.

6. Also add a **Stroke**. Set the **Size** to 6. I made the color blue (Figure 10.33).

7. Press OK, and you've built the effect.

10.32 Add Layer Style>Drop Shadow

There is one more step to take before going back to FCE. The effects have to be applied to the layer. The easiest way to do this is to add a layer underneath the effects layer.

8. Add a new layer to your Photoshop composition and in the **Layers** palette drag it below *Layer 2,* which holds the effects.

☞ *Tip*

Distinctive Logo: There are any number of different ways to give your logo a distinctive edge by using the power of layer styles. Rather than use the **Inner Shadow** and **Stroke** method, you could also use **Bevel and Emboss**. Change the **Technique** popup to **Chisel Hard**, and push the **Size** slider until the two sides of the bevel meet. This will give you maximum effect. Remember the logo is going to be very reduced in size. Also in bottom part of the **Bevel and Emboss** panel, try different types of **Glass Contour** from the little **Arrow** popup.

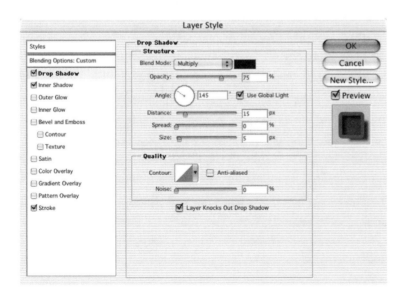

10.33 Drop Shadow Panel with Inner Shadow and Stroke

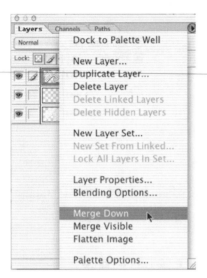

10.34 Merge Down

10.35 Logo with Composite Mode>
Multiply

9. Make sure *Layer 2* is selected. From the **Wing** menu, choose **Merge Down,** or use the keyboard shortcut **Command-E** (Figure 10.34).

10. Save your file and go back to Final Cut Express.

Layer 2 in the PS sequence *Logo.psd* will have been updated and include your new effects.

11. Open a new duplicate *Sequence 1* and drag some video into it. I used *Archers2*.

Now normally you're going to want your bug to run the duration of your sequence, which might be an hour or more. Because you can't drag out still image layers to an unlimited duration once they're in a sequence, you need to set the duration of the bug while it's still in the **Browser.**

12. The simplest way to work with this is to first open the sequence *Logo.psd*. Now drag your newly minted effects layer *Layer 2* out into the **Browser** (or the original *Layer 1* if you prefer).

This will, of course, be a copy of the *Layer 2* in *Logo.psd*. With *Layer 2* as a single-layer image, before you place the bug into the final sequence, you can change its duration in the **Browser.** Here you can make the duration of the still image anything you want—anything up to four hours anyway, which is the duration limit of any FCE sequence.

13. Set the **Duration** for the bug logo to whatever the duration of the sequence you want to cover. Now you can drag the layer into your final sequence.

14. The first step inside the **Timeline** is to fix the image distortion. Double-click on the logo layer and go into the **Motion** tab. Reset the **Basic Motion** and **Distort** reset buttons, the buttons with the little red **X**.

15. Next step you should change the logo's composite type.

There are a number of compositing modes that will work for this, but I like to use **Composite Mode>Multiply** (Figure 10.35). This will make the white of the logo almost transparent. For a slightly brighter look, try **Soft Light,** and for an even more transparent look, use **Overlay.**

16. At the current size the logo is probably a bit intrusive, so you might want to scale it down a bit and reposition it in the corner or your choice.

It will now be your unobtrusive watermark on the screen. Some like to use effects like displacements or bumpmaps in addition, but for something this small, I don't really think it's necessary. The simple transparency effect of a composite mode is enough. The one I created is at Marker 10 in Composite Stacks.

Day for Night

Color mattes don't have to be used only for backgrounds or graphical elements like we did in earlier lessons. They can also be used as a color filter. Day for Night is the now seldom-used technique of trying to shoot in daylight and make it look like a moonlit night. Old Westerns almost always used this technique. Basically, you stop down the camera and shoot through a blue or a graduated blue filter. Let's do something similar.

1. Start off by laying the clip you want to affect on **V1** in a new sequence.

I used *Village3* because it presents a typical daylight problem, the bright sky.

2. Darken the image, such as with **Color Corrector**.

I pulled down all the levels—**Whites, Mids, Blacks,** and even **Saturation**. Even with the levels pulled quite far down, the sky remains bright and pale (Figure 10.36). Next we'll use the **Color Matte** to add the blue night filter.

3. Create a deep, dark blue color matte and lay it on **V3**.

4. Create a **Custom Gradient** and place it between the two layers on **V2**.

5. Set the **Composite** mode on the color matte to **Travel Matte—Luma**.

All that's left to do is to make the gradient.

6. Open the controls, leave the default at **Linear** gradient, and change the **Direction** to 180.

Next you need to use the crosshairs to place the start of the gradient. There is a start point, but no end point for the gradient. If you start at the top of the **Canvas**, the blue will carry too far down into the image.

10.36 Darkened Image Bright Sky

10.37 Day for Night Gradient Filter

7. Scale down the size of the **Canvas** to something like 25%.

8. Place the start point for the crosshairs out in the grayboard above the image.

9. Tighten the **Gradient Width** so that it falls off more sharply.

10. Make the end color of the gradient somewhat less than pure black to give the image a cold, blue cast.

The sky should be dark blue, while the center of the image, should still show some light and color (Figure 10.37). The stack is at Marker 11 in *Composite Stacks*.

That brings us to the end of this packed lesson on compositing. We're almost ready to export our material from Final Cut and out into the world, which is the subject of our final lesson.

Lesson 11

Outputting from Final Cut Express

Remember that I said at the beginning that the hard, technical part of nonlinear editing was at the start, setting up and setting preferences, logging and capturing? The fun part was the editing in the middle, and the easy part was the outputting at the end. We're up to the easy part, the output. Because it's so simple this will be a short lesson.

The two basic ways of outputting are:

- Exporting, if you're going to another computer application or CD or DVD or web delivery
- Recording to tape, if you're going to traditional broadcast or analog tape delivery

Because it's probably the most common requirement for Final Cut Express users, let's look at outputting to tape first. We'll see exporting later on page 282.

There are basically two ways to get material from your computer to tape:

- **Record to Tape**
- **Print to Video**

Record to Tape

You can get your edited material back out to tape in several different ways. The simplest one, and probably the most commonly used way, is to record to tape. Before you do that you should always

- Make sure everything that needs to be rendered in the sequence is rendered.
- Make sure you are set to **FireWire** in the **View>Video** menu.
- Make sure you mix down your audio. Go to **Sequence> Mixdown Audio** (**Command-Option-R**).

Put the playhead at the beginning of the timeline, put your camcorder into VCR mode, switch on record with the VCR controls, and hit the spacebar. This is a fast, effective, and simple-to-use method.

It's probably a good idea to have some black at the beginning of your sequence and have the playhead sitting on it, so that when you begin recording, you're not recording a still image for a while. You should record at least 10 seconds of black before pressing the spacebar to begin playing back your sequence.

Using playback from the **Timeline** has some disadvantages; you don't get to put in bars and tone and neat countdowns and slates and black leaders and trailers, unless you physically add them to your sequence. If you want these features, you can use **Print to Video**.

Print to Video

Print to Video is now found under the **File** menu. If you have a sequence selected in the **Browser** or an active **Timeline**, you can call up **Print to Video** from the menu or use **Control-M**. This brings up the dialog box in Figure 11.1.

In this dialog you can set any number of options for program starts and ends. You can add bars and tone and set the tone level, depending on the system you're using. A number of different digital audio standards are used, if you can call anything that has variables as being a standard. Different systems use –12, –14, –16 or –20dB as digital audio standards. Analog uses a variety of other standards around 0dB. If you are going to send your video

Note

PtV Limits: Though you can loop FCE's **Print to Video** as many times as you want, the sequence had better be fairly short. The duration of any **Print to Video** recording is limited. It can't be longer than four hours, which is probably more than enough for most people.

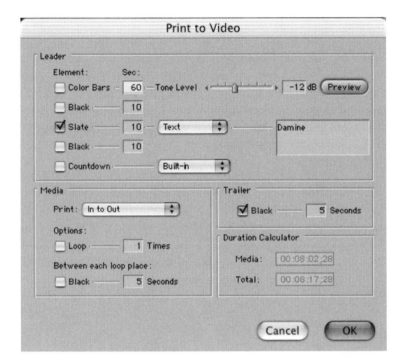

11.1 Print to Video Dialog

to a duplication house, check with them before selecting a tone level.

> **Tip**
>
> **Audio Mixdown:** One of the hardest tasks for a hard drive to do in digital video is finding, seeking, and playing back multiple tracks of audio simultaneously. Final Cut has a great feature: the ability to mixdown your audio tracks. From the **Sequence** menu, select **Mixdown Audio**, or press **Command-Option-R**. That's it. Wait while FCE renders out a single audio file that mixes down all your tracks. Your system will run more easily, and you're less likely to have dropped frames during that crucial playback to tape. I suggest mixing down every time you output to tape, whatever method you use.

The **Slate** popup lets you use the:

- **Clip Name**
- **Text,** which you can add in the text window
- **File,** which is any still image, video or audio file

So if you want to record an audio slate, selecting file and navigating to it with the little **Load** button will play the sound during recording.

You can use FCE's built-in countdown, using a form of Academy leader. Or you can use a countdown of your own by selecting **File** in the **Countdown** popup.

When you start **Print to Video**, FCE will write a video, and if necessary, an audio file of any material that needs to be rendered. Every time you use **Print to Video**, it will have to do this, even if you've just used **Print to Video**. After it's finished writing the video and audio files, FCE will prompt you to put your deck into record. Put your camcorder into record in VCR mode and press the record button or buttons. FCE will not do this automatically. Press **OK** and playback will start.

You can use either **Record to Tape** or **Print to Video** to make a VHS recording. Simply connect your DV camcorder or deck to your computer and then connect its analog output to your VHS deck. It's probably a good idea to have the VHS deck in turn connected to a video monitor or TV set so that you can see what you're recording. Then set the VHS deck in **Record**, and use the DV device as a digital-to-analog convertor to get your movie onto VHS.

Export

You can access the different formats and ways of exporting from FCE from the **File** menu (Figure 11.2). From here you can export to a Final Cut Movie or a QuickTime Movie, both of which offer a number of options.

Final Cut Movie

Let's start with Final Cut Movie, the first of the two **Export** options. When you export a Final Cut movie, Final Cut is listed as its creator type, so that if you launch the resulting movie, it will launch FCE. Because Final Cut is a QuickTime-based application, the exported movie will also play using the QuickTime Player and will work in any other QuickTime-based application, such as iMovie or iDVD.

You can export a sequence as a digital file into a Final Cut movie in several ways:

- From the active **Timeline** window directly from the sequence you're working in
- From an active **Viewer**
- From the **Browser** by exporting a sequence or clip

⭐**Tip**

In to Out: If you only want to record a portion of your sequence, select the portion you want to record by marking it with In and Out points in the **Timeline**. Then in the **Print to Video** settings window, select **In to Out** from the **Print** popup in the **Media** portion of window. When you press **OK**, playback will begin at the marked In point and run until the Out point.

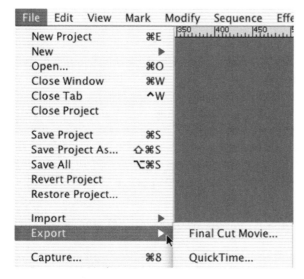

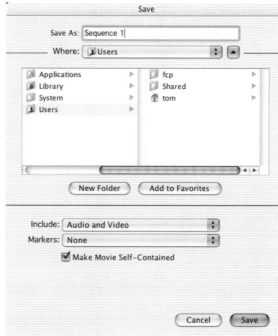

11.2   File>Export (above)

11.3   Final Cut Movie Export Dialog (right)

Click on the item and go to **Export>Final Cut Movie**. This brings up the dialog box in Figure 11.3.

Here you can rename your sequence, if you wish, and you can select whether you want to export **Audio and Video** or **Audio Only** or **Video Only** from the **Include** popup.

11.4   Exporting Markers Popup

Here you also have the option to export **Markers** through a popup (Figure 11.4). To export chapter and compression markers to iDVD3, select **DVD Pro Studio Markers**. Do not choose **Chapter Markers** from the popup. It won't work.

You should bear in mind a few rules about chapter markers:

- iDVD3 will no more than 36 chapter markers.
- Neither chapters nor compression markers not be closer than one second from each other.
- You can't have a chapter or compression marker within one second of the start or end of the sequence.
- A chapter marker is automatically created for the beginning of the export, and a compression marker is created automatically at the start of each chapter anyway. Select the popup of your choice and export.

The checkbox at the bottom of the dialog box, **Make Movie Self-Contained**, is an important one. This checkbox defaults to being on, but if you uncheck **Make Movie Self-Contained**, FCE will generate a reference movie. This is a relatively small file that points back to the original media source files. It will play the contents of the sequence as you laid them out. The reference movie will play back from the QT player, and it can also be imported into other applications such as iDVD or compression programs such as Sorenson Squeeze. The reference movie is treated just like any other QT clip inside these other applications. FCE and the importing application do not need to be open at the same time for this to work.

The real advantages to making reference movies are the speed in generating the file and the comparatively small file size. If anything in the FCE sequence needs to be rendered, it will still have to be rendered for the reference movie, and the audio files will also be duplicated as a mixdown of your tracks. You do, of course, need to have access to all the source media included in the sequence, because a reference movie only points to existing media source files on your hard drives. It's not a complete video clip in itself. Be warned: you cannot delete any of the media needed for the reference movie, or it will not play. It will be a broken Quick-Time file. If you send it to somebody on a CD, they won't be able to play it. It will only play on a machine that has access to the media.

Export to Final Cut Movie is an important tool because it is the only way to export a sequence from FCE without recompressing the video. All other exports, including export to QuickTime, will recompress the frames, producing some degradation of the video image, albeit very slight.

QuickTime

QuickTime is the catch-all for every form of file conversion and still export from FCE. I would have liked for **Still** export to be separated, but it's hidden in here as well (Figure 11.5).

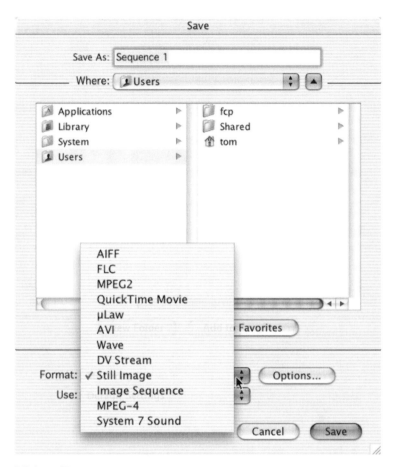

11.5   QuickTime Export

Video Export

Final Cut Express has a number of video export choices for QuickTime. The **Format** popup allows you to choose:

- FLC, an 8-bit format used for computer animations
- AVI, a PC video format
- MPEG2 export, which is only available if you have DVD Studio Pro installed
- QuickTime Movie
- DV Stream, DV audio and video encoded on a single for use with iMovie
- MPEG-4, a format designed primarily for cross-platform web compression

These are the video formats. Some, such as AVI and QuickTime, allow you to use a number of different codecs. DV Stream is used by iMovie, not by FCE. Do not export to DV Stream if you're going to a video-editing application other than iMovie.

In **Quicktime Export,** the **User** popup is contextual; that is, what is offered here is determined by what's selected in the **Format** popup.

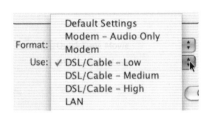

11.6   QuickTime Export User Popup

If you select **QuickTime** in the **Format** popup, the **User** popup offers a number of common Internet settings based on MPEG-4 (Figure 11.6). This is a really good place to start if you want to create a video to show on the Internet or put on your .mac home page.

If you want more control, choose MPEG-4 from the **Format** popup and then click on the **Options** button to bring up the **MPEG-4 Settings** window (Figure 11.7). The **Video** and **Audio** allow you full control over your media. It takes a great deal of practice and testing to become proficient at compression for the web. Try various data rates, frame sizes, and frame rates and compare them to the default web settings that come with selecting **QuickTime** in the **Format** popup.

Exporting with QuickTime allows you to use a variety of different codecs for compression, such as, among others:

- Animation

- Cinepak

- DV-NTSC

- Motion-JPEG A

- Photo-JPEG

- Sorenson Video 3

Codec stands for compression/decompression and is the software algorithm that a specific system uses to reduce the file size of the media. To export to other QuickTime codecs, such as the excellent Sorenson Video 3 codec, use the **Options** button and select the correct video and audio settings (Figure 11.8).

The default compressor is **Video,** but if you click on the **Video** button, you can choose the codec you want to use. For Quick-Time video on the Internet, you might set the **Compressor** to **Sorenson.** Try various data rate settings. 100KBytes/sec will give good results. Set the frame rate to 15fps.

Size should be set to 320×240.

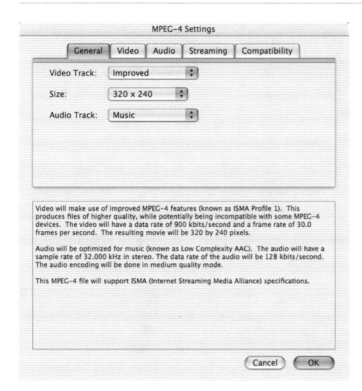

11.7 MPEG-4 Settings Window

11.8 QuickTime Video and Audio Options (below)

These settings will produce a fairly large file, suitable for use on high speed connections.

The **Sound** dialog box allows you to set an audio compression scheme as well as the sampling.

Photo-JPEG is used for file size reduction. An important codec is Animation, a high data rate, lossless compression codec often used to transfer material between various applications. One advantage that the Animation codec has that others don't is that it can carry alpha channel information with the video. This allows you to create a sequence in one application and bring it into FCE without loss and with its transparency information. Or you could export an FCE sequence that has transparency and bring it into another application such as After Effects, keeping the transparency you created in FCE. When you export with the Animation codec with an alpha channel, make sure that for **Colors** you select **Millions+**. The plus is the alpha channel.

To create high-quality web video, you'll need a separate application such as Discreet's Cleaner or Sorenson Squeeze. To create video CDs, you'll need an application, such as Roxio's Toast, that allows compression to the MPEG1 codec. This is a

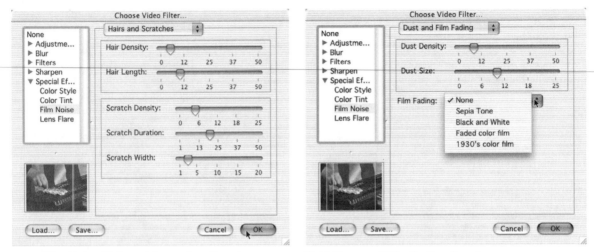

11.9 Film Noise Hair and Scratches Panel   11.10 Dust and Film Fading Panel

heavily compressed codec, but remarkable one in that it can actually play back off the very low output of a CD and still produce a full-screen, full-motion image. To create a DVD, you need another application such as iDVD or DVD Studio Pro. When exporting to iDVD, you should use either a self-contained or a reference Final Cut movie, and iDVD will do the compression to MPEG2 for you.

Exporting to QuickTime allows you to add filters to your clips or sequences. Most of the QuickTime filters are available directly within FCE, with one notable exception, **Film Noise** (Figure 11.9).

This filter adds an old-time film look to your video, as if it were scratched and dirty. A small QT movie runs in the bottom left corner showing you how much schmutz you've added to the picture. Here you can set amounts of **Hair and Scratches** that appear on your video, from very low to fairly well-destroyed. You can't control the grain, however, but you can add that in FCE before you export. In addition to **Hair and Scratches**, the popup at the top will take you to another panel where you can set the amount of dust on your video as well as tint the film. The sepia is quite subtle, and the 1930's color film is suitably garish (Figure 11.10).

Image Sequence Export

Two other types of QuickTime export are often used: **Image Sequence** and **Still Image**. Image sequences are useful for rotoscoping, frame-by-frame painting on the video image, and other animation work, and provide high quality output without loss. You can set any frame rate, and exporting will create one frame of video for every frame you specify. Make sure you first create a folder in which to put your image sequence because this can easily generate a huge number of files.

Still Image Export

Finally, the **Quicktime Export** allows you to export still images. This is how you get frames of video out to your computer for web or print use. Your stills will only be 72dpi, probably not good enough for fine printing. Photoshop plugins such as Lizard Tech's Genuine Fractals can help improve the image's appearance.

The **Options** button for **Still Image** export uses the same dialog box as **Image Sequence**, together with frame rate. Don't be confused; leave the frame rate blank.

The still you're exporting may very well be in rectangular pixel aspect ratio. This is not a problem if you're going back to a video application, but in print or on a computer display, the stills will look squashed. Photoshop will fix this problem for you. If the still image comes from DV, in PS go to **Image Size**. Switch off the **Constrain portions** checkbox, and either upsample the image by changing the size to 720×534 or, for better quality, downsample to 640×480. Either way, you'll end up with a 4:3 image in the correct pixel aspect ratio. Check **Resampling** and select **Bicubic** whenever you resize in PS.

If you're going to export stills for web or print work from video, especially video with a lot of motion in it, you'll probably want to de-interlace it. You can do this either in FCE before you export the frame. As we saw in "Video De-interlace" on page 248 in Lesson 9, you select **Video Filters>Video>De-interlace** from the **Effects** menu. Or you can de-interlace in PS as well. It's in the **Filters** menu under **Video>De-Interlace**. I normally do it in Photoshop because I think its **De-interlace** feature works better than FCE's built-in one, which simply drops one of the fields. In the Photoshop **De-Interlace** filter, you have an interpolation option, which works very well.

Audio Export

FCE can export to a number of different audio formats including:

- AIFF

- µLaw

- Wave

- System 7

If you select **AIFF** in the **Use** popup you'll get common audio file settings (Figure 11.11).

Notice that the selection does not include any of the DV sampling rates, although AIFF is the most commonly used format for audio files with Final Cut. Instead of the **Use** popup, use the **Options** button, which is also context sensitive and offers a wider range of options, including 32,000 and 48,000kHz, the DV sampling rates. AIFF export options also offers a large number of compressors to reduce the file size of the audio (Figure 11.12). Generally audio for video is not compressed, except for web use, where it's very effective.

11.11 AIFF Export Use Popup

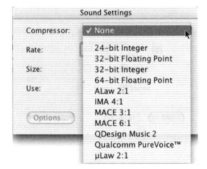

11.12 AIFF Export Options

Archiving

Now that you've finished your project you should think about archiving your material. Your original video tapes on which you shot the project should be your primary archive. Using the **Project** feature that we saw in the **Capture** window in Lesson 2 on page 47, you can recapture all the video for your project.

You need to store the project file itself. The best way to do this would be burn it onto a CD. On the CD you should also put on whatever graphics files you created for the project. Not the FCE titles, which are retained in the project file, but any Photoshop or other images you may have used. You should also save any music or separate sound you used in the project. And don't forget to save any **Voice Over** tracks you created. Everything other than the video clips that made up your movie should be burned onto your archive CD.

To restore the project, simply copy all the material back from the CD onto your computer. Open the project file and reconnect the existing files. Next run the capture process, clicking on **Project** in the **Capture** window to bring your video material onto the computer. The **Capture** window will prompt you for each tape it needs in turn. When all the material is back on your computer your project will be restored and ready to be re-edited.

Summary

We've now gone through the whole cycle of work in Final Cut Express, starting from tape raw material, either analog or digital, to capturing, editing, transitions, titling, special effects, compositing. Now finally we have returned our finished project to tape. It's been a long road, but I hope one that was exciting, interesting, and rewarding for you.

Index

The Authority on Digital Video Technology

DV MEDIA GROUP

DV PRINT

DVexpo EVENTS

DV.com ONLINE

www.**DV**.com

CMP
United Business Media

DV Media Group

Lighting for Digital Video & Television

by John Jackman

Get a complete course in video and television lighting. This resource includes the fundamentals of how the human eye and the camera process light and color; basics of equipment, setups, and advanced film-style lighting; and practical lessons on how to solve common problems. Clear illustrations and real-world examples demonstrate proper equipment use, safety issues, and staging techniques.
1-57820-115-2, $34.95, 222 pp

Nonlinear Editing

by Bryce Button

Build your aesthetic muscles with this application-agnostic guide to digital edi so you can excel in the art and craft of storytelling. Take stock of what feeds y vision and develop your abilities in employing timing, emotion, flow, and pac present your story effectively. Exercises and interviews with the pros help you hone your skills.
1-57820-096-2, $49.95, 523 pp, CD-ROM included

Producing Great Sound for Digital Video
Second edition

by Jay Rose

Produce compelling audio with this arsenal of real-world techniques to use from pre-production through mix. You get step-by-step tutorials, tips, and tricks so you can make great tracks with any computer or software. Audio CD contains sample tracks and diagnostic tools.
ISBN 1-57820-208-6, $44.95, 428 pp, Audio CD included

Photoshop for Nonlinear Editors

by Richard Harrington

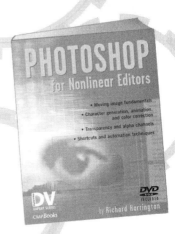

Use Photoshop to generate characters, correct colors, and animate graphics for digital video. You'll grasp the fundamental concepts and master the complete range of Photoshop tools through lively discourse, full-color presentations, and hands-on tutorials. Includes a focus on shortcuts, automation, and time-efficient techniques.
1-57820-209-4, $54.95, 302 pp, 4-color, DVD included

Creating Motion Graphics with After Effects

Volume 1: The Essentials, Second edition

by Trish and Chris Meyer

Create compelling motion graphics with After Effects v5.5. Boasting the same color-packed presentation, real-world explanations, and example projects that made the first edition a bestseller, this first of two volumes features a chapter to get new users started and a focus on the core features of the application.
1-57820-114-4, $54.95, 432 pp, 4-color, CD-ROM included

Boris Visual Effects for Editors

by Tim Wilson

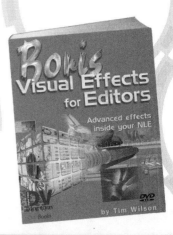

Master effects that include high-impact titles and advanced compositing. Packed with four-color illustrations, case studies, and tutorials, this book shows how to use and alter the most common features of Boris tools to do even more. Arranged by topic with an extensive index for easy reference.
Available October 2003
1-57820-220-5, $49.95, 240 pp, 4-color, DVD included

What's on the DVD?

The companion DVD for *Final Cut Express Editing Workshop* is a hybrid DVD. The DVD-ROM portion includes raw footage for the tutorial projects and sequences you can readily adapt to fit your own project's needs. It also contains nine minutes of DV media, 10 project files, 30 graphic files, well as:

- a folder containing QuickTime movies of each of FCP's video transitions
- CHV-FCE-Plugins demos and a free Silk and Fog filter
- Joe's Filters 3.5 Demo
- Carbon Copy Cloner 2.1.2
- Timecode Calculator

The DVD portion of the disk is a short introduction to Final Cut Express aimed primarily at iMovie users making the transition between the application. I go through some of the principle differences between the two applications and well as a few things to watch out to make the transition easier.